THE PROSE ELEGY

THE PROSE ELEGY

AN EXPLORATION OF MODERN AMERICAN AND BRITISH FICTION

JOHN B. VICKERY

Louisiana State University Press
Baton Rouge

Published by Louisiana State University Press

Manufactured in the United States of America
First printing

Designer: Laura Roubique Gleason
Typefaces: Minion Pro, text; Constantia, display
Printer and binder: Thomson-Shore, Inc.

LIBRARY OF CONGRESS CATALOGING-IN-PUBLICATION DATA

Vickery, John B.

The prose elegy : an exploration of modern American and British fiction / John B. Vickery

p. cm.

Includes bibliographical references and index.

ISBN 978-0-8071-3392-7 (cloth : alk. paper) 1. American fiction—20th century—History and criticism. 2. English fiction—20th century—History and criticism. 3. Grief in literature. 4. Loss (Psychology) in literature. I. Title.

PS374.G75V53 2009

810.9'353—dc22

2008031560

The paper in this book meets the guidelines for permanence and durability of the Committee on Production Guidelines for Book Longevity of the Council on Library Resources. ∞

CONTENTS

THE PROSE ELEGY

Introduction
MAJOR ELEGIAC CHANGES

In this study I examine the modern elegiac temper appearing in the work of a number of novelists, all of whom underscore the centrality of loss as theme and attitude. Novelists dealt with include high modernists from Joyce to Faulkner and Hemingway, each intent on forging his distinctive style; writers of social nuance as diverse as Henry James, James Agee, Sherwood Anderson, Ford Madox Ford, Truman Capote, and John Updike, voicing their apprehension and grief at the losses occasioned mankind by its own actions; and historically later chroniclers—such as Joan Didion and Malcolm Lowry—of a pervasive stoicism in the face of their sense that loss lies all around them.

The intent is to trace the shift from the traditional elegy's concerns to the attitudes evinced in the modern elegiac temper. The older pastoral elegy dwelt exclusively, as in Milton's *Lycidas* and Shelley's *Adonais,* with the death of an individual and how to cope with it. The twentieth century gradually transformed the elegy into a focus on the diversity of losses occurring in human life and a shaping of new (or different) elegiac responses to them. To the death of the individual, the modern elegy added most of the forms of personal, intellectual, and cultural loss suffered by mankind.

To point up this change, my study does two things. Its introduction considers some of the major ways modern authors have transformed the traditional elegy's basic triad: lamentation for the individual's death, confrontation with the fact of human mortality, and consolation for the inescapability of death. Then, individual chapters are grouped according to the several kinds of modern elegy: familial (chapters 1–4), marital (chapters 5–7), cultural (chapter 8), and philosophical (chapters 9–10). By exploring specific texts, they detail both the variety of losses preoccupying modern life and substantiate their being treated as elegiac.

Several key points follow from these losses. These include: the slow growth of individual characters' full awareness of loss's inevitability, the need for a deep-seated interrogation of past sources of elegiac support in living and mourning, the penchant for examining comparatively the cultural implications of diverse losses in other civilizations, the loss of the certitude of knowledge, and the growing distrust of the self as capable of providing the sort of consolation found in earlier elegies.

All of these bear on the ways in which the modern elegiac temper has modified the traditional elegy's basic triad of lamentation-confrontation-consolation. The first of these was inherently formal in character, functioning as the poetic equivalent of the public declaration of sorrow in funeral sermons. It frequently made lamentation the activity of all of nature (as in *Lycidas)* and indeed of the whole world known to the elegist (as in *Adonais*). After the initial expression of sorrow, the poet then came not only to face the reality of death but to confront the fact of the mortality of all living things. What life might entail for the mourner in the future now occupied his full attention. Death of the individual and the mortality of all created a gap in the mourner's consciousness that demanded filling by some authority—religious, social, or intellectual—capable of persuasively consoling him.

In contrast, the modern elegy reveals a hesitancy of attitude, a probing of intellectual boundaries, and an exploration of themes and conclusions hitherto only marginally related to the elegy. For it, individual contemplations of issues such as loss, memory, time, and survival augment the central focus of the traditional elegy. These topics have increasingly generated a need to seek less traditional forms of consolatory authority with which to invest the elegy. In the place, say, of Milton's religion or Shelley's philosophy, institutions such as the family and marriage and concepts like the self were turned to as possibly providing elegiac support in the face of the numerous losses that make up life.

How the modern prose elegy differs from its traditional poetic predecessors is a complex subject. Clearly the examination of prose works poses a different set of critical demands and expectations from those of poetic elegies. Thus, fiction's traditional reliance on a mimetic impetus, a teller or tellers of an extended narrative, and a physically larger text, for instance, obviously create significant variations on any emergent elegiac form. Nevertheless, as I hope to show, none of these materially alter the pervasiveness of the elegiac temper's presence in the prose authors considered here.

A preliminary way into the subject at hand is to consider several major differences. Thus, the extended formal lamentation of *Lycidas* or *Adonais* clearly is radically changed by the modern elegiac temper. Its move away from a formal and ceremonial response to death and human loss results in an erosive diminution of elegiac lament. For instance, Malcolm Lowry's *Under the Volcano* replaces Shelley's full-scale eulogistic obsequy with what is almost an anecdotal vignette describing its protagonist's body being pitilessly and indifferently cast into a ravine. An even terser version of elegiac lamentation is that of Virginia Woolf's handling of Mrs. Dalloway's demise in *To the Lighthouse.* Woolf removes even the last vestige of lamentation from her surprisingly factual, objective rendering of the death of a highly sympathetic character.

In general, the modern prose elegy both limits and redefines the traditional elegy's lamentation. James Agee's child narrator in *A Death in the Family* laments the actual death of his father almost silently, so foreign and sudden is the experience to him. At the same time, the transformative loss of his family as a supportive and comforting entity extends throughout the entire novel. In so doing, both the narrator and his family exhibit a subdued contrast between the traditional elegy and its modern counterpart. Thus, though mourned by family members in their individual ways, the father is far from eulogized unrelievedly.

Other novels give vent to even more abbreviated lamentation. Thus, after Dick Diver's climactic farewell at the beach, *Tender Is the Night* chronicles almost laconically his gradual loss of himself. In so doing, Fitzgerald shifts the emphasis from, say, Shelley's full-bodied lamentation for Keats to a subdued yet regretful pathos for his protagonist.

The muted sorrow felt for Dick Diver's pathetic end changes its key in Updike's *The Centaur.* Peter Caldwell struggles for roughly half his life to understand his father's true nature. Yet even when he has done so, he is not impelled to elegize his father formally or eulogistically. Indeed, Updike reverses the traditional elegy's lamentation for mortality by giving the prospect of death the aura of a comic foible. George Caldwell's obsessive concern with death by its very repetitiveness amusingly blunts the gravity of mortality.

Capote's narrator's personal memory of Holly Golightly generates an even more muted—almost subterranean—lamentation. His keen awareness at the waste inherent in her life renders impossible anything resembling a formal eulogy. For both Capote and Updike, memory—the recollection of things and persons no longer present—is itself inherently elegiac. Whereas the traditional elegy aspires to memory lasting forever, the elegiac temper of these writers recognizes that memories are actually prone to disappear in a relatively short time. As a result, they tacitly mount an elegy for memory itself as well as for the individual.

A final sort of lamentation found in the modern prose elegy is of an even more subdued order. Neither individual characters nor their public worlds appear to register any formal expression of grief at all over the losses suffered. Diffidence, detachment, irony, and doubt or uncertainty all conspire to mute the protracted lamentations celebrated in traditional elegies. A major instance of this, of course, is James Joyce. His detachment from his characters virtually requires him to decline to lament openly and unrestrainedly the losses they experience. With writers such as Joyce, extended public or formal lamentation is found to be pointless, given the actual nature of the world. Thus, in *Dubliners* Gabriel Conroy pensively recalls early in the story society's fond memories of its past conventions. Yet his efforts at recollection largely serve to indict those who like himself persist in verbally honoring what is irrevocably gone. Even the final paragraph of "The Dead" and the Anna Livia Plurabelle section of *Finnegans Wake*—key instances of Joyce's rhetorical skill—primarily treat formal lamentation as a stylistic artifice. And in so doing, they tacitly interrogate the intent and effect of extended lamentation.

Another approach to elegiac lamentation is that of diffusion rather than interrogation. *Under the Volcano* multiplies possible explanations for each individual's pitiable fate without ever fixing unequivocally on what it is that might occasion lamentation. In effect, Lowry ponders why individuals suffer specific losses rather than lamenting the fact that they do. In short, analysis preempts lamentation, which becomes at best the shadow of an impending event permanently postponed.

If formal lamentation is significantly reduced in modern prose elegies, the reverse is true of the traditional elegy's second major element. Confrontation with the fact of death and loss is materially heightened. The first and most immediate feeling of writers such as Didion and Capote is regret for the particular loss with which they are dealing. Quiet taciturnity is their response rather than the protracted, intense struggle to confront mortality found in the traditional elegy.

Both the earlier elegiac convention and its modern temper share, naturally enough, in the backward glance at a past unscarred by subsequent loss. The difference is that the nostalgia of the latter is coupled with diverse sorts of irony. In their several ways, most of the authors considered here adapt the backward glance in this manner. At the same time, they more sharply focus on the scope of the past being considered. Updike and Lawrence extend their glance the furthest back in time. For them, the past suggests an essentially ideal or, at least, a better human world standing sharply against the deeply flawed modern one they know. In so doing, they reverse, say, Milton's identifying the classical world and its myths as ultimately faulty and imperfect compared to Christianity.

Even less extended is the backward elegiac glance of Agee and Fitzgerald. Because filtered through a single central character, both their nostalgia and their ironies are more restricted in nature, more limited to the individual than an entire culture. Consequently, Rufus's exploration of the past and its meaning is less desperate than that of, say, Quentin Compson. Of even briefer duration are the backward glances of Dick Diver and Charlie Wales. Both look back on their past lives desperately aware of how past actions and decisions have created their own private nostalgias for a lost world.

All of these backward glances, unlike that of the traditional elegy, question the recollected past that antedates the losses being mourned. In so doing, they implicitly make furtive efforts to ameliorate the confrontation required. At the same time, these efforts tacitly lead to interrogations of the individual self and its ability to dispel the elegist's dealing with loss. In short, the modern elegists begin more or less consciously to entertain an intensely sobering likelihood. For them, sorrow is an inherent and enduring component of life rather than the fleeting and intermittent response it was treated as being in the traditional elegy.

Mourning and regret for past actions and events now come to be coupled with anxiety and foreboding concerning the future. Thus, in *The Portrait of a Lady* James is not only chronicling multiple forms of human loss; he is also tentatively envisaging the twilight shadows gathering around a civilized world. Some forty years later Ford's *Parade's End* intensifies the likelihood of cultural and personal collapse. Now, Christopher Tietjens faces not an unstated and uncertain future, as did Isabel, but one consisting of a barbaric vulgarity whose ruthlessness is matched only by its triviality.

How limited the future is and how intensified the anxiety it generates are traced by Faulkner and Capote. James and Ford stubbornly and determinedly persist in clinging to past cultural traditions as infinitely preferable to those they see coming. Faulkner, on the other hand, finds only too clearly the limitations of his cultural past. Thus, the deaths of Johnny Sartoris and Quentin Compson evoke basically ambiguous elegies. Their muted attitudes of sorrow are confined to regret rather than full-bodied encomiastic lamentations. With Capote, the elegiac voice is still able to haunt the mind by its portrayal of a future that is not so much threatening as emotionally blank. His narrator's elegiac confrontation is with the loss of vibrancy and excitement and the human waste of existence and time.

The final emotion aroused by the modern elegiac temper's confrontation with loss is that of doubt. A dominant attitude emerges of ironic, skeptical uncertainty as to whether a viable resolution of the trauma of loss is possible. This contrasts with the traditional elegy's reliance on a conventional authority such as that invoked in *Lycidas* for solace in bearing the loss that aroused the elegy's initial grief. How this doubt gradually hardened into deep-seated conviction can be seen in the more than fifty-year arc extending from Hemingway through Updike to Didion.

A Farewell to Arms builds steadily toward the death of Catherine and the stunned immediacy of her lover's grief. So intense and all-consuming is his grief that no possible resolution of it seems possible. Updike's charting of the decline and dissolution of the Maples' marriage directly contrasts with Hemingway's earlier treatment. The former de-escalates the intensity of the marital loss by treating it as the product of social habit. In effect, for him the elegiac becomes a normal, anticipatable, and quite possibly an inevitable phase of life. As such, it calls neither for bitter grief and lamentation nor for absolute resolutions.

Joan Didion's doubt about the efficacy of elegiac confrontation with loss derives less than does Updike's from philosophical acceptance and more from psychological struggle. She explores the possibilities of centering the elegiac resolution of human loss and losses in the self alone. Her assessment of the viability of such a resolution is twofold. In the foreground, she underlines the catastrophic waste inherent in the loss of an individual self. And in the not so distant background, she offers a trenchantly minimalist awareness of the consequences of living wholly and exclusively within the self.

In sum, then, the modern prose elegy alters the measure of significance attached to the traditional elegy's triad of lamentation, confrontation, and resolution. It mutes the first of these by diffusing, shortening, or virtually deleting the formalized frenzy of grief of, say, *Adonais.* Quiet regret, personal sorrow of an almost inarticulate order, and uninflected recording of death and other elegiac losses form the cornerstone of its response. Similarly, it reshapes its predecessors' confrontation with the ineluctability of loss both by extending and diversifying it. Stoical enduring of the immediate present, elevating the backward glance, and probing the future with apprehension are the modern elegy's principal ways of facing the challenge of how to survive. And finally, the traditional forms of authority such as religion drawn on by past elegists to afford solace and resolution of grief are by and large abandoned or at best fugitively embraced. In place of them, a persistent search for new forms occupies modern elegists. They explore romantic love, marriage, multiple cultures, philosophy, and the self as providing grounds for enduring mortality and all the other losses human beings face. And if their diverse probing of these possibilities appears to leave continuing doubts as to their ultimate efficacy, then that too becomes part of the modern elegiac temper.

1

ELEGIES OF FAMILY AND LOVE

1

LOSS OF THE IDEAL

James Agee's *A Death in the Family*

James Agee's unfinished novel *A Death in the Family* (1957) focuses primarily on the interplay between the nuclear and the extended family in order simultaneously to celebrate and critique the notion of the ideal or perfect family.[1] At the same time, all the actual family members mount throughout a diversified sense of the elegy as an extended mourning for a suddenly lost father.

Yet, ironically enough, many of the elegiac sentiments expressed over the sudden accidental death of Rufus's father counter or deconstruct those of the traditional elegy such as Shelley's *Adonais.* Of course, not all do by any means. Thus, Mary's stunned shock at the news of her husband's accident and her automatic reliance on her religious faith resemble in a lower key both Shelley's initial recoil from Adonais's death and Milton's culminating trust in "the dear might of him that walk'd the waves" (44, l.173). But customary ritualistic gestures such as the keeping of Rufus out of school and much of the family's behavior and mixture of attitudes almost make their intended solemnities into comical parodies of the conventional elegy. Both Rufus's baiting by his schoolmates and the extended sharp contrasts of philosophical outlook of family members call in question the efficacy of the elegiac convention. For instance, Shelley's fulsome eulogy of Adonais celebrates his fame, his nature as a "gentle child" (xxvii, 1) and "Lost Angel" (x, 7), his eternal perfection, and his role as immortal beacon for the still living. In contrast, Jay is seen from the outset by his family in a more quotidian light. Virtually everything about him—from being an overly fast driver, a poor risk as a prospective husband, not being a Christian like the bulk of the family, and his proneness to drink—testifies to his being ordinary rather than exceptional.

In the same way, the preparations for the funeral—notifying the adult family members, their conflicts of response and outlook, the seriocomic effort to explain their father's death to the children, and the chilling effect on them of Father Jackson's demeanor—deconstruct the elaborate ceremonial mourning found in Shelley's *Adonais.* Urania, Nature at large, and the host of others that "Came in slow pomp" (xiii, 8) to mourn provide a striking contrast with those assembled to witness Jay's death. The effect of such a realistic rendering of the victim's passing throws doubt on the eulogistic sentiments of the traditional elegy. By so doing, the psychic space required for the elegiac temper to take shape is created. As Rufus gradually says farewell both to his father and his childhood ideal of the family, that temper assumes preeminence.

The prelude to the narrative proper, "Knoxville, Summer, 1915," elaborates this broader kind of elegiac loss.[2] An adult narrator—part Rufus and part the author—elegiacally recalls a past time that is felt to have been sensuously idyllic and now to be irretrievably lost.[3] His recollections are wholly of a highly charged sensory past no longer available to him except through memory.[4] The dominant note struck is that of childlike sentiment keyed on the narrator and his voice of indulgent regret for an irrecoverable past.

This prelude is essentially a nostalgic recollection of childhood memories carefully selected by the narrator to summarize the central experiences of his childhood. Each recollection captures two different things. One is the details of daily lower middle class life recalled in their full immediacy. In contrast, the other is the highly charged significance attributable to them by a more mature and reflective spectator. One focal memory is of the neighborhood's fathers watering their lawns at twilight. Here the recall concentrates on the variety of local sounds made by water hoses, locusts, crickets, automobiles, horses and buggies, streetcars, and people walking on the streets. For the child, it creates a susurrus of tranquility tinged by regret for the scene's being a past one. Coupled with this is both a barely aware longing for its recapture and a recognition—caught solely through the style itself—that only by memory can such images of serenity be retained.

Another dimension of this focal memory is the child's sensitive awareness that the scene is rife with the movement of people and things: "People go by; things go by" (471). This leads him to two contradictory impressions, each of which, however, has a compelling, undeniable reality. On the one hand, he, or his later adult self, possesses a firm but sad recognition of the transitoriness of existence. Yet there is also an equally firm and reassuring conviction that no matter how slowly human time may move, it is also endless. These two impressions are melded into a single recollective experience. It prepares the child as narrator for the direct confrontation with his father's death and its more astringent elegiac response, which makes up the body of the novel proper:

> A street car raising its iron moan; stopping, belling and starting; stertorous; rousing and raising again its iron increasing moan and swimming its gold windows and straw seats on past and past and past, the bleak spark crackling and cursing above it like a small malignant spirit set to dog its tracks; the iron whine rises on rising speed; still risen, faints; halts, the faint stinging bell; rises again, still fainter, fainting, lifting, lifts, faints forgone: forgotten. Now is the night one blue dew. (471–72)

Rounding out the prelude is another seminal memory, this one centered explicitly on the family in a state of relaxed compatibility. It contrasts with the first memory's concentration on activity of all sorts, random and diverse sounds, and people doing all kinds of ordinary things. Here the extended family is lying down on quilts in the evening in the backyard, communicating through quiet desultory conversations "of nothing in particular, of nothing at all in particular, of nothing at all" (472). The child is struck by his physical smallness in comparison to the others. Yet rather than provoking anxiety or insecurity this sense only confirms his emotional tranquility. He has a feeling of belonging to a group that protectively cares about him personally. This remembered sense of personal security, however, segues swiftly into a sharp contemplation of "the sorrow of being on this earth" (472) and a prayer for the family's being blessed and remembered in their time of trouble and death.

The awareness of the mortality of individuals as well as of families leads the bifocal narrator (child and adult) to his final recollection. He remembers being put to bed amid security, love, and comfort only to recognize the family's inability to satisfy his deepest need. This recognition adds a fresh layer of significance to his elegiac temper:

> After a little, I am taken in and put to bed. Sleep, soft smiling, draws me unto her; and those receive me, who quietly treat me, as one familiar and well-beloved in that home; but will not, oh, will not, not now, not ever; but will not ever tell me who I am. (473)

What begins as an elegiac recollection of an idyllic childhood, compounded though it may be of tacit uncertainties as well as overt pleasures, modulates into several deeper perceptions. The first is a nostalgic celebration of the past as familial at its core, as essentially a natural, harmonious existence founded on the interplay of human beings and nature. This then segues into a personal sorrow for somehow not having all that one could or should have. And finally, there emerges an elegiac recognition that the familial past is inherently reticent about communicating an individual's specific or unique nature to him or her.

Clearly, Agee is suggesting that however supportive, protective, and nurturing the past, the family, and the natural world are or have been, they can never directly tell the child what he or she must learn personally. The boundaries established for the past, for former lives, for other lives, and for nostalgia itself are set down obliquely. They occur in the space between words and in the very order of the words of recollection. That is to say, it is the style of the prelude which embodies the challenge to be faced in the novel itself.[5] This challenge sees both nostalgia and sentimentality over the past as temptations that can vitiate the realities of self-awareness.[6] The task facing the narrator is to recognize both nostalgia and sentimentality for what they are.

Agee's novel begins with its prelude cast in the poetic mold of a self-consciously rhetorical style mourning the loss of childhood, family, and the past, all of which are felt to have been idyllic and ideal. Its heightened style suggests its affinities with the introductory lamentation of the traditional elegy. Then, the novel itself presents through the child narrator, undiluted by adult perspectives, a gradual and remorselessly realistic divesting of the family of its idealized traits. In this, it serves as an approximation to the confrontational stage found, say, in *Lycidas* with the comments of "The Pilot of the *Galilian* lake" (42, l. 109). Ultimately, it reveals the real focus of the family elegy to be the acceptance of loss as both inescapable and central to the human economy.

Chapter 1 initiates this process by dealing with the boy Rufus and his father Jay going to the movies after dinner. This habitual practice bonds the child to his father even more strongly. It also tangentially suggests if not a break with his mother at least a growing sense of his responses to life differing from hers at least in part because of their gender difference.[7] He, like his father, finds Charlie Chaplin funny while his mother recoils from what she regards as his vulgarity. Indeed, it is through the movies that Agee projects the polarities of life facing the child.[8]

Charlie Chaplin and William S. Hart, the silent film cowboy hero, dialectically balance one another as graphic symbols of his future. Social defeat or failure contrasts with physical adventure and success. The outsider, the victim of fate, is essentially looked down on despite his capacity to arouse humor and to endure an unfair and discriminatory world. He confronts the insider, the vigorous hero, who acts directly and effectively to conquer his antagonist. Rufus, of course, is unaware of the dramatic foreboding for his life implicit in these movie figures, but Agee assuredly is not. Nor is he concerned to choose between them morally as role models. Instead he makes Rufus's challenge that of integrating the use of nostalgia with the required strength of character to transcend the personal losses that accrue to him in life. By perpetuating without fixation his memories of his father and his family as they actually were, he can compensate for the losses inflicted by death, differing sensibilities, intellectual choices, and spiritual sentiments.

Balancing the artificiality of the movies is the direct immediacy of his subsequent accompaniment of his father to a tavern. Here the bonds of love between them are felt more acutely because they are sharing a purely male environment. At the same time, his love is coupled with uncertainty because he feels the unalterable weight of the child-adult distinction. No matter how close he feels to his father, he cannot eradicate the imbalance or asymmetry of the parent-sibling relation. Nor can he avoid the intuitive recognition of the need to consume Life Savers to prevent his mother's discovering where they have been. Thus, just as at the movies, he feels a faintly emerging sense of fissure between his two parents and between them and himself. With this, Agee begins to separate the lyrical nostalgia for the ideal vision of the family found in the prelude from the actualities and ambiguities inherent in the dramatic actions of the real family.

The separation of parent from child begins concomitantly with Rufus's most intense feeling of kinship with his father. On their somewhat reluctant way home after the movies, they make their customary stop to sit on a rock in the shade of a tree in a vacant lot. Here, for both father and son the feeling of privacy and isolation, of being cut off from the rest of the world, builds a further sense of the uniqueness and secrecy of their bond. It carries for both of them a deep and profound sense of contentment. For a moment, they have a sense of complete freedom from all of their immediate personal, social, and familial obligations.

It is this feeling that arouses the authorial narrator's deep and pervasive nostalgia for childhood, the sense of a past sad pleasure recoverable only through and in the act of memory. Rufus's satisfaction with this moment of tranquility is deepened from simple childish pleasure to recognition of the intrinsic difference between individuals and hence to the limitations inherent in family relationships:

> He felt that although his father loved his home and loved all of them, he was more lonely than the contentment of this family love could help; that it even increased his loneliness, or made it hard for him not to be lonely. (481)

The same feeling gradually envelops Rufus as, after his father's death, he is exposed to the full significance of the concept *family.*

In the prelude, Rufus believed that *family* inevitably entails such qualities as compatibility, nurturing, protection, compassion, and, above all, love. This conviction implicitly starts on its realistic course of erosion in chapter 2. It begins with a late night telephone call from his uncle Ralph to his father reporting Jay's father possibly to be near death. Quickly, however, the emergency is perceived by Jay to have been inflated by Ralph's customary windy drunken sentimentality. Jay's initial "cold sad darkness" (485) at reflecting on his parents is quickly displaced by a strained argument between the brothers. This arises from Ralph's intoxicated state and his indulgence in stereotypical sentiments concerning family, death, obligation, thankfulness, and so on. Clearly, in the real world of real families, there are more grounds for tension, conflict, and strain in personal relations than appear in the idyllic prelude with its powerful though subdued elegiac temper.

This chapter's being a thematic cornerstone for Agee rather than simply a casual sketch of a secondary character is seen in Jay's other responses to the situation. First, there is a repressed spillover of his irritation with Ralph onto his wife Mary. This is aroused by her softly raising a cautionary suggestion that perhaps he should wait until morning before starting for his father's bedside. Old minor resentments flare momentarily in his mind before being replaced by dual assessments of his father's character. On the one hand, his father has always been essentially a useless burden to his family. Yet he has also been marked by a substantial gaiety of manner and a natural kindheartedness. "He meant so well" (490) summarizes for Jay both his father's nature and the irritation it arouses in him. None of these sentiments concerning his brother, father, and even wife are expressed in the child Rufus's presence. As a result, they function as a covert foreshadowing of the dramatic actions to be initiated by Jay's accidental death. In this regard, they form a parallel to Mary's remark when he is about to depart: "if worst comes to worst, Jay, you might be gone longer than we hope" (496). Taken together, they indicate that the "worst" Rufus will have to face is a dual loss. In addition to the premature and unanticipated death of his father, the loss of his childhood dream of the actual nature of *family* is to make up the whole of his elegiac experience.

Such a loss of family is in Agee's eyes an inescapable part of human maturing and a natural, though highly painful, phenomenon. It is not, therefore, exclusively or even primarily an illusion foisted on the innocent young by a cynical and hypocritical adult ethos. However much the adults may encourage the idyllic view of the family as a context for the child's life, the child too desires to retain the almost perfect security provided by the family. For Rufus, this security is made up of immediate sensory familiarity, emotional comfort, and a limited measure of knowledge. This frame of mind is what makes the elegiac response to the idyllic concept of the family such an intense mingling of recollected pleasure and painful regret, one felt by more than just children in the process of growing up.

Chapter 4 shifts the novel's gender focus and in so doing broadens and deepens the thematic complexities inherent in the realities of *family.* It centers on the mother's responses and reflections back home waiting for morning. In comparing her in-laws' marital relationship with her own and the various individuals involved, she manages to suggest both the variety and the alternative forms of *home.* She develops fleetingly the sense that human beings are always leaving one home for another. At the same time, she is aware that the security inherent in the concept of *home* affords one the opportunity and freedom to critique others and other places. In so assessing them, Mary conveys something of the difference between the personal (private) and the social (public) reactions to people and situations that permeates the novel as a whole. What she does is to reflect the narrator's awareness of secrecy and privacy as somehow necessary in his role as a child.

Her contemplation of her father-in-law echoes Jay's sense of him as goodhearted but essentially irresponsible. Unlike her husband, however, she implicitly raises the difficulty of really and truly knowing another human being while grappling with the moral issue of whether there should be a limit to generosity and self-abnegation. Haltingly but still perceptively, she concludes that society would theoretically argue for no limit since this is for it essentially an abstract or hypothetical problem. The individual, on the other hand, grudgingly insists on the primacy of the family. In so doing, its inherently selfish component stands revealed. This enables her to recognize that the father is the one central barrier between her and her husband. She has no real liking or deep personal concern for him:

> Her thoughts for him were grave and sad, but only as they would be for any old, tired, suffering human being who had lived long and whose end, it appeared, had come. (509)

Pity and a generic sorrow dominate her feelings for her father-in-law, while her primary concentration is "on his son's grief and her inadequacy to it" (509). This is the focus for her true elegiac concern.

Gradually it emerges that the real source of the gulf between Mary and Jay, the elegiac source of loss felt by Mary here, lies in her Roman Catholic religion. Their religious difference occasions "silence and withdrawal" (510) on his part and apprehension on hers over raising the children as Catholic. Her religious sensibility tells her that keeping the family one and unified and closing the marital gulf is her responsibility. At the same time, she recognizes psychologically that making the children Catholic and closing the gulf with Jay are antithetical and contradictory actions. The chapter ends with her crying not for the anticipated death of Jay's father but for her dilemma and its irreconcilabilities.

The systemic antitheses she discovers point to the existence of insoluble family tensions rooted in the very social fabric itself. When set against the idyllic view of the *family* expressed in the prelude, Mary's perspective opens up for the child Rufus an ultimately dizzying vista of moral, personal, and social complexities. Inevitably, they create for him an elegiac attitude toward even his mature recognition of the nature of the "family."

The next three chapters gradually presage some of the complexities awaiting Rufus. Chapter 5 opens next morning with the children being told of their father's sudden departure and the reason for it. At its core is the children's utter lack of comprehension of the nature of death. This lack is dramatized by their persistent questioning of their mother on the subject. Once again, Mary finds herself facing an insoluble dilemma in family life: protecting the children from the harshest fact of human life—its mortality—and satisfying their natural and persistent quest for knowledge. Balancing the inherent pathos of the scene is the mock-comic, prototheological series of questions raised by Rufus, which leads to his harried mother's dismissal of him for upsetting his younger sister. This launches him into a "sudden solitude" (514) in the very midst of a core familial situation. The irony of this is escalated by his apology to his sister going awry and arousing her renewed and louder outburst of tears. Thus, his brief, pathetic experience of a kind of metaphysical isolation from the family is compounded by a social separation from it that leads to his quasicomic expulsion from it.

Chapter 6 rings the changes on the differing and shifting concepts of *home* that reflect the ambiguities and complexities inherent in *family.* Jay discovers what he had suspected earlier: his father's health is not as precarious as alleged and Ralph has once again overreacted in his customary fashion. The entire chapter is given over to a dramatic sketch of Ralph's characteristic behavior and nature. It sharply intrudes a powerfully realistic sense of weakness, failure, role-playing, and self-inflation into the family drama. Implicitly it provides a savage critique and qualification of Rufus's idyllic view of his family. Instead of all family members being protective, nurturing, and compatible as Rufus has assumed, the reverse is true. Ralph is self-important and egotistical, bogusly confrontational, self-indulgent, incapable of self-control, and morally weak. In short, the chapter serves to dramatically foreshadow yet another facet in the dissolution of Rufus's idealistic and idyllic notion of the *family.* Not only ideas or beliefs such as those concerning religion but also the natures of individuals within the family serve to render it an infinitely more complex institution than the child realizes at the beginning.

A subtler form of erosion of the idyllic appears in chapter 7. The introduction of his aunt, Hannah Lynch, immediately presents a disturbing challenge to Rufus's consciousness. Though she and Mary are closely attuned religiously, nevertheless she inadvertently brings to the novel's perspective on *family* a problem for Rufus's moral sense. She does so through appealing to his pleasure in her company and offering to satisfy one of his current deepest desires, the possession of a cap. His childlike passion for it signifies the utmost in personal pleasure as well as a tacit public recognition of his growing older. In effect, she tempts him to indulge a desire of which he knows his mother does not approve, thereby creating for him an incipient ethical dilemma. Her phone call to Mary at the beginning of the chapter has made it clear that the two women possess other familial tensions including personality differences, ways of handling finances and expenses, and ways of handling social situations. None of these, however, is insisted on by either woman, for both tacitly regard them as no more than casual incidents of ordinary familial stress. Nevertheless, it is clear that Hannah's general demeanor sharply contrasts with that of Rufus's immediate family.

By her polite attitude toward him, her briskly efficient shopping methods that please him, and her offer to buy him a cap, she inadvertently creates for him an aura of underlying and intensifying temptation. As a result, a dilemma unconsciously develops in the child's mind as to which sort of family life he should prefer. Should he opt for a life of duty, self-abnegation, and denial of purely emotional desires, or should he reach out for a life of simple aesthetic pleasures, freedom from boredom, and the surge of sudden surprise, delight, and excitement at the unexpected realization of a long-sought dream? That is, the threat to the child's idyllic vision of the family can come not only from within the immediate family but also from a radically different way of living provided by a member of the extended family. Rufus never has to face this challenge directly because of his father's death, his aunt's sensitive rationality, and his own temperament. Each in different ways allows him to be aware of the differences between pleasure and moral obligation without having to choose between them.

Between parts 1 (the living father) and 2 (the dead one), three editorially determined interludes occur.[9] In effect, they bridge the narrator's awareness of the elegiac potential inherent in the story and the child's growing familiarity with the realities of *family.* They also point up the sharp difference between actuality and sentiment inherent in those realities. At the same time, their being cast entirely in italics clearly associates them with the opening prelude of "Knoxville: 1915" and its point of view.

The first interlude reverts to the anonymous point of view of the introduction and its tone of reverie. It suggests the author is reflecting on his own personal experiences out of which his narrative is finally to be shaped and brought into being. At the outset, the voice is suspended in a virtually timeless realm of anonymous contemplation (the narrator is identified simply as "he"). Leaves, street lamps, and curtains create a congeries of silent elements standing against the diverse sounds of the human world (autos, a train engine, horses and buggies, creaking chairs, and voices). The scenic harmony creates its own kind of prelude to consciousness. By so doing, it associates the mood with the authorial sense of "*perfect peace*" (533; Agee's italics). In effect, this sense antedates his struggle to create a story that will accurately capture the personal feelings that existed prior to and that motivated the generating of the narrative.

The first phase of this interlude yields to an almost anonymous lyrical voice poetically invoking and interrogating the surrounding darkness, which is regarded as thoroughly gentle and virtually a love object. The darkness is felt to hold all the sensory and emotional things the voice has experienced and loves: children of his age, older ones, his father and mother, all of whom dispel fear and loneliness. The second phase also is cast in lyrical rhythms, but it echoes those of the 23rd Psalm:

> *I hear my father; I need never fear.*
> *I hear my mother; I shall never be lonely, or want for love.*
> *When I am hungry it is they who provide for me; when I am in dismay, it is they who fill me with comfort.* (533; Agee's italics)

This phase clearly invokes the image of a child requesting preternatural aid. And this in turn mirrors the elegiac poet's calling on his Muse for support and assistance in confronting the significance of death and loss. For Agee, like Milton, the Muse invoked is in Christian accents and the invocation is couched as a prayer to an amorphous phenomenon, Darkness. The prayer gradually modulates into an invocatory request that darkness come close to him. It becomes a tacit appeal that he be relieved of the responsibility of and for individual consciousness. He fugitively longs to be absorbed into an amorphous abandonment of personal identity. Such abandonment holds out an ideal of tranquility, a state devoid of the need for decisions and choices, and with that of seeming rejections and disclaimers.

Gradually the child's idealization of the idyllic notion of *family* comes to be set against the reality of actual family life. Similarly, the child's longing to abandon effort and choice is countered by his being launched into an exploratory dialogue with darkness, which now is clearly identified with death, nothingness, and the self. Darkness is no longer beneficent, no longer a freeing from responsibility. Now it implicitly reproaches the child's naïve initial conviction that darkness is totally supportive of him. He recoils from its revealing itself as nothingness, which appears as "*fanged and mortal*" (535; Agee's italics), an "*inconceivable chasm of invulnerable silence in which cata-*

clysms of galaxies rave mute as amber" (535; Agee's italics). Gradually, darkness increases its ominousness even while continuing to tempt the child to submit to the consequences of his prayer for suspension of personal responsibility:

> *Only a moment ago, I was your friend, or so you claimed; why this sudden loss of love? . . .*
> *Only be steadfast: for now, my dear, my darling, the moment comes when hunger and love will be forever satisfied.*
> *And darkness, smiling, leaned ever more intimately inward upon him, laid open the huge, ragged mouth—*
>
> Ahhhhh . . . !
>
> *Child, child, why do you betray me so?*
> *Come near. Come very near.*
>
> Ohhhhhh . . . ! (536; Agee's italics)

He faces the fact of his own inescapable mortality that lies hidden beneath the temptation of surcease from a struggle to achieve the impossible. In so doing, the child encounters the final stage of death's temptation: that he may actually not desire to escape his mortality but rather may wish to seek it out actively. In short, the transformation of temptation from an external overture to an internal desire is the most insidiously destructive form taken by the abandonment of personal effort to deny death. It is the trauma of this recognition that leads to the dual elegy facing him. Simultaneously, it makes the death of his father both an overpowering shock to Rufus and the source of his struggle to come to terms with the true nature of "family."

How traumatic for the child this experience is actually appears in two events. The first is the psychic split he experiences in which "*the child was torn into two creatures*" (536; Agee's italics). One of them cries out to his father, while the second segues from the anonymity and generality of "the child" into Rufus himself. His second scream fuses with the revelation that Rufus is merely an infant able to talk in his crib. With this, the author's autobiographical child narrator merges with his creation, the character Rufus whose point of view and reactions to the family tragedy are to dominate part 2.

These two events signal two further points: one narrative and the other thematic. Each involves one of the dual point-of-view voices, Rufus's and

Agee's. In the first case, the cry signals Rufus's return from sleep and a particularly bad dream or nightmare to the familiar world of nurturing support. This is identified with the voices dimly heard talking just as he fell asleep. The second point is that Agee too recognizes the need to continue to struggle with and against mortality. This struggle ultimately entails seeing that the idyllic idealized world of *family* when seen by the adult is but a dream like that experienced by Rufus. Though it too begins as a warm comforting place of supportive trust, it also turns into an entrapment in a dead end of passivity and tranquilized semiconsciousness ultimately indistinguishable from death and nothingness.

The remainder of the interludes sketches the archetypal or typological features of the elegiac struggle to recapture the child's ideal notion of *family.* First, there is the father's reassurance that the child's fear of the dark stems from a natural dislike of lonesomeness. His solicitude stems from his recognition that the attaining of one's full self depends on having a child with whom one can retrieve one's own earliest selfhood through the act of memory. Second is his consequent recognition that at the center of everyone's life is a lack or loss, which produces guilt, regret, and shame. All of these cohere into a rationale for the supportive feature of *family* life.

Complementing the father's role is that of the mother, which focuses upon the present and the conscious surface of life. Her pregnant condition suggests both the origin and growth of the *family* concept. Gain to the family of a new member is accompanied by a temporary personal loss of parental sexual intimacy. For his mother, the connection between this gain and loss can only be intimated to Rufus through the evasive term *surprise.* Thus, the full complexity of *family* as a concept lies beyond the child at this point.

Her pregnancy also gives rise to her casual, almost accidental misunderstanding of Jay's covert allusion to be a criticism of her housekeeping. This scene, thus, generates two things essential to the ideal concept of *family.* The first is the centrality of mutual sexual desire; the second is a gentle willingness to understand deeply another human being. At the same time, this scene introduces the fact that even the ideal family possesses gaps in understanding and lacks in sensitivity.

The mother's singing him to sleep brings him, strikingly enough, his first awareness of apprehension and loss of security. On the one hand, her singing gives him pleasure both in her company and the sound of the songs. On the other hand, the songs contain phrases that he doesn't understand, leading him to think that knowing their meaning will only increase his fear. Indeed, it is the singing of both parents together, despite their different ways of doing so, that produces for Rufus a sense of completeness and finality in the family setting which is the prelude to a dreamless sleep.

In the third interlude, Rufus encounters full-scale change and with it some additional qualities involved with *family.* His mother's pregnancy dominates the family world, but to him it is a mystery, which leaves him discomfited and uneasy. Fissures in family harmony appear both externally and internally. The former occurs with his Uncle Andrew's angry and short-tempered response to his uninformed query having to do with changes in his mother's appearance. Internal fissures are dramatically revealed in the different attitudes taken by the father and mother to direct disclosure of the expected birth. These are developed further with the arrival of Victoria, a black servant present at Mary's earlier pregnancy. Anger, mystery or secrets, and the intrusion of societal attitudes involving race and human relations all intrude into Rufus's conscious world. They, however, produce unsettlement, puzzlement, and apprehension rather than any clearly discerned meaning. These are elements not ordinarily associated by him with *family.* They suggest implicitly that the ideal *family* is a concept constructed by selectively disregarding the full range of human reactions and emotions and the world or society at large.

Part 2 (chapters 8 through 13) commences the slow but inexorable involvement of Rufus's family in the death of his father, Jay. This death initiates the family's diverse and multifaceted effort to deal with the tragic consequences of the accident. In doing so, it presents a societal form of the elegiac in which varied conventional responses to sudden death vie to cope with the event and with its impact on others, notably Mary, the wife. Disbelief, psychological denial and other avoidance mechanisms, sorrow, differing views of life from the tragic to the stoical to the sentimental, from the piously religious to the dogmatically rationalistic, all endeavor to frame answers to human mortality. In a low-keyed, basically realistic manner, these serve further to undermine the lyric interludes, which make up Rufus's idealized image of *family.* Gone now is an unblemished harmony of nurture, support, and protection. Instead, there is a dissonance of dissent, stereotypical utterance, misplaced sentiments, and ineffectual efforts to decide in a single-minded fashion what Mary, the pivotal figure, should feel, think, and do.

Agee structures this part not as a bitter, ironic attack on the family but as a quietly realistic portrait of how people do in fact respond in a crisis. Chapters 10 and 11 achieve his characteristic tableau effect by creating successive dramatic scenes between limited numbers of characters (two or three at most). Each scene focuses on a topic of central importance to the individual characters. The final effect is one of geological strata gradually accumulating to form a mélange of feelings, thoughts, and wishes. These tableaux create a realistic depth of experience by exploring the minds of the principal characters and by concentrating on the mundane, homely details of everyday life. In this way, the tragedy of Jay's death achieves a detached, slow-motion effect.[10] Coupled with it are the fugitive motions of memory recalling past scenes that stand in vivid relief against the static uncertainties of the present.

This societal effort to create an elegiac temper in the face of death is set against the personal elegy of Rufus's gradual acceptance of loss as he steadily matures following his father's death. With this maturation, he pays his necessary farewell to the idyllic view of *family.* He does not, however, simply dismiss it out of hand. Instead, it is taken from him by time, the reactions of others, and historical circumstances. In its place, as part 3 reveals, there emerges an elegiac burden created by the loss of the ideal family. This somber acknowledgment is borne largely unwittingly by Rufus as he fitfully disengages himself from his idyllic childhood view of his place in the family and, even more importantly, in the world.

Between the societal elegiac response of part 2 and the personal one of part 3 are three more editorial interludes. These, however, focus not, as did the earlier ones, on the idealized *family.* Instead, they revolve around Rufus's memories of actual historical experiences in which he encounters both challenges to and unexpected support of his personal identity. They consist largely of contacts with the external world both within and outside of the family. The first of these consists of Rufus as a preschool child watching others go to school and seeing them as "*a whole world*" (639; Agee's italics). His view reflects his deep, passionate desire for sharing in a communal unity. The threat of the loss of such a world triggers or tempers his elegiac feelings whenever it occurs or is anticipated as likely to occur.

The diverse but characteristic responses of the schoolchildren introduce him to the pleasures, confusions, and sadness of the social world at large. Thus, he is puzzled, like the very young Stephen Dedalus, at their responses to his name and his saying it.[11] What Agee underlines here is the puzzlement of the honest, direct individual in a dishonest, indirect world, of the innocent child among pseudo-adults. His overall reaction is most fully captured in the authorial observation: "*The more alone he felt, the more he wanted to feel that he was not alone, but one of them*" (643; Agee's italics). In embryonic form, this sentiment contains the core of the elegiac temper. It is compounded of a sense of loss generated by total isolation and a longing for a transformation of a painful situation into a supportive one.

Similarly, he finds himself confused and puzzled by the racially loaded questions that they ask him in rhymed riddle form. These point up a child's necessarily limited knowledge and the impact of ignorance on him. In a threatening and disturbing manner, such questions intensify the shaping of his elegiac temper. At the same time, they add to it the irony inherent in the fact that the true ignorance is not so much his as it is the other children's. The confusion of ignorance and innocence is created by them and suffered or endured by him.

As this interlude unfolds, it gradually becomes clear that life is seen to be a game played by a group that first identifies a fool and then makes him a scapegoat. That Rufus is elected to play the fool is clear both to the other children and to him. His acceptance of this role recalls his easy delight in and identification with Charlie Chaplin during the novel's opening. The other children operate as a pseudo–lynch mob aiming at satirico-comic rather than tragic results, while he, like Charlie, serves as a helpless because unwitting victim. Verbal teasing constitutes the first phase of this childish ritual. The second stage of his transformation into a fool is dramatic in that he sings and dances to a childish tune, one that he likes immensely. Gradually, the children cease to make direct fun of him; this, however, leads him to have an increased suspicion of their motives and so to be more reluctant to perform. To keep the game going, the children now have to resort to a third stage—that of bribery—to get him to continue to play the fool. At length, the older boys finally become "*obscurely ashamed, as well as bored*" (649; Agee's italics) by their behavior. At some level, they recognize implicitly the links between their game and that of the more violent adult version. Because they are aware that such violence lies morally beyond them, they cease their game.

Rufus's gullibility, desire for acceptance and recognition, and innocence are those of early childhood and the process of shedding them is the lifelong struggle for maturity. At the same time, it entails the individual's initial encounter with change and loss of security. In so doing, it lays the ground for the formation of the elegiac temper with its grieving for an earlier form of existence in which all was well, opponents did not exist, and opposing attitudes did not appear. Serenity and security become either precarious elements of the present or passionately longed for features of the past and memory. Antagonisms and intellectual and ethical puzzles replace them. Threats to personal identity and the arousal of apprehension, fear, and competing points of view become the staple of existence.

Yet as the second scene of the interlude makes clear, the movement toward maturity has its own pleasures and compensations. These balance its harshly disturbing introduction of insecurity, conflict, and the persistent need for decision making. Here Rufus is older, is in fact the oldest child, who is permitted to stay up with the adults prior to a family trip to visit his great-great-grandmother. Now, however, the idealized world of *family* is already part of the past of early childhood. Tensions and ineptitudes merge with nurturing and protection. Thus, his mother expresses a persistent concern—almost a form of quiet nagging—over the speed of his father's driving. In turn, Ralph exhibits a confused uncertainty about directions and the difficulty of finding their way. Together, they introduce uncertainty and false disclaimers of confidence into the family conversation. All of this serves as a prelude to a kind of pre-elegiac visit as family members engage in a conventional bemoaning of the hundred-year-old lady's physical and mental lapses. This iteration of changes and losses is modulated from the critical to the reflectively elegiac by virtue of his mother Mary's historical perspective, which explicitly links the old woman with the nation.

In this scene, Rufus focuses largely on time as a factor in the maturing into an elegiac temper. He contemplates a series of temporally conditioned factors: the old woman as a historical fact; the ancestral family home—never before visited by him—located in a remote, barely accessible mountain area; his mother's temporal equations linking herself, the grandmother, and the United States in a way that foregrounds the issue of time; and finally, his meeting his oldest living relative in person. Both time and the old woman are difficult to grasp and to respond to because of their uniqueness and unfamiliarity.

The boy Rufus experiences the impact of very old age in contrasting ways. First, he senses "*the sadness of time dwelt in the blue-breathing, oily center, lost and alone and far, deeper than the deepest well*" (660; Agee's italics) as he stands close to her preparing to kiss her at his father's behest. This sense of fear, strangeness, and infinite remoteness is quickly followed by the delight of a suddenly discovered love aroused by her personal and pleased response to him. With this, he feels, perhaps for the first time, both comfort derived from the awareness of time's immensity and awe at its inherent sorrows.

The final scene in this interlude carries a quite different tone though it continues the general motif of Rufus's gradual indoctrination or education in the ways of the world. It focuses on the aesthetics of nature as a counterpoise to familial humor and jokes, the complexity of language, the ethics of trust, and the need for sophistication (or suspicion) in dealing with all of them. The view from the train of the Great Smoky Mountains of Tennessee arouses conventional expressions of admiration and awe from Rufus's parents. These are anticlimactically undercut by his quasi-relative Aunt Kate's phlegmatic and unimpressed response and by his sister's "*very heavy and earnest*" (663; Agee's italics) aping of her parents' attitude. The aesthetic experience is essentially diminished in import by the individual responses. Prominent here is the failure of Catherine to laugh off the joking of the others at her overly solemn attention to the mountains.

Both in this and in the dinner table joke played on Rufus by Kate's husband the concern is with being able to make the correct or appropriate social response to an unfamiliar social situation. Here Rufus experiences a twofold reaction. First, he has the feeling of being in on a joke or funny situation and second, of having the joke played on oneself. Coupled with this is the quite different attitude of his mother to the two jokes: she is the one who chides Catherine for not taking it appropriately and then later defends Rufus furiously and excessively against Ted's good-humored baiting of Rufus.[12] Sharing the joke on someone else makes Rufus feel part of the family group, while having a joke played on him predictably isolates and humiliates him.

Ironically enough, Agee is clearly counterpointing the mother's two reactions as well as the differences in the two parents' reactions to the targets of the two jokes. The mother's reactions successively urge her two children in opposite directions. She encourages her daughter to greater maturity by expanding the child's sense of the various uses of language. In contrast, she seeks her son to remain innocent and childlike by continuing to be ignorant of the range of words available to those who are mature. Similarly, the father's response to Catherine's beginning to pout is quietly sympathetic whereas the mother's is openly critical and almost dismissive. Later, the father attempts to qualify the mother's outburst in defense of her son and to share, at least marginally, Ted's suggestion that Rufus needs "to learn what to believe and what not to" (665).

These simple incidents capture in an understated way the child's dramatic transition from innocence to experience. This is embodied principally in changes in the two parents' roles. At first, the mother is dominant in the family through her nurturing role. Later, this shifts to the father's assumption of control. He does so via his willingness (however reluctant and uncertain) to expose his son to the ways of the world. In particular, these ways are exhibited through the diverse uses to which language can be put. Such shifts in personal alignment signal a kind of intellectual replacement of the idealized and idyllic *family* by the actual one found in the real world of persons who live and die. This also completes the novel's shaping of an elegiac temper to the loss of a child's perspective on his first and basic world, that of the family.

Part 3 (chapters 14–20) details the convergence of Rufus's incipient and unconscious elegiac attitude to life with the sudden, accidental death of his father. His experiences following the latter reveal the vast difference between actual events (as in part 2) and verbal conventions such as those of the elegy (as in the prelude and several of the interludes). This contrast is dramatically captured in chapter 14 when his mother attempts to tell him of his father's death in a circuitous conventional fashion thought appropriate with children: "He isn't going to come home ever any more. He's—gone away to heaven and he isn't ever coming home again. . . . God let him go to sleep and took him straight away with Him to heaven" (668). To her circumlocutory efforts to provide sympathy and support for an event she anticipates they will have difficulty understanding, Rufus answers with a bluntly direct question which verbally equals the sudden immediacy of the accident itself: "Is Daddy *dead*?" (668; Agee's italics).

The balance of part 3 is devoted to Rufus's experiencing the various ways in which society and the real family attempt to memorialize and so to cope with the father's death. These ways make use of social conventions intended to signal to the world at large the advent of death: the children's being held out of school; the pre-funeral arrangements complete with the meeting with an austerely severe Roman Catholic priest from another city; the final public viewing of the body; the funeral; and the post-funeral reception. Here Agee repeatedly sets the formalities inherent in these rituals against the realistic and unpredictable actions and comments of those involved, particularly the children. The effect is to undercut the solemnities of the religious conventions with the naturalness and ordinariness of the individual human reactions. Actually, the two responses also correspond roughly to the ways in which the traditional elegy relates to the modern elegiac temper.

Throughout, Rufus and his sister respond as children both to the accident and the adults' rather clumsy efforts to explain it and to prescribe the ways in which they should behave. The result is a mélange of comic, pathetic, posturing, argumentative, and puzzled scenes that capture the full range of their efforts both to behave appropriately and to struggle against actions and expectations beyond their comprehension. The gulf between the two is seen in chapter 15 when their aunt Hannah endeavors to explain their father's accident fully. While she stresses the theological concept of God's will as the determining factor in the accident, Catherine serio-comically misunderstands the term *accident.* Instead of an event of tragic significance, she thinks the word indicates that her father had a bowel movement in his pants, which is her household, familial sense of the term.

The same sort of polarization of the tragic and comic, the solemn and the grotesque is found in chapter 16 and Rufus's responses to being held out of school. He feels it is both an honor and a privilege to be exempt from such a daily duty. Nevertheless, he also regrets his absence from the spotlight of the imagined attention he would receive from his teacher and classmates. Later, after vigorously discussing the death with other children on their way to school, he ruminates on their remembered comments, which brutally present a more horrific and catastrophic perspective on his father's death.

On the one hand, he feels ironically that his parading of the fact of his father's death is more a celebration of his importance as a living experiencer of death than a remembrance of the deceased: "I tell them he is dead and they look up to me, they don't tease me" (691). On the other hand, he regrets this behavior and wishes to be forgiven by his father's soul. Taken together, these two attitudes mirror the elegy's traditional pattern. Thus, the latter celebrates regret and loss for something valuable in the extreme, while the former reflects the conventional elegy's aspiration to be accorded special recognition by its act of memory. If the former is the subtext, then the latter clearly contains the text of the child's regret and efforts to redeem both him and the event upon which he is focused. It is with Rufus's uncertain effort to register his sense of loss that his slowly emerging elegiac temper appears, admittedly somewhat sentimentally, to his consciousness:

> He still looked at the chair. With a sense of deep stealth and secrecy he finally went over and stood beside it. After a few moments, and after listening most intently, to be sure that nobody was near, he smelled of the chair, its deeply hollowed seat, the arms, the back. There was only a cold smell of tobacco and, high along the back, a faint smell of hair. He thought of the ash tray on its weighted strap on the arm; it was empty. He ran his finger inside it; there was only a dim smudge of ash. There was nothing like enough to keep in his pocket or wrap up in a paper. He looked at his finger for a moment and licked it; his tongue tasted of darkness. (692)

Rufus's personal effort at the elegiac gesture is made without words, an act that in itself counters the traditional elegy's celebration of its subject. It functions as a simple self-correction of his ordinary feelings about his father and his limited knowledge of the death and its significance. As such, it contrasts sharply with Father Jackson's socially formal manner, austere and dismissive behavior, and the argumentative tone of voice he uses with Rufus's mother. The certitude of the religious ideologue contrasts negatively with the hesitant but genuine efforts of Rufus to create an elegiac memorial with and for his father. Sensory recollection of his father's aromas, emptiness, nothingness, and darkness graphically constitutes the static elements of his silent effort at the elegiac.

Balancing his personal but unuttered elegy is the undertaker's expressed recollections of Jay as "one of the finest men that ever lived" (710). Walter Starr's remark captures the elegy's formal praising of the subject but in such a conventional, prosaic fashion that its effectiveness is persuasive with the child. In a sense, it brings down to a more ordinary level the traditional nature of the elegy in its "let us now praise famous men" mode. Nevertheless, his heartfelt compassion for the children and the situation contrasts admirably with the priest's self-satisfied, unctuous formality of manner and rigidity of doctrine.

Essentially, these two guardians and custodians of death represent polar opposites to life. The priest is the defender of religious faith, a professional whose logic is indifferent to personal feelings and desires. In contrast, the undertaker is the proponent of secular humanity, a businessman whose sentimental feelings are his own and who espouses them out of charity for the children. This polarity tends to balance the religious-stoical split between Mary and her father. It suggests that Mary's devout belief structure requires modification fully as much as does her father's dogmatically held philosophical stoicism. Both lack a truly viable way of viewing the world. To achieve such a view is what confronts Rufus in part 3. The uncertainty of his having attained it is suggested at the end of the novel where Rufus joins his uncle Andrew for a walk filled with yet new puzzles for the child.

As they start out, Rufus expects to learn something, to be told something, and hazards guesses appropriate to his age. He anticipates that it is something that he has done wrong or that it is about the funeral itself. His concern over local and specific issues, of course, is appropriate to his age. But Agee wants also to show that Rufus's apprehensions are ultimately directed to larger issues, which will confront him for the balance of his life. In starting to probe these issues, Rufus is introduced to them by a family member who has never been part of the nurturing ideal of *family.* Andrew is something of a stranger to him as compared, for example, to his Aunt Hannah. His willingness to differ with his sister Mary's religious devotion puts him squarely with the realistic view of *family.* That is, families are likely to be congeries of distinct individuals with markedly differing attitudes. These are prone to generate tensions and outright conflicts as well as the inability to provide unequivocal support for one another. In short, to Rufus, Andrew is an outsider, a representative of society rather than *family,* as they commence their walk.

What brings them somewhat together is not so much mutual support as mutual bafflement by the funeral and the issues it generates. Finally, Andrew shares with Rufus two incidents that disturb him considerably. The first is the landing of a butterfly on Jay's coffin just above his heart, its fluttering with life all the way into the grave itself, and then flying up into the sky. The second is the priest's refusal to perform the entire burial service because Jay was never baptized. Andrew confesses that for him the butterfly incident is as close to a miracle as a nonbeliever like himself can come. Rufus is puzzled by his uncle's remarks—for instance, he doesn't comprehend the concept of miracles—but he is pleased because he feels it redounds well to his father whom he has been envisaging as lying in a coffin: "It would always be dark there. Dark as the inside of a cow" (735). This barely comprehended incident relieves Rufus's sense of loss without removing his awareness of it. Strikingly enough, this is essentially what in verbal form the traditional elegy seeks to do: fuse remembrance with solace.

Set against this elegiac attitude of grief relieved, the mourner's self restored, and the death accepted is Andrew's violent, angry, satiric criticism of the priest's action at the burial. Cast in the sardonic tone of the unbeliever, Andrew's remarks produce a final confusion in Rufus's mind, which balances his sense of peace achieved by the butterfly incident:

> Everything had seemed so nearly all right, up to a minute ago, and now it was changed and confused. It was still all right, everything which had been, still was, he did not see how it could stop being, yet it was hard to remember it clearly and to remember how he had felt and why it had seem all right. (738)

Andrew's two remarks confuse Rufus as to right and wrong, his own feelings and their appropriateness, and Andrew's relation to his own family and its religious affiliations. Rufus sees these issues only in terms of love and hate. So he cannot determine how the various feelings and attitudes fit together or how he himself stands in relation to Andrew and the family. Here he confronts the struggle between his ideal and real families. The former exudes an aura of total harmony and support, while the latter is marked by disagreements between father and daughter, brother and sister, brother and brother, and even father and mother. In effect, Andrew has explicitly created for Rufus a moral dilemma with regard to death, religion, family, love, and hate. This is one he, like his author, will face for the rest of his life as he struggles toward maturity and the full understanding of the elegiac temper.

2

FAILURE AS A LOSS

John Updike's *The Centaur*

Though published only five years apart and marked by a number of shared aspects, *A Death in the Family* and John Updike's *The Centaur* (1963) nevertheless have quite different approaches to the elegiac temper and the nature of the family. The former deals with the actuality of death in the family and concludes with a sober acceptance of the inevitability of loss as an inherent factor in life. The latter, on the other hand, considers familial death as a seriocomic possibility and ends with the celebration of story as a timeless, immortal function of the human mind.[1] The one confronts deprivation while the other resolves loss through the endless possibilities of narrating it. In so doing, they draw on contrasting phases (confrontation and resolution) of the traditional elegy while enacting radically different formulations of each.

Both too possess a realistic substrate, but there the resemblance ends.[2] Agee's novel dissects a child's notion of the family as ideal while casting it as recollections existing only in the individual person's memory. In contrast, Updike sees the family throughout as a complex and tangled set of personal relationships in which from the outset discontent and dissatisfaction play as large a role as do nurturing and support.[3] He rescues his characters from the fact of mortality through postulating their having a mythic dimension that allows narrative patterns to be repeated endlessly in different guises. This multiple patterning extends beyond the memory of any one character.[4]

Rufus begins, as we have seen, with an idealized view of the family appropriate to his age. Peter Caldwell, on the other hand, starts out with a critical, disenchanted view of his family, particularly his father.[5] As the two narratives unfold, they move, in effect, in opposite directions. Rufus gradually discovers that the world he is ultimately to live in is one of tension and conflict rather than nurturing harmony and that his family, like all others, is materially conditioned by it. For him, life becomes essentially a coming to terms with reality and historical experience. Peter, in contrast, is enmeshed in daily tensions largely revolving around an endemic love-hate relationship with his father.[6] From it, he aspires to art as an ideal, transcendent release and counterweight to the strains enacted by lived history.[7] Only as an adult looking back at his father's life does he find a perspective that enables him to understand and, at least to some degree, accept failure (both his and his father's) as a central part of human existence.[8] Failure becomes a kind of key to personal success, which is seen as the willingness to sacrifice one's own ambitions and ultimate desires. For Peter, life is essentially a struggle to achieve freedom from history without accepting the limitations of a purely aesthetic perspective on reality. He accepts these limitations when he recognizes his mythic role in the narrative nature of existence, as with his identification with Prometheus in chapter 6.

This contrast in character development and narrative advancement also reflects the two authors' differing senses of their craft and their historical relationship to modernism's changing attitudes. Agee's struggle, ultimately unresolved, is to settle the differences between his own authorial desires and Rufus's desire for identity and selfhood. It captures in many ways the problem of early modernism as enunciated in Joyce's *A Portrait of the Artist as a Young Man.* In this form of modernism, the struggle to define the self, its relation to history and art, and the reliance on the epiphanic moment of quasi-transcendent awareness dominate its concerns. All lead to works whose open-endedness reflects a search for an insight that will "explain" life. The explanation sought by both Joyce and Agee seeks to justify the deep elegiac emotion occasioned by the loss of the simple sensuous awareness of childhood. It is through this search itself that the protagonist comes to recognize that loss is a constant of life. As a result, its multiple natures prevent its restriction to a single meaning. Instead the persistent presence of loss compels the mind and imagination to grapple with its brute actuality. For Updike, the authorial contest with his material is less an ongoing personal, psychological one. Instead, it is a theological or philosophical one in which the intellectual hierarchy and the scope of reality is determined. What is required, Updike implies, is the tough-mindedness to determine the legitimate boundaries to the actions of the human mind and the discipline to accept these boundaries as actual. For him, the tenets of modernism are not so much determinedly aspiring as quietly reflective of the consequences of their successor, postmodernism. He writes, in *The Centaur* at least, under the shadow of self-reflexivity, fiction making, and internal contradiction.

Set against these forces, Updike establishes myth as the original form of narrative and storytelling as an ineluctable power and requirement of the human mind. A storyteller is essentially engaged in rendering the conceivability of the inconceivable. *The Centaur* addresses this task directly in its first two chapters by a mixture of ironic comedy and dispassionate satire.[9] It is no accident, however, that the second chapter concludes with Peter's incipiently elegiac reflection about his father: "for the first time his death seemed, even at its immense stellar remove of impossibility, a grave and dreadful threat" (93). For it is with the third chapter that the elegiac temper of the novel is first invoked. This is established by the narrative shift from George Caldwell and the contemporary world to Chiron and the classical realm of Olympus.

Chiron's world contrasts with that of George in several ways: in terms of setting (forest versus urban); of aesthetics (natural beauty versus technological squalor); and psychological tone (harmonious reverence and tranquil relationships versus a multitude of tensions and apprehensions). Shaping each of these is the immense temporal gap between the two worlds. It is so huge as to lie virtually beyond the mind's ordinary ability to grasp or entertain. Updike's use of classical myth invokes a paradise existing in a past so distant that it arouses a nostalgic longing for a kind of existence irrevocably lost in the deepest recesses of time.[10] This contemplation of the immensity of time assumes that Chiron's ancient world actually existed historically in the manner described. Yet it is in the revelatory questioning of this assumption that Updike welds together myth and narrative art as a single nature. For, once Chiron's experiences are seen to be questionable as historical or pre-historical events, the resemblance between them and those associated with George Caldwell is altered dramatically. They are seen to be less analogous entities differentiated largely by the concept of time. Instead, they become homologous actions, two essentially distinct instances of narration or storytelling performed by a single author at the same historical moment. In short, the focus becomes not history as much as fiction, not actuality but invention. As a result, mimesis stands forth as but one way of telling a story.

Chapter 3 provides a full-scale example of a radically different manner of storytelling. Thus, it creates a twentieth-century redaction of the opening scene of pastoral elegy:

> Chiron hurried, a little late, down the corridors of tamarisk, yew, bay, and kermes oak. Beneath the cedars and silver firs, whose hushed heads were

> shadows permeated with Olympian blue, a vigorous underwood of arbutus, wild pear, cornel, box, and andrachne filled with scents of flower and sap and new twig the middle air of the forest. (93)

Here the pastoral dimension of the scene achieves its elegiac quality indirectly, through the perception of nature's sympathy with Chiron's role of teacher.[11] This affords an implicit contrast with George's pedagogical relationship with his milieu and students in chapter 1. The harmony between teacher and subject, teacher and students evokes a world dominated by simplicity, desire for knowledge, and devoutness. As such, it creates a disjunction in the contemporary consciousness between then and now, ideal and real that is dominated by a conviction of irretrievable loss.

What has been lost extends, however, far beyond the academic fixation on a commitment to learning. At the close of the chapter, Chiron's lecture on "'the Genesis of All Things'" sets up a polarity between Eros and Death. The former "'set the universe in motion'" and made "'the world as harmonious as a beehive'" (99), producing a kind of Golden Age. The rule of Uranus that follows it presages the diminution of Zeus and the other Olympians, the disruption of world harmony, and the dwindling of the pleasures of living. It is the loss of love and the centrality bestowed on death as ultimate that drive Updike's narrative vision and the consciousness of both father and son, George and Peter Caldwell.[12]

George's virtual obsession with his own mortality arouses his wife's exasperated irony, his son's apprehensive worry, and the reader's comic awareness.[13] Taken together, these make up a satiric view of a foreshortened elegiac temper itself. From this standpoint, the seriousness of the possibility of George's death is undercut by the absurdity of its actual likelihood. The result by implication is a balanced perspective on the elegy as a form. Its impulse to key on the catastrophic is restrained by the mirth at George's mock-egotism and his proneness to exaggerate the traumatic nature of his immediate future. In short, mortality is seen as a serious topic warranting concern but not as something demanding daily focus. To treat it obsessively, as George does, is to stultify one of the chief features of the elegiac—its concern with the uniqueness of the fact of death—and to transform mortality into a mordantly comic stalking-horse.

In contrast, then there are Peter's efforts as an adult to understand his father. His struggle to capture his father's true nature—the hero as ordinary man—requires him to acquire a genuine elegiac temper. This occurs most clearly in chapter 8, which bi-focally relates several of Peter's adult musings. First, he recalls his habit of visiting the local museum with his mother when he was a child. Then he reflects about the relationship between himself as an adult and his black mistress. Finally, he recalls a far earlier childhood memory of his father and himself taking refuge in the Hummel's house during a fierce snowstorm.

Essentially what the museum experience gives him is a feeling of dread for "the quantity of death" (267) memorialized by the museum. This feeling, however, is also balanced by an aesthetic sense of "seizing something and holding it fast" (267), of somehow feeling that time, change, and mortality can be suspended. When he turns to his present existence, he somewhat self-consciously declares his love for his mistress while admitting that they are irrevocably to be denied complete fulfillment. Ultimately, he is driven to place his adult life against that of his father and to ask "*Was it for this that my father gave up his life?*" (270; italics in original). However much he claims to value his life as an artist, a free spirit, and a lover, its ultimate significance can only be questioned when it is compared to his father's remembered presence. What he recalls most vividly about his father is his laughter, mourning, and ability to puzzle:

> I miss only . . . the sudden white laughter that like heat lightning bursts in an atmosphere where souls are trying to serve the impossible. My father for all his mourning moved in the atmosphere of such laughter. He would have puzzled you. He puzzled me. (269)

The baffling nature of the departed parent and his commingling of joy and sorrow continue to haunt the son increasingly as his own aging impels him to self-assessment. In measuring himself against his father, Peter implicitly acknowledges that it is the father, not he, who is the hero.

The seed of this recognition is planted in his mind as a child after he and his father have passed the night in Vera Hummel's guest bedroom. Waking in the morning, he finds himself alone and his father gone. Quickly, he is drawn into an adolescent fantasy in which miraculously he has an improved, normal standard of living and Vera Hummel is his wife. Permeating this world, so dramatically different from his ordinary world, are two contradictory feelings. The first is that his family's customary manner of living is due to the fact that his father "had never rid himself of the idea that he might soon be moving on" (273). And the second is that his father's absence resonates with Peter's concerns over George's health. He immediately becomes apprehensive that the absence is permanent rather than temporary, and that this means a fundamental loss for him, which he greets with horror. Thus, the fact that his current life with all its embarrassments is his father's fault is balanced by the recognition that without him he is helpless, not yet an adult able to cope on his own.

Peter's initial response to this duality of feeling is to retreat further into his romantically unreal fantasy of love and Vera Hummel. From it, he is ejected by the sudden arrival of his father, whose absurd appearance comically and instantly dispels Peter's adolescent dream of romance: "My father looked in his bullet-head cap and snow-drenched overcoat like a man just shot from cannon" (278). It is replaced by the child's relief at being released from the unbearable prospect of the loss of a parent. In a brief moment, Peter is transformed back into his callow, insecure, high school self: "'Where have you *been*?' I asked. My voice ignobly stumbled on a threat of tears" (278; italics in original). George appears as a "testimony of adventure," a figure on whom "Mrs. Hummel's attention had shifted" (278) completely. Reluctantly, Peter is driven to see his father's trip around town, his possession of all the news about the storm, his typical humorous response to life, and his self-deprecation as the embodiment of his father's energy, curiosity, and admiration of others. In short, he sees the heroic dimension possessed by the ordinary man who through self-sacrifice persists in living. With this, he accepts the difference between himself and his father, resumes his role as son and child, and abandons his romantic fantasy. Thus, he declines to emulate his father in kissing Vera good-bye. He is an aspirant to the heroic, Promethean dimension of his nature. His father, on the other hand, has already become Chiron through his pedagogical commitment, his acceptance of his role as solicitous father, and his willingness to sacrifice his own ambitions and aspirations for the welfare of others.

As a result of this action, the adult Peter will ultimately recognize that life is not a matter of choosing between his and his father's attitudes but of perceiving the symmetry of their roles. He comes to see both to be appropriate and justifiable over the course of a person's life. Thus, the chapter ends with Peter making two dramatic changes. He renounces his preconceived personal point of view about the external world, other human beings, and himself. And simultaneously, he accepts the fact that knowledge and learning are not imposed by but received from experience:

> it came upon me that I must go to Nature disarmed of perspective and stretch myself like a large transparent canvas upon her in the hope that, my submission being perfect, the imprint of a beautiful and useful truth would be taken. (293)

The truth to which Peter aspires is found in chapter 9, which reverts to Chiron's ancient pastoral world interfused with elements of George's contemporary one. Chiron-George finds that his humorous way of coping with his experiences generates a joy that lies at the very core of life and is its basic value. Consequently, his often-expressed conviction of his enslavement to forces stronger than himself and his sense of failure evaporate. Gone is his sense of living a straitened and severely conditioned existence. It yields to the centaur's realization that "in giving his life to others he entered a total freedom" (296). With this, the centaur and the man, the ancient and the contemporary, are able to face the maw of death. Each recognizes that ultimately he will have to enter and pass through it, and to accept fully and forever the fact of mortality. As the Greek passage of the conclusion makes clear, the relationship of father and son is finally defined on both mythic and mimetic levels. The acceptance of death by the father figure reveals the parent-child relationship to be successive rather than competitive, as post-Oedipal rather than Oedipal. Similarly, when the son comprehends his own mortality, the father is released from his seemingly eternal role as teacher, mentor, guide, and ruler and so dies but only *as a father,* as a function, not as a distinct and separate human being.

3
GENERATIONAL CRITIQUES
Virginia Woolf's *The Years* and William Faulkner's *Sartoris*

Agee and Updike privilege, as we have seen, the elegiac form and the family as subject. Virginia Woolf in *The Years* (1937) brings both under critical scrutiny as part of her questioning of the direction and future of the twentieth century. She implicitly yet drastically revises the concept of the elegy itself while bringing the elegiac temper into a mainstream position among modern ways of viewing the world and accepting its realities.[1] The result is a subtle extension of the innovative and experimental thrust of her fiction. She achieves this while simultaneously appearing to return to Georgian, Edwardian, and even Victorian methods of responding to the family as a fictional subject and thematic focus.[2] In effect, her ultimate modernist innovation is to eschew its techniques while maintaining its perspective and attitudes.[3]

Woolf's effort to integrate the elegiac temper into an overall worldview revolves around the passage of time through both family and society. As the novel's title indicates, it is for her the constituent element in life.[4] The very opening of the novel suggests this:

> Slowly wheeling, like the rays of a searchlight, the days, the weeks, the years passed one another across the sky. (2)

Various units of time serially in motion suggest the inexorability they possess for the dispassionate observer. Simultaneously, as individual units they function as sudden, sharp, brief moments of light illuminating the natural dark of the world. They confer no absolute or perennial truth; instead, they momentarily show but a ceaselessly new, or fresh, or different aspect of the human condition.[5] The implication is that human history is neither a factual "given" nor purely an invention.[6] Rather, it consists of an interrelation between the physical scene, the external world of public society, and the one who examines it reflectively with the aid of whatever light can be brought to bear.[7] Through multiple and varied glimpses of what can be seen, the thoughtful individual may draw some inferences that can shape a limited but genuine sense of the nature of reality and the world in which he lives.

A number of these perceptions bear on the family as a social unit. They, however, do not even entertain, as Agee does, the possibility of the family being an ideal. Nor do they focus, as Updike does, on either a parent or sibling making extended efforts to understand others. For Woolf, the family is not primarily an integral social unit bonded by similar traits, interests, and desires. Instead she sees it as a group of individuals linked basically by the accident of biology and sustained by social custom. Of the three families figuring in *The Years*—the Pargiters, the Malones, and the Digbys—none of them, despite being blood-related, share similar emphases of outlook, interest, or socioeconomic status. What enables them to interrelate socially are the customs of individual and group politeness. Beyond this, they exist almost as existential monads, certainly as individuals locked in their own natures. They are unable to communicate with or to understand others in any essential or intimate fashion.[8]

The starkness of Woolf's view of social reality is muted both by her attitude toward it and by her fictional techniques. The inability to understand others fully is, for her, not so much a failing of human beings as a metaphysical condition inhering in the human condition itself.[9] Consequently, it generates neither a critical spirit leading to irony and satire nor a regretful sense of failure entailing a tragic or pathos-ridden response.[10] Instead, it is merely an inescapable fact about human beings and as such is to be simply endured rather than publicly mourned or lamented.

Any inclination to mount such lamentation is thwarted by Woolf's episodic technique, which provides glimpses rather than detailed explorations of scenes and interpersonal interactions. It functions much like the searchlight of time. For a moment, it brings into view a limited aspect or aspects of the concrete reality of an individual and then passes on to another aspect of another individual.

As a result, the traditional priority given to character in the novel is significantly altered in *The Years*. It shifts away from the concreteness of individual character to the greater abstractness of the group entity, the family. This is not to say that the individuals in the novel do not matter or are not important, for they are assuredly central to its themes. Instead they do not generate foci central to the series of actions presented. This concentration on the family as a character is the source of much of Woolf's innovative effort in the novel and is what makes *The Years* a different kind of experiment from her immediately preceding novels. It is a subdued rather than an attention-calling experiment. As such, it almost deliberately courts the risk of losing the interest of its readers.

One sees this in virtually the very first scene of the novel, where the Pargiter family gathers for tea and to await their father, the old colonel, Abel. The domestic scene involving the various children is marked by a quiet amiability and a mild pretentiousness on the part of the older sisters who strive to emulate their invalid mother's adult manner. None of the characters are developed sufficiently for them to be established as central to the story. Instead the thematic focus of the scene is upon their individual interests and concerns. These are set against Abel's rough but false patriarchal jocularity and his wife's suddenly worsening physical condition. In this way, the conventional Victorian scene celebrating the family and the pleasures of domesticity is subtly suggested. At the same time, it is ironically undercut through being preceded by the disclosure of Abel's inept foray into infidelity with his mistress, Mira.[11] The erosion of the conventionally ideal scene is strengthened even further when Delia goes to sit with her seriously ill mother. There, surprisingly enough, the daughter "longed for her to die," seeing her mother "as an obstacle, a prevention, an impediment to all life" (22). She is incapable of feeling affection or pity, opting instead for a political fantasy in which, accompanied by Parnell, the Irish leader, she addresses a crowd.[12]

Similar deflections of sibling concern for their dying parent are engaged in by the other brothers and sisters. These range from Rose's adventure fantasy to Eleanor's contemplation of the lot of the poor as a separate, distinct class and then of marriage as an alternative to her current existence within the family. The dominant focus of each is the individual self and its aspirations and desires. This attitude limns in the inherent selfishness or diffidence of all the family members concerning others. At the same time, any indictment of their responses is muted and qualified. For instance, Eleanor's actions suggest that her family life is a straitened, circumscribed, and limited existence that only her patience enables her to accept. Hence, to focus on one's self is seen as not so much selfish as a natural response to dissatisfaction with familial existence.

From the outset Woolf grounds both her and her characters' assessment of the family as a social unit in the realities of human drives and interests.[13]

In this, she is quite unlike Agee, who has Rufus and his narrator experience the transition from an ideal to a realistic view of the family. Nor does she follow Updike's strategy of focusing on father and child as characters in order to trace out the relations of understanding and misunderstanding dominating their lives and defining the nature of their family. Her episodic technique requires her to focus not on characters as individuals. Instead, it allows her to deploy them to make up a kind of meta-character, namely, the family named Pargiter.[14]

The representative nature of the family is underscored in two ways. First, the conventional, almost stereotypical careers its members adopt point up the typical quality of the Pargiters. Second, it is implicitly seen in relation to other families more or less of the same era and class, namely, the Malones and the Digbys. The Pargiters consist of markedly diverse individuals: a parent of military background in service to the empire; a son who goes to India as an officer; a daughter who embarks on a lifelong career as a political activist embracing causes like Ireland's struggle for freedom, the suffragette pursuit of the vote, and antiwar efforts; a son who adopts the law as a profession while pursuing a determinedly bourgeois life; another son who becomes a classics scholar and professor while remaining a bachelor; and finally, an eldest daughter who dutifully remains a spinster caring for her father while sublimating her desire for personal freedom through international travel after his death. Similarly, the Malones and Digbys, while different from the Pargiters as families, are essentially more like one another than they are radically different social units.[15] Their siblings differ from the Pargiters in degree but not in kind. As a result, *The Years* makes of the family a kind of microcosm of society itself; it is the ground of human existence that defines what life actually is.[16]

Essentially, the concept of the family provides the novel with an epistemological unit larger and of longer duration than the individual. At the same time, Woolf pays sedulous attention to the differences obtaining between family members. Her dispassionate view reveals that the family is basically a congeries of individual persons. They are loosely linked by shared past experiences but have scarcely any intimate or personal familiarity with one another. Nor is there any unity of outlook to the family or its members. In short, at some fundamental historical level the family has, for Woolf, little claim to be elegiacally lamented. It neither is the occasion for celebration, as it was in Victorian times, nor does it command regret for its ostensible social diminution, as more modern times seem to imply.

The reason for this is largely found in the individuals themselves. None of them, and indeed no character in the entire novel, is seen by Woolf to possess the quality of historical uniqueness or personal distinction that would warrant their being singled out for conventional elegiac regard. In a word, they are the summation of ordinariness, with each begetting as much criticism as praise or regard. A prominent aspect of the traditional elegy develops out of a conviction of the notable value of the person being celebrated and on an impulse to lament its subject's death or loss.[17] Consequently, a worldview that refuses to find either public or private entities worthy of such regard is either going to eschew completely the elegiac attitude or else significantly to alter its focus and method of handling.

Woolf carries out her radical alteration of the elegiac view of life and the human world by examining the connections she uncovers between time, death, loss, and reality. Time, in *The Years,* is a combination of continuity and change, neither of which is seriously lamented though they are acknowledged in the consciousness of individual characters.[18] This polarity of impressions—time is always with us and yet is always changing—arouses for Woolf neither a sense of irremediable sadness nor a deep conviction of the value of making new the world in which human beings live.[19] Together, they simply create one of the basic conditions within which we must function. Any regrets we feel at the passage of time are but individual moments of consciousness, which never cohere into a uniform public or social point of view.

How this works itself out in the novel is seen by Woolf's juxtaposition of two ostensibly contradictory techniques. One is the structuring of the novel into eleven sections, ten of which carry an annual designation. The other is the presentation of scenes and thoughts in terms of episodic consciousness and social reality.[20] The first of these points up the serial, cumulative nature of time, while the latter reflects its multiple and variable nodalities. The one is interpersonal, the other essentially individual or personal in character. The author privileges neither. Instead, she evenhandedly acknowledges the awareness of both. For her, a disinterested observer concerned with whatever truth can be formulated about the world of human beings accepts each.

The effect of her scrupulous detachment is to call into question both the habit and the emotions attached thereto of privileging either the past, as does the elegy, or the future, as does the utopia. At the same time, the relevance of both past and future is found in the present, which essentially is revealed to be a discontinuous mélange of moments of consciousness. This mixture consists of change and difference possessing little sense of permanence or value. In short, the present is not associated with any long-term or public point of view that can integrate change into itself.

Thus, in moving chronologically from, say, 1890 to 1918, *The Years* acknowledges the historical and social relevance of and differences between the reigns of Queen Victoria (1837–1901), her son Edward VII (1901–1910), and her grandson George V (1910–1936). Yet it does so without mourning sorrowfully for the loss of any one of them. The same is true of the last and longest section of the book. Its title "Present Day" catches the special relation existing between present and future. The same quiet irony surrounds the conversations of Eleanor and Nicholas. She is the spinster embodiment of the old and he the foreign advocate of the new. Their exchanges merge a Lawrentian social skepticism and probing of the individual consciousness with a Wellsian naïve optimism regarding the future. The former opines, "We cannot make laws and religions that fit because we do not know ourselves" (304) while the latter declares, "Here's to the New World!" (315). The derivative nature of these views is attested to by their simple formulation and naïve enthusiasm of expression.

It is as if Woolf stands apart from both her literary predecessors and successors revealing indirectly and coolly their critical shortcomings when set against the thirty-odd years covered in her novel.[21] Such radical polemics and rank endorsement of new ideas and thoroughgoing change are part of her historical world and so deserve inclusion. But they do not embody an authorial perspective any more than do the idle, casual conversations that make up so much of her novel. They are ironically assigned their very limited value through the skepticism inherent in Woolf's language and tone. The result is a profound and skeptical interrogation of both the past and the future.[22] Neither is deemed appropriate to arousing the traditional elegiac voice compounded of regret and praise directed at a particular historical moment or character.

The same unblinking refusal to elevate death to an elegiac occasion is seen in the author's handling of personal or familial, social, national, and political instances of the passing of individual lives. The first is that of Mrs. Pargiter who, as we have seen, occasions in one of her daughters the opposite of the grievous sense of anticipated loss that Woolf generates in *To the Lighthouse* for Mr. Ramsay. The earlier novel resonates with the conventional elegiac tone no matter how much anger and frustration he also arouses in his family. In contrast, the emotional bedrock expressed in *The Years* is the modern elegiac temper. It consists of a new social reality marked by detachment from and irritation with the unspoken demands of others for sympathy, pity, and understanding. At Mrs. Pargiter's funeral, it is the detachment from elegiac feeling that dominates. Delia's random thoughts contrast society's funerary customs with her own personal desires and perceptions. She is struck by the contrast between the casualness and brevity of society's observance of death and the solemnity and impressiveness of the traditional burial service. In the former, death is recognized by customary gestures yet is seen as but a small part of the entire social reality. In the latter, Delia is momentarily and fleetingly stirred by the musical language of the burial service. Her struggle to gain genuine feeling for her mother's death is animated by the poetry of the service. Ultimately, however, it is lost when she detects in the minister's voice a sense that "he seemed to pass from the known to the unknown; from what he believed to what he did not believe" (91).

This same movement from aspiring to believe to renouncing of significance she encounters in the interment itself. At first, she recognizes that this is her last opportunity to elegize her mother and for a moment feels that "she was possessed of something everlasting; of life mixing with death, of death becoming life" (92). Finally, however, she concludes that the minister or priest "had robbed her of the one feeling that was genuine; he had spoilt her one moment of understanding" (93). The final perception she has of her mother's death is the antithesis of the traditional elegiac attitude: "None of us feel anything at all, she thought: we're all pretending" (93).

The more public instances of death—the passing of Charles Stewart Parnell (1891) and of King Edward VII (1910)—are essentially social signposts for the characters. Each extends Woolf's sense of the futility of the conventional elegiac attitude. Parnell's death begets a variety of contradictory responses that mirror the personalities and attitudes of individual characters. In so doing, they deny the possibility of a formal elegiac lament. Thus, Delia's response is judged by Eleanor to be a political one that results in the thwarting of her high-minded commitments. Her dedication to an ideological cause and her idealistic celebration of abstract concepts such as justice and liberty are essentially shattered: "This would be the end of all her dreams" (121).

Set against her sense of ideological disruption is her father Abel's personal note of satisfaction: "A shock of something like relief, of something that had a tinge of triumph in it, went through him. . . . Well, he said to himself, he's dead—that unscrupulous adventurer—that agitator who had done all the mischief. . . . Anyhow he was dead and that was an end of it" (123–24). Abel does, admittedly, qualify his view of Parnell, but it is underlined by Woolf's tacit and ironic comparison of the private and sexual lives of Abel and Parnell. Nevertheless, he concludes that "it would make no difference, Parnell's death, coming now" (124) and so excludes it as a possible subject for elegy. In so doing, it counterpoises his denigration and dismissal of Parnell against his daughter's extolling of his merits and Eleanor's instinctive sympathy for Delia's grief as an individual supporter.

Only with Abel's sister-in-law Eugenie's response to the news of Parnell's death is there a powerful personal emotion expressed. It, however, is founded not on his political loss but rather on his romantic loss deriving from his illicit relationship with Mrs. Kitty O'Shea. Eugenie's and Abel's responses focus on quite different aspects of Parnell's role in Edwardian society. Nevertheless, without materially judging either one Woolf starkly sets forth their contrast:

> "She ruined his career for him," he said with a little snort.
> "Ah, but how she must have loved him!" she murmured. (128)

Only in Eugenie's reflective observation does Woolf hint at how she is radically revising the elegiac temper of her time:

> "How people suffer! . . ." she murmured, looking at the flower. "How they suffer, Abel!" she said. She turned and looked straight at him. (128)

Suffering, whether through the ruination of a public career or by the torments of a personal passion, is the common lot of mankind. For it, a subdued elegiac feeling of regret is appropriate even though it is extended to all mankind rather than the customary individual elegiac subject. Even more radical an alteration of the elegiac tradition is found in the brevity of Eugenie's remark. It is not that she is inarticulate. Rather her comment is all that can be said without launching into the quick sands of rhetoric, poetry, sentimentality, and panegyric when set against the full scope of the years that make up human time.

It is, however, exactly such quick sands that Woolf ventures to engage when she takes up Eleanor's selling of the family home. This action follows her father's death and entails her parting from the family's aged servant, Crosby, and their old dog, Rover. The last good-bye to the empty house and to one another arouses the pathos of loss, the fondness of old memories, the collapse into unrestrained tears, the desire to retain a part of the past, and the inevitability of final separation. As Woolf sketches the scene, all of these are carefully probed for their boundaries and legitimacy. One is aware of the Dickensian bathos enveloping it as well as the legitimacy of the feelings aroused. Thus, Eleanor's and Crosby's feelings are carefully differentiated even as their appropriateness is made clear. For Eleanor, "the mixture of emotions was positively painful; she was so glad to be quit of it all, but for Crosby it was the end of everything" (232). For Crosby, loss of the role of faithful servant for forty years to a family whose "doings had made her entire world" (232) leads to unrestrained grief on which ultimately and necessarily "Eleanor shut the door and went in" (233).

The consequence of such an emotionally charged moment for which there can be neither extenuation nor transcendence is a sternly profound one. It reveals the utter impossibility of its reality and significance being exaggerated. That life contains many such experiences is obvious to Woolf. That they lie beyond the ability of language to capture their truth fully, or perhaps even partially, is her conclusion in *The Years.* Only by deliberately using words bathetically or, at least, recalling past bathetic uses, can, Woolf suggests, the full reality of such human experiences be captured.

Nowhere is this better seen than in the account of Rover's final days attended by the dutiful, caring Crosby who then proceeds to Martin Pargiter's flat to pick up his laundry. His last embarrassed glimpse of her from his window extends sentimentality as far as it can go. This scene is then curtailed with a swift dispatch that suggests the necessary limits to be placed on rhetoric and language in the full scope of a human world:

> he saw Crosby come up the area steps with a parcel under her arm. She stood for a moment, like a frightened little animal, peering round her be-

> fore she ventured to brave the dangers of the street. At last, off she trotted. He saw the snow falling on her black bonnet as she disappeared. He turned away. (240)

Both Martin's and Eleanor's responses to Crosby—the conventional old, loyal servant consigned to a pitiable retirement—are laconic but quietly emphatic rejections of the traditional elegy and its focus on the pathos of the individual death.[23]

Woolf replaces this traditional spirit with, in part, the modern concentration on loss and its numerous varieties. Yet even here she hews to her disciplined and clear-eyed sense of the nature of social reality. She insists on the avoidance of any hint of emotional overreaction or rhetorical exaggeration in responding to any particular human loss. Thus, most of the instances of loss in *The Years*—the inevitable signs of physical aging, societal change including the decline of the empire, and the disappearance of confidence in fully knowing an individual—are chronicled in a tone of muted recognition that accepts but does not mourn them. Loss, like death and the inexorable passage of time, is a constituent element of human life. For Woolf, mourning of individual instances is a private not a public matter; it is an action scrupulously limited in duration and controlled in expression. The sense of surprise, shock, anger, desolation, and grief, which conventionally and historically have contributed to the elegiac response to loss and death, are not so much rejected as understood to be fruitless. They change nothing in empirical reality; they are indeed "natural" but fundamentally unconsidered reactions to the moment. In a way, they approximate for Woolf what the philosopher Gilbert Ryle called "category mistakes."[24] These are erroneous ways of construing reality, which when scrupulously and objectively examined can yield more accurate views of the world in which human beings live.

The view of life dramatized by Woolf in *The Years* is one of a succession of frames within which change, loss, and death recur repetitively but in different forms and guises. For her, this, quite simply, is the nature of reality and the human world. To lament it eloquently and passionately, as does the conventional elegy, is to make one's response purely an aesthetic one. When one considers the role of aesthetics and the arts in her novel, one finds Woolf, the consummate artist, taking a rather surprising view of them. In the last analysis, the arts are for her essentially incidental and limited by the temporal horizon within which they lie. It is true that the references to Renan, Wagner, Antigone, and Dante's *Purgatorio* do function as symbolic signposts for members of the family.[25] But for Woolf they also convey the limitations of the symbolic for communication among all human beings. Among the cognoscenti their function is allusive. But among the servants like Crosby, the upwardly mobile academics like the Robsons, and trades people like Mr. Duffus, they are recognized neither as symbolic nor as signposts to anything except possibly a culturally superior class.

The ultimately incidental nature of the arts to human society is captured most graphically in Eleanor's response to Dante: casual recognition followed by a halfhearted effort to comprehend, which ends in a desultory conclusion to return to it when she has more time.[26] It is perhaps no accident that the one actual artist in the novel is a consummate egotist with "a queer face; knit up; nerve-drawn; fixed" (388) who "could not free himself, could not detach himself" (389) but in Ixion-like fashion "was bound on the wheel with tight iron hoops" (389). In effect, Woolf recognizes that the arts cannot be philosophically fundamental but only historically relevant to a certain segment of the world and human society.

Within the frames of change, loss, and death, elements such as repetition, endings, and beginnings operate recurrently to underline the inherent boundaries or limitations of the world in which we live.[27] They generate the only elegiac temper Woolf feels it is possible to recognize, one that is essentially epistemological in nature. It is founded on the absence of an absolute, timeless knowledge about the meaning of the physical world, the nature of the self, and how to control or govern society. Such an absence reduces human consciousness to an interrogative mode about its content.[28] Essentially it silences the act of mourning that was prompted by the impulse to desire a world other than the one we have. The grim stoicism of such an outlook is muted only by recognizing the persistence of time as a means of recording the passage of human life.[29]

The witnessing of endings is minimally rendered by Mrs. Pargiter's funeral service: "The ceremony was over; rain was falling" (93). In the same fashion, Eleanor's witnessing of the return home of a young bridal couple captures the persistence of optimism and futurity in human affairs: "And now?' she asked, holding out her hands to him" (469). These two scenes encapsulate Woolf's recognition that neither beginnings nor endings are unique or absolute. Both are basically generic repetitions compounded of regret for the past and hope for the future. They are as inescapable as time itself. Taken together, they encompass the elegiac temper and the meaning of *The Years*.[30] The sheer simplicity of this temper enables Woolf to conclude the book with an equally simple conclusion. Looking back on the enormously varied renderings of the natural world in which human beings are consigned to live their years, she only remarks: "The sun had risen, and the sky above the houses wore an air of extraordinary beauty, simplicity and peace" (469).[31]

William Faulkner's *Sartoris* (1929) both continues Woolf's critique of the family and counters her minimalistic bleakness of outlook. *The Years* diminishes the family's importance by a leveling process, which reduces its members to the same status as all other persons. *Sartoris,* however, sees the family as slowly disintegrating over several generations in ways that both grieve and satisfy its audience. Woolf's treatment of the family follows logically from Faulkner's bifocal response to the decline of the Sartorises. While he still leaves them on a pedestal, albeit a decaying one, she stonily focuses on the Pargiters' ordinariness. Unlike the Sartorises, they are in no way exceptional as compared to their confreres. Both families, however, are significantly distanced from the idealized family of Agee and his child narrator. Thus, they embody the century's gradual dissolution of the family as a central source of meaning, value, and security.

Faulkner's charting of the decline of the Sartoris family is particularly striking when compared with his handling of the Compsons in *The Sound and the Fury.* The latter he views largely as a personal or individual historical unit. The Sartoris family, on the other hand, stands as a societal unit that possesses a dominant elegiac element through its being exclusively a lamentable consequence of Southern history.[32] Involved in this element are two essential tendencies. One is to embrace a psychology of risk taking and living for the moment. The other is to engage in cultural histrionics by making the social unit carry more weight than it can. The poignancy of such an attitude is captured movingly in the authorial reflection at the very end of the novel:

> For there is death in the sound of it [the name Sartoris], and a glamorous fatality, like silver pennons downrushing at sunset, or a dying fall of horns along the road to Roncevaux. (380)

By aligning his nineteenth-century Southern family with an ancient French romance, such as *The Song of Roland,* and the Holy Roman Empire of Charlemagne, Faulkner suggests a historical continuity between them.

Among other things, both deal in quixotically heroic battles with an inexorable fate. By so doing, he seeks to suggest some of the origins of his and the South's dogged defense and insistent celebration of the Civil War. In effect, he argues that principles or convictions are more important than life itself and indeed are worth dying for. Woolf, on the other hand, a stress that the actualities of life determine the principles by which mankind endeavors to live. For her, principles are drawn from the facts of life and are few in number and scarcely earth-shaking in their distinctiveness. She basically reduces principles to points of view whereas Faulkner insists on celebrating them as "old truths" operating absolutely rather than relatively.

At the same time, Faulkner's own view differs from that of his characters as is seen in Miss Jenny's telling and retelling of her husband's death in the war. She sees it as a heroic effort to repel an invader and to preserve a prized way of life. His view captures explicitly the way in which retelling a story is capable of ennobling and making important the casual prank of two young men. The persistent retelling transforms an event from "a harebrained prank" to "a gallant and finely tragical focal point to which the history of the human race had been raised" (9). The formation of legend in this way, he suggests, is to provide an elegiac response to human folly, risk taking, and raw headstrong courage.[33] Thus, deep sorrow or lament is felt for the loss of life, the destruction of a future, and the irresponsible disregard for the feelings of others. At the same time, this grief is blended with a passionate celebration of a single-minded willingness to sacrifice time, life, and the possibility of success or survival for what amounts to nothing but impulse. And the repetition of the tale provides an oral solace by smoothing the raw edges of loss while burnishing the irresponsibility into exasperated admiration. Finally, by this process the full-scale legend generates an elegiac temper toward the incident itself as well as the cultural context in which it existed historically.

Faulkner's ambivalence toward his fictional family, his native region and its history, and his sense of the pitiable feeling it arouses in him is caught graphically in Bayard's talk about war and violence. According to the anonymous narrator, it embodies "doomed immortality and immortal doom" (126). These phrases provide the two constituent elements of his elegy for the South and its people. The first phrase focuses on the ever-present nature of time; it makes of the absence created by death a fate undesired but inescapable. This is conveyed through memory's perpetual presence in human consciousness and its persistent recollection of human folly or mistakes or disastrous decisions. Thus, by his first phrase, Faulkner makes of immortality something almost Swiftian in its consigning mankind to a state of not being able to forget its follies.

Such a satiric view is transformed into an elegiac one by the second phrase, "immortal doom." With it, Faulkner deftly balances the focus on memory, accident, and personal responsibility by invoking the timeless presence of anticipation, fate, and freedom from personal or societal responsibility. The phrases in tandem make clear the grounds for his ambivalence. On the one hand, the universe is conceived of as an endless succession of disasters ordained by some metaphysical power or force or agency. And on the other, such a world is sure to generate a feeling of frustrated sorrow and a readiness to express deep-seated lament for the victims of it. In short, Faulkner's elegiac temper, in contrast to Woolf's, is the product of the inevitability of ultimate human defeat rather than the recognition of the real limitations of the universe and its human populace.

By the same token, Faulkner's view is distinct from the nineteenth-century naturalistic perspective. The difference lies in his insistence on man's commitment to a gallant and persistent struggle with the adversities inflicted on him by the nature of his world. A fine instance of this is the extended set passage praising the mule as an embodiment of the South's resistance to "the hopeless juggernaut of circumstance" (278) that led the South to lose the war and to survive Reconstruction through patience and determination alone. Out of this figure of a single cotton gin mule engaged on its mindless and endless task, Faulkner provides an early instance of his capacity to elevate the trivial or commonplace to the extraordinary and compelling:

> Some Homer of the cotton fields should sing the saga of the mule and of his place in the South. He it was, more than any other one creature or thing, who, steadfast to the land when all else faltered before the hopeless juggernaut of circumstance, impervious to conditions that broke men's hearts because of his venomous and patient preoccupation with the immediate present, won the prone South from beneath the iron heel of Reconstruction and taught it pride again through humility, and courage through adversity overcome; who accomplished the well-nigh impossible despite hopeless odds, by sheer and vindictive patience. Father and

mother he does not resemble, sons and daughters he will never have; vindictive and patient (it is a known fact that he will labor ten years willingly and patiently for you, for the privilege of kicking you once); solitary but without pride, self-sufficient but without vanity; his voice is his own derision. Outcast and pariah, he has neither friend, wife, mistress, nor sweetheart; celibate, he is unscarred, possesses neither pillar nor desert cave, he is not assaulted by temptations nor flagellated by dreams nor assuaged by vision; faith, hope and charity are not his. Misanthropic, he labors six days without reward for one creature whom he hates, bound with chains to another whom he despises, and spends the seventh day kicking or being kicked by his fellows. Misunderstood even by that creature, the nigger who drives him, whose impulses and mental processes most closely resemble his, he performs alien actions in alien surroundings; he finds bread not only for a race, but for an entire form of behavior; meek, his inheritance is cooked away from him along with his soul in a glue factory. Ugly, untiring, perverse, he can be moved neither by reason, flattery, nor promise of reward; he performs his humble monotonous duties without complaint, and his meed is blows. Alive, he is hailed through the world, an object of general derision; unwept, unhonored and unsung, he bleaches his awkward accusing bones among rusting cans and broken crockery and worn-out automobile tires on lonely hillsides while his flesh soars unawares against the blue in the craws of buzzards. (278–79)

This breathless recitation of the place, nature, traits, and role of the mule is transformed into a valedictory memorial to the South's past. By such a memorial, Faulkner celebrates that past on which he himself stands and out of which his fiction emerges. And in so doing, he assumes the very role he summons up at the beginning of this set piece, that of "some Homer of the cotton fields."

This set piece is central to the elegiac design of the novel as is further underscored by the scene that immediately follows it. Bayard and Narcissa's visit to the cotton gin suggests that *Sartoris* is an elegy not only about the past but also the present. Bayard and Narcissa embody the death of the present itself insofar as it contains all of the familiarities from the past. Narcissa, sitting alone in the car, is "lapped in the ripe odors of the failing year and all its rich, vague sadness" (279). Her reaction, however, is not that of despair or desperation so much as of quiet acceptance of the elegiac conclusion. This implicit anticipatory farewell to the familiar that Faulkner dramatizes ultimately comes to focus on Bayard and Narcissa as increasingly she senses the inevitability of his movement toward death. Returning from possum hunting, they kiss, only for her to find that "his lips were cold and upon them she tasted fatality and doom" (289). Thereafter, she waits for him at home where "they would lie so, holding to one another in the darkness and the temporary abeyance of his despair and the isolation of that doom he could not escape" (289). His doom is both psychological and historical. It stems from the wartime death of his brother, he himself being a member of the Sartoris family and its heritage of recklessness, and his having been born in the South.

Narcissa sympathetically contemplates the ironic contrast between Miss Jenny's lifelong behavior and manner and those of the Sartoris men. In so doing, she embodies Faulkner's elegiac yet almost dispassionate assessment of his Southern heritage and its multigenerational emphasis on family. As Miss Jenny's life is "closing, not into the future, but out of the past" (357), Narcissa feels her own chilling assessment of the Sartoris family develop. Motivating it is her feeling that the saving of her unborn child is at stake. Only by severing the family's generational inheritance of rash headstrong actions and attitudes can her child avoid the fate of his father.

She ascribes the family's self-destructiveness to different attitudes held by the two genders:

> she thought how much finer that gallantry which never lowered blade to foes no sword could find; that uncomplaining steadfastness of those unsung (ay, unwept too) women than the fustian and useless glamour of the men that obscured it. (357–58)

What Narcissa makes of this perception, however, is but part of the problem. Miss Jenny and the other Southern women of her generation are indeed models of "uncomplaining steadfastness" (358), but by this very trait they also make of themselves ultimately helpless enablers. Even more sinister in familial terms is the fact that, as Narcissa states, Miss Jenny is almost unconsciously trying "to make of my child just another rocket to glare for a moment in the sky, then die away" (358). The emphasis on family remains constant even though the gender contrast inherent in it carries still the shape of disaster and tragedy.

Sartoris is a bifocal vision of the elegiac occasion, one that simultaneously celebrates and mourns the idea of the family as a historical record of mankind. Integral to this record is its heroism and determination, its willingness to sacrifice and to survive, as well as its follies of pride and vain gloriousness. The several burial epitaphs chronologically reveal the efforts of family survivors over generations to condense the elegiac record to simplicity and directness rather than rhetoric and bombast.

The effect of the several epitaphs is that of a twofold elegy: one for the family members who have died (largely by their own decision or hand or choice) and one for the human persistence in keeping such records. Essentially, the novel struggles to answer the question, "Why remember and mourn human folly and self-destructiveness?"

In the final paragraphs of the novel, Miss Jenny answers in one way and Faulkner in another. She declares simply and categorically, "It always does me good to see all those fool pompous men lying there with their marble mottoes and things" (379). Faulkner's more complex narrative response involves recognizing that remembrance and recollection of "glamorous and old disastrous things" (380) entails a response to glamour, disaster, fatality, and death. It is itself part of an outmoded game and "an old dead pattern" (380) on the verge of cessation. It signals the possible end of this kind of human folly through the diffidence, detachment, and the dream of "quietude and peace" (380) held by Narcissa. At the same time, her name itself suggests the limitations of such an arbitrary personal evasion of the elegiac challenge. These same limitations lead to the emergence of the even more disastrous behavior and games she is to play in *Sanctuary.*

4
FAMILIAL DISINTEGRATION
James Joyce's *Dubliners* and F. Scott Fitzgerald's "Babylon Revisited"

James Joyce's *Dubliners* (1914) stands midway between Woolf and Faulkner in its elegiac rendering of the impotence and failure of the family as a central social unit. Like Woolf's *The Years,* it generates a restrained, dispassionate objectivity toward the disintegration of the family.[1] And like Faulkner, it periodically introduces a highly wrought style (most notably in "The Dead") that utilizes all the resources of rhetoric to convey its perspectives on the family and its members. What it adds to their stances is the Celtic sentiment for the fact of loss—personal as well as cultural and societal—considered simply as loss, as deprivation, as absence of the once familiar.[2]

Death opens and closes *Dubliners* and dominates the families rendered therein as well as the city in which they live. Family and city taken together define the loss being glossed by Joyce.[3] The occasion and its instigator meld into a sorrowful depiction of a world that overlays a world that was. In the course of the series of stories, a full range of losses is documented, many of which would arouse no lament nor sorrow were it not that now their subjects are no more. In effect, Joyce, like Woolf, is exploring new ways of rendering the elegiac temper even while, like Faulkner, he both alludes to and uses older, more traditional verbal techniques of presenting it.

The first story, "The Sisters," opens in the same way as the last story, "The Dead," closes. Each displays a rapt concentration on death. The boy in "The Sisters," though fearful of death, is also fascinated and drawn to its presence. His youth and lack of experience drive his attraction. Conversely, the close of "The Dead" locates Gabriel Conroy, the would-be elegist for the family, as he is about to be absorbed into a narrative elegy for each human being, both living and dead.

Between these poles of attraction to and absorption into death, Joyce in many of the other stories rings a series of changes on elegiac emotions. The variety of ways in which he registers pity, sorrow, grief, and lament exposes the shortcomings of conventional expressions and modes of regret for losses suffered or witnessed. Thus, "Eveline" ends in its last paragraph with a paralyzed reaction to love and its loss. It mutely testifies to a woman having foregone the possibility of a family life for herself:

> He rushed beyond the barrier and called to her to follow. He was shouted at to go on but he still called to her. She set her white face to him, passive, like a helpless animal. Her eyes gave him no sign of love or farewell or recognition. (48)

For the character Eveline, the only elegy she can mount is the denial of freedom, life, and personal choice. It is Joyce himself who writes a contemporary elegy for a girl rendered incapable of a full emotional response.[4] He does so through tracing her individual, personal history. It is one of ceaseless stifling in a limited, restricted "family" of one, her father. The latter functions as he feels a society dominated by a doctrinaire religion has dictated that he should. Thus, the family she has known is the opposite of the one fondly remembered by Agee's Rufus.

The dissolution of the ideal family envisaged in *A Death in the Family* stands, however, as a shadow over the actions and thoughts of many of Joyce's characters. This is true even in stories like "Two Gallants" or "Counterparts," which cannot themselves be regarded as elegiac in nature. The shadow is that of the loss of cultural sustenance and support capable of enabling the individual to live a free, independent, and fulfilling life. And what deepens the elegiac cast is precisely the failure of these characters to be aware of the loss even of the "idea" of the family as a sustaining cultural unit.

Many of the characters' lives are so straitened, thwarted, and frustrated that they threaten to occasion pity and a sentimental pathos for them. Underlining this temptation is the perceived impossibility of their changing or breaking free from their inherited world. Only Joyce's detachment and style of "scrupulous meanness" keep the stories from erupting into full-blown elegiac laments for their characters' essentially unrealized lives.[5] Frustration of both a repressed and suppressed order is the cornerstone of the Irish urban scene and the incentive both for its sentimentality and elegiac potential.

In a way, a story such as "A Painful Case" reveals part of why Joyce opts so sedulously to control his narratives' potential for pathos. Not to choke back his stories' impulse to pathos would threaten them with becoming mired in the sentimentality inherent in Irish or Dublin society and with invoking the conventional and formal elegiac voice. His strategy in "A Painful Case" is rather to deploy the devices of elegy to enable the point-of-view character, James Duffy, to elegize internally and self-indulgently. Images of a dark autumnal world, personal sadness and suffering, and self-directed sorrow and regret are summoned up to create what Duffy histrionically conceives as his own state of being—immutable loneliness:

> He gnawed the rectitude of his life; he felt that he had been outcast from life's feast. . . . No one wanted him; he was outcast from life's feast. . . . It passed slowly out of sight; but still he heard in his ears the laborious drone of the engine reiterating the syllables of her name. (146)

In so doing, however, Joyce's rhetorical restraint creates a savage situational irony.[6] Mr. Duffy's ego-centered elegiac temper serves to indict him as not deserving an elegy by anyone. Only in the story's final paragraph when "he began to doubt the reality of what memory told him" (147) does his egotism fail him as the reality of his actual life engulfs him:

> He could not feel her near him in the darkness nor her voice touch his ear. He waited some minutes listening. He could hear nothing: the night was perfectly silent. He listened again: perfectly silent. He felt that he was alone. (147)

With this, Joyce generates his own elegiac temper for the dangers of elevating the individual ego at the expense of expressing genuine human sympathy. It is a dispassionate temper content to mourn the losses inherent in the situation only through chronicling them without explicit comment.

Given Joyce's careful insistence on the order of the stories in *Dubliners,* there is little ground for surprise that "Ivy Day in the Committee Room" should immediately follow "A Painful Case." They provide contrapuntal perspectives on Dublin's conventional invocation of elegiac attitudes. "A Painful Case" provides a personal but by no means unique manner of summoning up the conventional elegiac attitude for critical inspection. The story both exposes the shortcomings of this attitude and at the same time redefines it through impersonal but not detached irony.

In contrast, "Ivy Day in the Committee Room" indicts the public or societal manner of displaying the elegy for ignoble ends.[7] Joseph Hynes's conventionally sentimental elegy on Charles Stewart Parnell unconsciously exposes both the oft-repeated glib use of Parnell's name and his ill-fated career.

To invoke him in this fashion is to elevate the self-opinion of his admirers and supporters who stood by in mute helplessness when action and vigorous speech were needed to save Parnell's political career and reputation.

Even more savagely than Woolf, Joyce suggests very clearly that the existing public elegiac tradition is conservative or reactionary in the worst way. It reinforces the prevailing Irish social conventions of self-exculpation, scapegoating of others, and rank political opportunism in order to reveal them as the shallow sentimentalism they are.[8] In effect, doggerel such as Hynes's "The Death of Parnell" is pitiable enough simply as verse. In Joyce's eyes, however, it is also culturally destructive through verbal stereotyping and contributing to a disintegration of public taste and literary standards. It laments the fallen hero for the wrong reasons in the wrong ways. It is small wonder that Stephen Dedalus should cite "silence" as the first of his weapons to be used in defending his personal integrity. The closest that Joyce himself can come to silence while still acting as an artist is the last sentence of the story.

In a quietly understated response to the emotional, unthinking enthusiasm of the others for Hynes's poem, Joyce has Crofton answer a request for it to be praised. He does so with an impersonal, restrained utterance that thoroughly undercuts the enthusiasm so as to expose its excessiveness and irresponsibility:

> "Good man, Joe!" said Mr. O'Connor, taking out his cigarette papers and pouch the better to hide his emotion.
>
> "What do you think of that, Crofton?" cried Mr. Henchy. "Isn't that fine? What?"
>
> Mr. Crofton said that it was a very fine piece of writing. (170)

Through the simple act of switching from direct to indirect discourse, Joyce manages economically and trenchantly to distance himself from the public espousal of a conventional elegiac sentiment. By so doing, he renders it suspect both as artistically effective and socially appropriate.

Only with the final story, "The Dead," does Joyce present both genuine and fraudulent instances of the elegiac.[9] The latter is found in the representative elegiac temper of Dublin, which consists of a group of persons limited and dominated both by the presence and the absence of family. The fraudulent instance surfaces in portions of Gabriel Conroy's speech commemorating his aunts. It is a conventional and sentimental invocation of the past and its memories designed to move its audience in predetermined and stereotypical ways. Even its abrupt, ostensible refusal to continue to focus on the past is designed to suggest an elegiac attitude underlying the societal and joyous celebration of the aunts and their hospitality.

The genuine form of the elegiac reveals a more individual view of the central fact of the human condition, namely, its personal mortality. It emerges in the style deployed in the last few pages of the story as Gabriel and Gretta prepare for bed in the hotel where they are staying after the aunts' Christmas party. This scene is the product of several factors. These include: the end-of-party social conversation; Gabriel's fascination with his wife's listening to a final song; his intimate memories of their life together; and his mounting but ambivalent sexual desire that ultimately is thwarted by her tale of a lost love. From the ordinary and public to the personal and private is the setting against which the elegiac moment emerges. By doing so in all its heightened style, it signifies the disintegration of Gabriel's egoistic focusing on his own anticipated desire and its fulfillment. Real passion expressed simply and directly through Gretta's account of the death of Michael Furey supplants Gabriel's ego-driven sexual impulse. Love unrealized and hopeless in its intensity replaces love as a physical consequence of a familial relationship.

The centrality of the family and its emotional privileging are supplanted by loss and mortality throughout *Dubliners*. In the final pages of "The Dead," the family is shown to be intellectually bankrupt as a subject for the conventional Irish elegiac mode. There, Joyce's handling of the elegiac temper creates a coda for Gretta's tale, for the story and for the collection as a whole. Human mortality underlies all human activities. Consequently, the only thing more significant than the end of the individual life is the awareness of that fact. Out of that arousal occasioned by a consciousness alert to the full possibilities of language, Joyce creates his own individual elegiac temper.[10] It is one molded out of the contemplation of the past and the invocation of the present for the sake of an unknown future.

> A few light taps upon the pane made him turn to the window. It had begun to snow again. He watched sleepily the flakes, silver and dark, falling obliquely against the lamplight. The time had come for him to set out on his journey westward. Yes, the newspapers were right: snow was general all over Ireland. It was falling on every part of the dark central plain, on the treeless hills, falling softly upon the Bog of Allen and, farther

> westward, softly falling into the dark mutinous Shannon waves. It was falling, too, upon every part of the lonely churchyard on the hill where Michael Furey lay buried. It lay thickly drifted on the crooked crosses and headstones, on the spears of the little gate, on the barren thorns. His soul swooned slowly as he heard the snow falling faintly through the universe and faintly falling, like the descent of their last end, upon all the living and the dead. (287–88)

Through repetition and variation, the euphonious prose solemnly intones the inevitability of an ending for every individual consciousness, even that of its author. By the very act of composition, he testifies to his own participation in an elegy for himself as well as mankind in general. Through the bravura nature of his style, he calls attention to his creative talent so that he in effect underlines the grounds for elegiacally lamenting the ultimate and inevitable loss of such a skill.

For Joyce the elegiac temper revolves around the inescapability of mortality. And with this recognition, even human institutions such as politics, religion, and family are diminished in significance. For F. Scott Fitzgerald, however, the elegiac focus falls on the implications of that inescapability for those still consigned to life. They are called upon to struggle to come to terms with that fact, to confront their past actions, and to aspire, with little more than a desperate hope, for some means of escape or extenuation before their lives end. No more than for Joyce does the family in Fitzgerald afford a shelter against the realization of absence, loss, and death.[11]

Perhaps this insight is captured most economically in his short story "Babylon Revisited," which deals with the story of Charlie Wales's effort to regain what is left of his family. The plot develops both sequentially and as a kind of layering over of a regret for a dissolute past, for weakness of character, and for the unforeseen nature of one's personal fate.[12] Charlie laments his past, entailing as it does his destruction of his family through the death of his wife and the loss of his daughter. He does so partly out of sorrow and grief for actions he can barely understand. Foregrounding his lamentation is his confronting his past culpability and his endeavoring to redeem the past for the sake of his future. Here he endeavors to follow the traditional elegy's pattern of lamentation-confrontation-resolution. Only with his failure to resolve the loss he faces is this pattern thwarted. In place of spiritual and psychological transcendence, Charlie is left with the unbearable prospect of his personal isolation being extended forever. By exposing him to such a prospect, Fitzgerald poses but does not answer the modern elegiac temper's challenge of how to survive without solace.

In the course of the story, Fitzgerald transforms the despair and self-pity of the weak for their weaknesses into a legitimate human lament. The absurdity and foolishness of past actions is seen from the present while the lack of forgiveness and understanding in familial affairs is shown to be cruel, petty, and self-stultifying. Fitzgerald makes his main character cling with a pathetic romantic sentimentality to the idea of family as crucial to his redemption from loneliness. What Joyce regards with consummate irony and Woolf with quiet stoicism, Faulkner and Fitzgerald view with a kind of romantic tragic desperation. The latter two recognize that the notion of the family as something to elegize is past and thus lost, and yet they still passionately desire its presence. The loss of the family as an elegiac subject is a fact to be accepted for Woolf, while for Joyce even its former privileging is grounds for ironic dismissal. For Fitzgerald and Faulkner, however, its past viability still lingers in memory at the same time as its destructiveness and hopelessness persist with almost equal fervor.

5

THE LOSS OF ROMANTIC LOVE

Ernest Hemingway's *The Sun Also Rises* and James Baldwin's *Giovanni's Room*

Two novels stressing romantic relationships as the occasion of change and elegiac loss are Ernest Hemingway's *The Sun Also Rises* (1926) and James Baldwin's *Giovanni's Room* (1956). Both, though in differing ways, mark a radical modern approach to and view of romantic love between individuals. The one focuses on heterosexual love displaced, while the other stresses homosexual love thwarted by events and time. Yet each conveys an elegiac temper haunted by loss and confronted by the challenge of how to cope with the systole of loss and the diastole of challenge. Neither author entertains death as a suitable or possible response to his protagonist's romantic fate. Hence, the focus for the resultant elegiac temper is the challenge of how to deal with loss, not death.[1]

The Sun Also Rises deploys its elegiac nature through character relationships (principally those of Jake Barnes and Lady Brett Ashley), narrative point of view, geographical settings, and its restrained and then-innovative style. The relationship between Jake and Brett is defined by his war wound and consequent loss of sexual potency.[2] It is, however, played out against a view of romantic love that deflates the conventional view of pre-war times by elevating the physical over the emotional and consummation over commitment. Brett, not Jake, is the one who articulates the intensity of her sexual desire and the one who makes that desire the critical core of their relationship. Her behavioral attitude is an unspoken and uneasy combination of serious pre-war commitment and postwar casual infidelity. This inherent contradiction engenders suspicions about their relationship being the critical situation she views it to be.

Early in the novel as they discuss love, we find sets of feelings that are polar opposites. He thinks being in love is "an enjoyable feeling" while she regards it as "hell on earth" (27). Despite this, they are linked by their mutual attraction, bound together emotionally but unable to consummate it physically.[3] The intensity of this attraction moves their mutual loss or deprivation from a vulgar joke to the pathetic or potentially tragic.[4] The narrator is recollecting or reminiscing over all permanent past losses occasioned by the war. Consequently, he sees this shift both as one toward the elegiac but also as affording a perspective on such losses.

Jake makes two brief responses to Brett that point up Hemingway's dual focus on consequences: "Don't we pay for all the things we do, though?" (26) and "Nobody ever knows anything" (27). The first of these calls attention to the crucial nature of human actions for one's personal future. The second declares consequences, among other things, to be largely unpredictable. Taken together, they spell out a view that holds that one is always responsible for oneself regardless of not knowing in advance the results of one's actions or inactions.

Hemingway suggests this inevitably creates an elegiac situation as the basis for human life. For him, the paradigmatic form of such a situation is war, which so often results in the intersection of sudden death and frustrated love. It is sad that one should have to pay for, be held accountable for situations one has not consciously or deliberately planned. Yet this is the case whether or not it arouses emotions of regret, anger, or the deepest grief. All such emotions are the products of pathos, which figures so prominently in much of Hemingway's fiction. What transforms these emotions into the elegiac temper is the narrator's insistence on coping with the paradigmatic human situation while accepting its inevitability.[5] For Hemingway, like Faulkner, the hero is not the individual who surmounts and conquers his critical situation. Instead he is the one who endures it without losing self-control and abandoning himself to its pathos.

Jake's struggle to control and to mute his sexual loss makes up much of the novel's dramatic center, but it is not simply as a function of character that it acquires its elegiac quality. Crucial also is the narrative point of view, which grafts onto the character's feelings and responses the author's disciplined perspective. Three instances chart Hemingway's development of Jake's initial elegiac response to his loss: his reaction to the homosexuals in the bar, his walking home alone past Marshal Ney's statue, and his crying while in bed. The first of these is Jake's response to Cohn's question: "This whole show makes me sick is all" (21). It indicates how far he is from the absolute self-control for which he strives.[6] At the same time, his view of the homosexuals is not simply a homophobic response characteristic of the age, its culture, and perhaps the author. Within the context of the novel, Jake's comment is also an expression of his bitter resentment at those who frivolously squander the physical sexuality that he no longer possesses. His intense awareness of his own loss drives him to a laconic outbreak of self-pity expressed obliquely and almost in spite of himself. This awareness is heightened by the customary *outré* behavior of the homosexuals. For Jake, it spells out their unawareness of or indifference to what they are physically capable of, namely, making love to a woman. To him, they are trivializing this capacity by taking it so casually. He knows all too well that sexual intercourse gains in importance in direct proportion to its loss.[7]

The second instance, his walking home alone after leaving Brett and Count Mippipopolous, dramatizes starkly his isolation and uniqueness. They constitute the basic ways in which he is cut off from the rest of the characters. All the restaurants are closed or closing, streets are essentially deserted, and only he is moving toward yet a sharper form of isolation—home alone to face his physical loss. His passing Marshal Ney's statue (one of Napoleon's greatest generals) ironically extends the scope of that loss. The statue historically contextualizes both his personal loss and the broader, general disaster of World War I.[8] In a manner reminiscent of Eliot's *The Waste Land,* it suggests that war has always been an instrument of human loss. Concomitantly, its residue is public proclamation and admiration accompanied by private sorrow and deprivation. Sexual impotence is but the most dramatic and romantic—almost sentimental—form of that grief and loss.[9]

The third instance—Jake's momentary emotional collapse while in bed and completely alone—deflates his earlier efforts at self-control, self-delusion, and cynicism. Here he segues into a mini-elegiac response that moves through several stages. It passes from his ironic memories of the war and his wounding "on a joke front like the Italian" (31) through his cynical regret at first meeting Brett—"I suppose she only wanted what she couldn't have" (31)—and on to his skepticism over the transcendental solace of the Roman Catholic Church—"Not think about it. Oh, it was swell advice. Try and take it sometime. Try and take it" (31). The psychological movement is from the individual "I" to the dual "we" before concluding with the impersonal "they" or institutional "it." All three cases, however, are informed by pity for himself and irony for others. As such, they provide a poignant prelude that underscores the tragic finality of his loss:

> Then all of a sudden I started to cry. Then after a while it was better and I lay in bed and listened to the heavy trams go by and way down the street, and then I went to sleep. (31)

Like Agee in *A Death in the Family,* Hemingway here uses street noises as emotional interrupters and soothers of his point-of-view character. Similarly, the simplicity of his sentence structure, like that of *A Portrait of the Artist as a Young Man,* mimes the perspective of a child trying to articulate a phenomenon beyond his comprehension. Both the noises and the mode of expression serve to draw Jake back into the world of others and everyday society and so to thwart his descent into self-pity and bathos.

Subsequently, the cycle created by these three scenes is charted in a concentrated and accelerated fashion. The arrival of a drunken Brett, the obvious pointlessness of her conversation with its pretense of self-control, and Jake's bifocal assessment of and response to her reiterate the struggle he is facing. They underscore the hard-won character of the elegiac temper by economically suggesting the swiftness with which Jake oscillates in his emotional responses. Motivated by his own sexual loss, he veers between contempt for and love of Brett. Then he entertains the ambiguity of whether or not she is anything more than a sentimental loss. Finally, he concludes with the realization that his ultimate loss, symbolized by the day-night contrast, is something he has in common with other human beings. What he has lost is his being just like everyone else. Consequently, he is left to face the challenge of being isolate and unique.

The geographical settings coupled with Hemingway's stylistic control rescue Jake and the novel from the inclination to sentimentality and bathos.[10] Moreover, they provide both the character and the text as a whole with an overall elegiac temper. The countryside of Basque Spain is marked by the beauty and domesticity of a simple, easy, and quiet aura. As such, it creates an elegiac contrast to Jake's and the others' Parisian life. The peasant world is one of natural acceptance of one's lot fused with a timeless, unchanging physical setting. For Jake and the other characters, representative as they are of the entire postwar era, it is one they have lost or left behind in their propulsion into "a lost generation." Gertrude Stein's phrase is the elegiac slogan of the postwar era and its inhabitants. It is both the way they wish to see themselves and Stein's ironic view of their attitude.[11]

Hemingway's descriptions of the natural settings as Jake journeys to Pamplona stress tranquility in the midst of isolation, which is exactly the state Jake is trying to achieve psychologically. At the same time, they summon up a picture of an idyllic, innocent world of simple harmony in which people live at ease with themselves and others. In short, it is an Edenic world symbolizing that in which Jake lived, or thinks he did, before the losses initiated by the war, the dislocation of expatriation, and the moral changes wrought in individuals and their society. The vestigial remembrance of such a world impels Jake to endeavor to regain it physically by entering a universe similar to that which Hemingway and Nick Adams inhabited in northern Michigan. Yet all that is achieved is Jake's consolidating of his ironic detachment and stoical self-control. Both of these, however, only simulate the longed-for Edenic tranquility and harmony of existence. At this point in the novel, the elegiac temper is that of the author, not of Jake the character. Only when Jake is able to confront directly and dispassionately both his physical loss and the illusion-ridden nature of Brett is he able to match Hemingway's elegiac perspective by his final words "Isn't it pretty to think so?" (247).

Between the close of chapter 4 and the end of the novel, many of the scenes are implicitly devoted to two tasks. First, they strip Jake of his defenses against loss and then, they develop in him what he needs for possessing a completely elegiac temper. Scenes such as his entering the Roman Catholic Church and engaging in prayer eliminate traditional elegiac resolutions of loss and remove the welter of psychological defenses he inevitably mounts. His praying in the church suggests he is aware at some level that his initial defenses of irony and stoicism are insufficient. At the same time, it reveals that his religious impulse is thwarted by his skepticism concerning its value or usefulness for him. On one level, the scene questions whether ultimately there is any form of mourning or lamentation that is effective or useful or helpful. Yet on another level, it serves to heighten and to confirm the author's awareness of its futility.[12]

Jake's momentary but recurring attraction to religion questions the efficacy of mourning one's loss or losses. Simultaneously, it suggests that the elegiac consists of more than lamentation. Thus, his anger at and needling of Cohn as they wait for Brett's arrival in Pamplona reveals another function integral to the elegiac. To a degree, it serves a role similar to the satire often found in Renaissance elegies such as *Lycidas*. It attacks an obstacle that distracts from the grieving narrator. Further, it exposes the corruption of that segment of society that ignores the seriousness and significance of the losses being lamented.

Cohn's smug self-satisfaction at having had sex with Brett betrays a retrogressive prewar attitude toward romance and sexual relations. It stands in sharp contrast to the view of such relationships held by the "lost generation" and its postwar perspective on change. Cohn's later hangdog, idealistic sense of abandonment and dejected betrayal occasions only the pity and exasperation reserved for someone hewing to an outmoded convention. For Jake and the others, the legitimacy of mourning and grief is unquestioned. What can be challenged is the way in which and the attitude with which one mourns and expresses the grief. Cohn's way is to impose his attitude on others who, in any case, do not share his personal sentiments. In sharp contrast, Jake and Hemingway adopt a stern, almost compulsive restraint of expression and with it the avoidance of arousing pity on the part of others.

At the same time, Hemingway is concerned to view the elegiac temper in perspective and from more than one angle. This is seen clearly in the description of the bus ride through the countryside taken by Bill and Jake on their way to the river and fishing:

> We were going through farming country with rocky hills that sloped down into the fields. The grain-fields went up the hillsides. Now as we went higher there was a wind blowing the grain. The road was white and dusty, and the dust rose under the wheels and hung in the air behind us.
>
> The road climbed up into the hills and left the rich grain-fields below. Now there were only patches of grain on the bare hillsides and on each side of the water-courses. (105)

The neutrality of attitude and impersonality of feeling in such passages take Jake outside of himself, the loss he has suffered, and the consequences it imposes. The neutrality of the setting conveys the important fact that Jake's loss is not the totality of human experience no matter how central it may be to him. That is, the loss can be gainsaid or overcome or put in context without in any way denying its legitimacy and the tension it creates. The natural setting's ostensible indifference to his loss, nevertheless, reflects the importance of the problem facing him. This permanent undertow of the elegiac is suggested here exclusively by the rhythm of the author's sentences and the gradual movement of his imagery from rich farmland through thick dust to bare hillsides and barren landscape. Sooner or later, these sentences intone, one must face the bare and barren lineaments of existence, and what matters is whether one does so with an elegiac temper or not.

The culmination of Hemingway's balanced, judicious placing of the elegiac in the context of the idyllic natural world occurs with the arrival of Jake and Bill at the country inn in Burguete. There they attempt to counter the bitter cold and the wind and the pictures on the wall, all of which record dead animals and birds. They do so in the most basic of ways: eating, drinking, and reading in bed. All of these convey the nature of the idyllic available to Jake: a pleasurable, asexual companionship founded on the natural essentials of life. While this is a pleasant state, it proves on reflection to be a limited condition desirable only for a brief period:

> After supper we went up-stairs and smoked and read in bed to keep warm. Once in the night I woke and heard the wind blowing. It felt good to be warm and in bed. (111)

Clearly this feeling good counters Jake's night experience in Paris, but the presence of the wind testifies also to the continuing presence of turmoil in his life and psyche. Hemingway focuses on the pleasure of the experience in contrast to a haunting background implication. No matter how pleasurable, it is not the equivalent of love requited. And so it takes on an elegiac quality of regretful sadness at its second-best nature, at being good, but not as good as love and intimacy with another human being.[13]

A similar qualifying of the immediate pleasure of an experience also informs the dinner scene involving Jake, Brett, Mike, Bill, and Cohn. After Mike's bitter diatribe at Cohn before the meal, Jake finds himself surprised that "supper was a pleasant meal" (146) and recalls what he deems to be similar wartime dinners. When the present is set against the past, an elegiac mood is created by Jake's mistaken belief that "it seemed they were all such nice people" (146). He is recalling a time of crisis and elevated feeling, of truly living while facing imminent death. It stands in contrast to the present occasion composed of nasty drunks, recollected perfidious sexual encounters, and a silly snobbery of manners and social behavior. This juxtaposition of past and present underscores Jake's largely unconscious longing to recover a lost state of being and awareness. Hemingway's noncommittal style of rendering Jake's mistaken interpretation of events extends the elegiac perception to the perceptive reader. And what is perceived are the lengths to which the elegiac temper extends in connection with Jake's life. His sexual loss is but the initiator of an extensive sadness that suffuses not only his existence but also his perceptions of that existence.

Only when Jake is able to see that not only his life but all of life is profoundly elegiac does he gain a livable perspective. In a mortal world, a lament for irremediable loss can be both appropriate and inescapable. By recognizing this, Jake gains a profound insight into his personal fate, one apart from his earlier deliberate, willed efforts at self-control and disciplined repression. The breaking down of his defenses against the dissolution of his desperate mental concentration is begun by the geographical settings he occupies. It is finally completed by the juxtaposition of the world of the fiesta against the ritualized actions of the bullfight and its participants.[14]

Though these two are closely associated, in Hemingway's view they are actually polar opposites. Jake sets out for the fiesta in an effort to escape the fact of his sexual loss. He indulges in an inflated version of his Paris life—hedonistic, self-indulgent, ironic, and covertly superior to others because largely self-controlled and repressive. The fiesta becomes a time when "it seemed as though nothing could have any consequences" (154). This makes it the antithesis of Jake's view that everything has consequences. It is a time when his impotence can be ignored if only because of the concentration on group frivolity, anarchic alcoholic excess, and interaction with strangers.

Here the elegiac temper is sustained only by recognizing that it is illusory to view the fiesta as consequence-free, a transvaluation of values, and a carnival of pleasure alone. The fiesta, as its anarchic ritual of abandon and celebration makes clear, is only a seeming not an actuality. It constitutes a limited and unusual period of time rather than a permanent condition.[15] Thus, when Jake asserts that "everybody behaves badly" (181), he reveals an ironic awareness of the elegiac nature of existence. He now senses that perfection does not exist and that he is no different from the others in being lost. By this loss, he gains a growing awareness that he is unique from his fellows only in the kind of loss he has suffered, not in his having suffered a critical loss. With this, his freeing himself from egotistical suffering and regret is impending. And it occurs when he goes alone to San Sebastian after the fiesta.

The critical experience in Jake's coming to terms with his loss is the bullfight. The true nature of the elegiac temper is now seen to be something existential or metaphysical rather than psychological. Here Jake's passion for the public ritual of the bull ring is a displaced surrogate for the sexual contest denied him by his war wound: a commitment by two beings to struggle toward fulfillment in a deathlike exhaustion. Romero's isolation and loneliness are set off against Jake's. Both are warriors, lovers in distress, and ultimately losers of Brett. The one endures unconsummated love and rejection while the other suffers consummated love and abandonment. Both are deserted or abandoned by Brett out of love or charity or morality realized too late and thus destructive.

Romero's and Brett's flirtatious linking of death and friendship via the bulls spells the end of Jake's love for her and the final stage of his elegiac condition. Now he is totally isolated, beyond even friendship, much less romantic love. This is underscored by his estrangements even from the other aficionados and acquaintances of Romero. They no longer respect Jake because they think he is endangering Romero's life by encouraging his association with Brett. To their mind, he has allowed himself to be superseded as her lover without even a struggle or personal war. Jake's tacit disregard for the legitimacy of these views testifies to his indifference toward his own ego. In its place lies his growing identification with Hemingway's own sense of the metaphysical nature of the elegiac temper.

Evidence of this change of perspective is to be found in the veritable tidal wave of scenes of death, wounding, loss, and elegiac feelings that henceforth cascade around Jake. These range from his witnessing the departure by train of the family of the man gored in the street, through Romero's consummately heroic performance against his bulls, and Belmonte's contrasting performance, to Mike's tales about Brett and her past. In the face of these, Jake finds that "in the morning it was all over. The fiesta was finished" (227). All he has to do now is settle his accounts: the financial one with his fiesta friends and his own emotional one based on what he has witnessed involving the bullfight.[16] Thus, he goes alone to San Sebastian where he performs his elegiac farewell to the fiesta world of escape and illusory freedom from the constraints imposed by life itself. He isolates himself temporarily from everything but the natural world. He does so in order to divest himself of the effort to belong or be a member of the ordinary world, the world of social intercourse. His swimming and diving are acts of purification, which can work only metaphorically, not literally.[17]

They function as both a crucial interlude and preparation for his being able to live the elegiac temper. This is implicitly established by Brett's telegram asking for help and his response: "Well, that meant San Sebastian all shot to hell. I suppose, vaguely, I had expected something of the sort" (239). This ironic, sardonic summation of their relationship suggests his distancing of his feelings from what can and must be done. Their final conversation in Madrid brilliantly contrasts her pseudo stoical attitude with his genuine self-control. The effort required is revealed by his almost compulsive drinking, which suggests the intensity of pain he feels at the ending of their relationship.

It is, however, the narration of the scene rather than the characters themselves that generates the metaphysically elegiac reverberations in the situation. Only with their last words and the presence of the policeman is the elegy of their relationship invested with a profound and deep irony that encompasses the whole world pictured in the novel:

> "Oh, Jake, . . . we could have had such a damned good time together."
> "Yes, . . . Isn't it pretty to think so?" (247)

Her statement captures her self-pity and the conventional elegiac longing for something desirable that has been lost. His remark, in contrast, ironically deflates the illusion she is still maintaining as well as its underlying conviction. She still believes that the occurrence of one event (his war-inflicted impotence) can totally destroy lives. His metaphysical elegiac temper suggests the opposite. For him, if losses of this sort could completely and actually destroy individual lives, all lives would be destroyed, for everyone suffers loss in some measure. Consequently, if all lives suffer losses of one order or another, and individuals continue to live in spite of them, then one is already living the ultimate elegiac temper and not merely aspiring toward or searching for it.

Here is the real point of the policeman directing traffic. It embodies Jake's vision of the place of his impotence in the total scheme of things and his recognition of its actual value as a form of loss in the world.[18] The multiple ironies inherent in the policeman's wearing khaki and raising his baton remind us of the military and the war in which Jake suffered his loss of manhood. More, however, is implied than simply the casual and callous irony of virility set against impotence. The policeman's control over social intercourse results from institutional symbolism of uniform and baton, not from sexual prowess or ability. Jake's feeling Brett's body accidentally pressed against his underlines his deliberate need for sexual control in the face of incipient physical passion. He is unable to control or order his personal, inner life without a perpetual conscious struggle. In contrast, the policeman is able to control the social, public life of society automatically and unthinkingly. Despite his loss, Jake is free to live only when he possesses the elegiac temper. It enables him to choose the word *pretty* to characterize Brett's backward glance at the possibility of their romantic idyll.

Giovanni's Room was published some thirty years after *The Sun Also Rises,* yet in a number of ways it deliberately appears to recall its predecessor. Instances of this include: the use of Paris as a scenic backdrop and generator of an elegiac perspective, the reliance on a sexual dilemma as a focus for the dramatic action, the interjection of Spain as an interlude that permits escape, reflection, and ultimate withdrawal from a painful relationship and situation, the symbolic role of a policeman with a baton, and the intermittent reliance on religion either via the Church or God. Thus, it appears likely Baldwin was deliberately invoking Hemingway's novel as well Camus's novel, *L'Etranger.*[19] Yet in using these two earlier novels as models for *Giovanni's Room,* Baldwin thwarted his intent to generate a work of unrelieved elegiac temper. In a way, it is precisely where he departs from his models—in manner of narration and philosophic perspective—that he creates virtually insuperable obstacles to his work's ability to resonate with the full elegiac temper of his predecessors.[20]

The structure of *Giovanni's Room* consists essentially of four distinct parts: the protagonist David's early life in America with his family and friends; his life in France and his heterosexual relationship with Hella; his meeting of Giovanni and their doomed homosexual or bisexual affair; his return to Hella and the collapse of their relationship as a result of the impending execution of Giovanni.[21] These parts are arranged so as to create a cycle of David's memories. This cycle begins with his childhood and adolescent, first homosexual contact before moving on to his similar full-scale extended relationship with Giovanni. The contact with Giovanni entails his struggle with his sexual identity and his resistance to the homosexual world at large. Ultimately, the cycle concludes with David's final acceptance of his sexual nature, his concomitant loss of Hella, and his isolation from everything while surrounded only by his memories and guilt for all of them.

The sense of loss, sorrow, guilt, and death suffusing the novel is more than enough to make it a highly viable candidate for an elegiac work. Unfortunately, technical choices and authorial attitudes combine to force the novel into an uncertain mixture of the pathetic and the tragic. The form of narration chosen together with Baldwin's tensions, anxieties, and ambiguities concerning his own sexual identity conspire to produce a disjointed effect.[22] Only a remote suggestion of the elegiac creeps in directly through the style and more indirectly through the protagonist's dramatic situation and its sociocultural implications.

By electing to use a first person narration, Baldwin, unlike Hemingway, is unable to create sufficient detachment from which to view David's gradual and reluctant discovery of his homosexual drive.[23] His unwitting and naïvely unaware attraction to males and his moralized rational intelligence's recoil from and rejection of it create a theme of essentially pathetic and tragic implications. The narrative "I" in such a situation is impelled to respond in two ways. He can either mourn his fate or see it in inflated terms as a virtually unique event in human history. The former invokes self-pity for his sexual situation while the latter requires a tragic perspective that fills the protagonist with fear or terror.[24] The narrator is too close to the events of the narrative to be able to assess their significance with anything approaching objectivity. As a result, he veers between two compelling emotions. He feels that he is unable to select whatever will provide a stabilizing force in his life. At the same time, he takes on himself an all-consuming guilt and responsibility for the fate of others.

On the one hand, the narrator toys with a Hemingwayesque kind of determinism while also investing himself with an existentialist conviction of absolute personal responsibility. The former argues that his lack of culpability follows from the necessary ignorance of the future. Against it stands his belief that his desertion of Giovanni makes him totally and perpetually guilty and absolves everyone else of blame for anything.[25] However plausible such a contradiction may be from a psychological standpoint, it cannot create the elegiac temper of acceptance and confrontation with the consequences. Instead, it suggests the narrator-protagonist has not achieved the stoicism and self-control of Jake Barnes. The latter finally realizes that to live a necessarily limited life is still to live a life, and all the losses attendant thereon compensate to some degree for not having died. In its place, Baldwin indulges in an almost self-indulgent rhetorical posturing by his protagonist. In effect, this replaces the tragic hero's controlled acceptance of his fate with a denial that guilt can be escaped.

Baldwin's mixed feelings about his own homosexuality are perhaps reflected in two things: the identity of David, the protagonist, and the repeated narrative differentiation between the overt homosexual world and lifestyle and the casual bisexual relationship of David and Giovanni.[26] In making his involved narrator a white, blond, Anglo Saxon male, Baldwin is able to project his own dilemmas onto a world with which he was already at odds.[27] In effect, he is able to demonize it with his own demons. Such a projection would have sought to free him from facing the realities of his own situation by transferring it to a representative of a world of which he felt himself not a part. At the same time, in tacitly concurring with two contradictory thrusts of the narrative, Baldwin evades the central issue of sexual identity that he explicitly raises.[28] On the one hand, the narrative recoils from the overtly homosexual world as corrupt, squalid, and destined to end in loathing. Yet at the same time, it seeks to lend strong support for the "true love" of David and Giovanni.

Similarly, the American and European sections of the book set up polar views regarding sexual identity. Not only naturalistic but also religious or metaphysical explanations are propounded to explain or justify David's homosexuality.[29] The American section of the novel has a curiously flat quality. It is almost as though the author was content to rely on conventional plot elements to sketch in a required preliminary setting whose central role is to function as something from which escape is predetermined. A dead mother, a casually indifferent father, a bizarrely warped aunt, and melodramatic incidents together with the narrator's adolescent wild, rebellious nature all have a dispiriting stock quality. Many of these elements carry a clichéd sense of the dramatic that suggests the author is less than passionately interested in what he is doing.

Yet seen in context, many of the scenes and dramatic incidents do contribute subtly to the development of the theme of a protagonist being very gradually drawn into the homosexual world that is to be his ultimate destiny. This is a theme that could have, at least potentially, a significant elegiac component. Thus, David's childhood nightmares of his dead mother embracing him and almost swallowing him alive work as submerged incest dreams whose function is to move him toward his later homosexuality. By concealing the underlying nature of these dreams beneath grief for her death, Baldwin fugitively entertains a potentially elegiac theme. It, however, is never followed up in the novel largely because of the protagonist's narcissistic egoism and the author's use of first person narration.

Similarly, the presence of David's Aunt Ellen contributes to the naturalistic "explanation" of his latent homosexuality. Her incongruities of dress, demeanor, and attitude build in him a sense of her standing always on the edge of social disaster so that she creates intense anxieties in him. Consequently, he reveals the shaping forces of his past and his character in ways unperceived by him but fully comprehended by the author. The effect is to create a minimalist sort of pathos for David, one that verges on an incipiently elegiac temper. It consists of the pity for the immature person (David) felt by a spectator (Baldwin) who is at least partially involved.

This feeling is intensified through Ellen's jealousy over the father's girlfriend, Beatrice. Her essentially savage reaction suggests her own sexual frustration and her repressed incestuous drives with regard to her brother. It also conveys the revulsion of the narrator for heterosexual relationships of this sort. They provide him with a rationale for expanding his recoil to all heterosexual relationships. As a result, they incline him to an almost instinctual preference for homosexual contacts. Later, when David imitates his father's drinking behavior and quarrels with Ellen, he enacts a version of her perverted or warped relationship with his father. This becomes to his mind a paradigm of the only sexual relationship possible between heterosexuals. Yet even here there is implicitly operating a defense mechanism allowing him to escape responsibility. Thus, his subsequent engulfment in open homosexuality can, under the naturalistic explanation, be attributed to the actions and behavior of others such as his father and aunt.

Later in the novel, the European experience involves not a naturalistic but a philosophic rationale for his gradual absorption into the world of homosexual relationships. Such a rationale is scarcely an explanation in the ordinary sense of the term. Instead, it consists of metaphysical assertions that resonate with deeply felt but logically unjustified emotions. When David, early in the novel, recalls Giovanni and their "nights in bed" (6), he does so with an existentialist emphasis on the consequences of personal freedom: "no penalties attached—it was this last fact which was our undoing, for nothing is more unbearable, once one has it, than freedom" (6). The dreadful freedom of the existentialist is here reduced to a belated recognition that the freedom to do what one wishes is catastrophic to the self of the one engaging in it.[30]

It is not so much the facing of the moral abyss created by his desertion of Giovanni that animates David's self-flagellation over the latter's death sentence. Rather it is his avoiding the elegiac temper's recognition that the past is irredeemable and that all that can be done is to bear it. David repeatedly declares himself to be overwhelmed with guilt, regret, sorrow, and loss, but in the end he takes refuge in religious concepts such as "the heavy grace of God" (248), repentance (see 7), and "possible salvation" (214). These are more appropriate to the childhood preaching background of the author than the casual secular existence of the protagonist. As the novel closes, David is unable to aspire to the elegiac condition even as Baldwin himself was never able to attain or perhaps even to desire it.[31] In short, Baldwin's existentialism, if that is what it is, is quite unlike, say, Katov in *Man's Fate,* who possessed a clear-eyed recognition of what it is that needs to be done. David cannot sacrifice himself for the sake of his friend: "The burden of his salvation seemed to be on me and I could not endure it" (168). Nor, in fairness, is it at all clear how David's electing to stay with Giovanni rather than running off with Hella could have ultimately saved Giovanni. From the narrative's perspective, Giovanni was as likely to leave David at some future time as to be left.

The elegiac potential of the plot and the central characters' aspiration to an elegiac attitude constitute two instances of the elegiac in the novel. Other instances consist of physical settings and fleeting comments of characters, all of whom are more or less engaged in role-playing of one order or another. Thus, Paris in the early morning after a night's drinking arouses a sense of elegiac revulsion for a world in which men sleep under bridges, lovers aimlessly wander the streets, and drunken homosexuals indulge in expressions "of contempt and self-contempt" (65):

> I looked out, beyond his heavy profile, which was grey—from fatigue and from the light of the sky above us. The river was swollen and yellow. Nothing moved on the river. Barges were tied up along the banks. The island of the city widened away from us, bearing the weight of the cathedral; beyond this, dimly through speed and mist, one made out the individual roofs of Paris, the myriad, squat chimney stacks very beautiful and vari-colored under the pearly sky. Mist clung to the river, softening the army of trees, softening those stones, hiding the city's dreadful cork-

> screw alleys and dead-end streets, clinging like a curse to the men who slept beneath the bridges. (66)

This is an infinitely sad vision of a desperately old world in which everything has been done before and nothing any longer is worth doing at all. The implicit threnody captured here by David is intensified in its elegiac aspirations by its following almost directly after David's encounter in the bar with the mummy like figure of death and corruption. As a blend of Le Grande Guignol theatricality and the camp world of the homosexual, it stands as a baroque symbol of the significance of his first encounter with Giovanni.

The same juxtaposition of dramatic action and scenic reflection occurs just after David has left Giovanni for the last time. Their lover's quarrel is marked on both sides by extreme, exaggerated accusations and mute defensive responses full of hysteria, intensity, and multiple evasions of the truth. It reveals the stark reality behind the romantic pathos Baldwin tries to engender. Such affairs are destined to be relatively brief, to end messily and with pain for all concerned, and to depend on immaturity, role-playing, deviousness, and self-distortion. Against the stridency of the present and the human beings involved lies an autumnal urban scene rife with elegiac features. It conjures up the passing of time, the decay of nature, the growth or intensification of impending gloom and darkness, the aging of people, the commencement of rain, and the absence of sunshine. All work together to create an elegiac tableau. Against it, the impending, resumed heterosexual relationship with Hella is played out as an exercise in melancholy and futility.

A similar scene follows immediately after David's seduction by Giovanni. David, having left him for Hella, now faces the fact of her departure after she has learned the truth about his sexual identity. Here, not in Paris but in a small village in the south of France, the scene modestly and elegiacally reflects his post bisexual experience: unrelieved cold weather; unreasonable expectation of a surprise visitor (it is deliberately not made clear whether it is Hella or Giovanni for whom he longs); his intense personal isolation and loneliness; and the implicit sense of a rupture in his local social contacts. All culminate in his memory of Giovanni and "that claustrophobic room in Paris" (105) and the prospects of a future life. They are set against the stark finality of his elegiac recognition of their permanent separation: "I suppose they will come for him early in the morning, perhaps just before dawn, so that the last thing Giovanni will ever see will be that grey, lightless sky over Paris" (105).

With this, there begins David's time of reflection, self-assessment, and elegiac regret at the almost inevitable pain of existence. The fragmentary, disconnected, and unfocused character of this reflection by a first person protagonist thwarts the novel's ability to achieve a sustained elegiac temper. The reflection is composed of a series of foci that move toward the elegiac without ever really confirming it as a dominant point of view. Thus, the Parisian spring, when the central bisexual relationship develops, is recollected by David as a backdrop to the isolated, hidden, strained, tension-filled life of the two male lovers. It serves to intensify the elegiac tone directed at a past relationship composed of caring and betrayal as opposed to the claustrophobia inspired by Giovanni's room.[32] A further intensification is created by the gradual dwindling of sorrow in David's mind and his rising egoistic desire for personal freedom.

This personal recoil is followed by David's brief attempt to analyze his relationship to his nationality and other Americans. His critical contempt concentrates on his countrymen's apparent uniformity and reluctance to risk breaching the boundaries of circumspect sexual conduct. Of these, the one is a cliché and the other an effort at self-serving arrogance. Ultimately, however, he recognizes that at bottom the American identity consists of "power and sorrow, both unadmitted, unrealized, the power of inventors, the sorrow of the disconnected" (130). This muted elegiac response to America, however, is fleeting. For David, it is perceivable only as an expatriate living the life of a stranger and foreigner.

Baldwin's abbreviated redaction of Henry James's international theme implicitly demands a sharply critical assessment of his simplification of the differences between Americans and Europeans. In effect, Baldwin joins a snapshot version of the Jamesian motif with *The Sun Also Rises*. His effort to emulate Hemingway's sociocultural elegiac feeling for expatriation, contextual displacement, and personal isolation diffuses its energies by oscillating between brief cultural analysis and personal self-pity for his protagonist.

The difference between Baldwin and Hemingway is starkly seen in the contrast between the walk home through Paris streets taken by the two protagonists. The walk for Baldwin arouses some of the same elegiac overtones it does for Hemingway, though in a more muted and abbreviated fashion.

Where it differs is in its extreme focus on David's ego and its projection onto the meeting with Sue. Jake's minimalist objective rendering of his surroundings is dedicated to keeping his egoistic feelings in check. David's egregious sense of predatory sexual contact reveals his confusion and immaturity despite his conviction of his practicality and common sense. His effort at seduction is totally self-serving and consciously so, while Brett's almost reluctant pursuit of Jake is driven by genuine passion, which she can neither abandon nor direct. Baldwin's is a more indulgent world lived in by people who unconsciously role-play a superficial game of sincerity and significance. They do so in order to convince themselves they are engaged in truly meaningful activities, challenges, and crises that must be met.

This is particularly true of David, Baldwin's protagonist and more or less alter ego.[33] His multiple reflections range from the trivial to the too easily genuine. An instance is his thinking with regard to Sue: "Somewhere, at the very bottom of myself, I realized that I was doing something awful to her and it became a matter of my honor not to let this fact become too obvious" (146). It is this invoking of the concept of honor that captures the quintessential difference between Hemingway and Baldwin. For Hemingway, honor entails a stoical, cynical acceptance of the actual and the determination to cope with it through the development of an elegiac temper. In contrast, for Baldwin, honor is essentially a word invoked as part of the self-inflationary actions of the individual ego bent on justifying the breaking of ordinary societal and sexual boundaries. Just as with Giovanni, David's sexual encounter left him back in a "dark, tiny room" from which he "wanted only to get out" (147).

Essentially, the image of the room symbolizes the human self as a mysterious, sinister place in which people enact their own individual futilities and efforts to escape. Its darkness and chaotic, constantly-in-transition condition are not confronted by David when he first meets Giovanni, who challenges him to free himself from his past accustomed attitudes and to explore a new and radically different way of life. The tragedy for David, as for most rebels against the status quo, the established, the customary, is that he is never able to envisage the full range of cultural consequences embodied in this challenge. Simply to list some of these consequences is to sketch the complexity inherent in it: to risk seduction by a sophisticated lover; to venture into the unknown mystery of the full range of potential human relationships; to surrender an old, false sense of self as a consciously aware entity; to abandon a father's heterosexuality for an emancipated version of another relative's thwarted and perverted sexual drive; to entertain sex as a casual, temporary, fleeting encounter rather than as a symbol of commitment, love, and permanence; to reject American Puritanism for European hedonism and ironic skepticism about the possibilities of human nature; to deny Christianity's trust in deferral of satisfaction and achievement in favor of a classical "carpe diem" philosophy. All of these are implicit in Giovanni's challenge, but David responds only to the immediate surface one of a long repressed personal gratification.

What David never realizes is that its very extended repression only heightens the sense of immediate excitement and self-realization beyond what it can confer permanently after the immediate moment has passed. The seriousness of his action emerges only later after Giovanni has lost his job as a kind of sexual reprisal by Guillaume. The full consequences now appear of David embarking on the relationship almost as a game or diversion. His casual curiosity about boundary breaking is now seen for what it is, an exploration of the underside of the self. Then, he recognizes that it has turned into a trap of indeterminable duration. Verbally at any rate, David never does wholly face the reason for this. The reason lies in his self, its weakness or indulgence, its willingness to ignore possible consequences in order merely to break the boundaries of ordinary bourgeois society. He never considers that a casual and misplaced impulse is capable of producing such incredibly deep pain and suffering. So seen, *Giovanni's Room* is an implicit and strong indictment of psychological hedonism, its implications and possible consequences. Yet finally, it is one that fails to achieve its full power as a result of its author's inability to detach himself sufficiently from the narrative theme.

This inability stems from the reliance on first person narration, which ultimately warps the elegiac potential of the theme into mere personal pathos. As he tries to comfort Giovanni over his job loss, David feels that "Judas and the Savior had met in me" (162). With this, he signals the consequence of the first person narration—the shift from the elegiac to the pathetic or, as viewed by the narrator, the tragic. David's undeniable personal pain and sorrow are set against his landlady's revelations of the effects of war—family deaths and financial impoverishment in old age—on her and her family. Consequently, the nature of the elegiac is succinctly limned in so as to broaden its implications from the personal to the societal: "It is sad, is it not, to have worked so hard all one's life in order to have a little peace in one's old age and then to have it taken away?" (101) Against such a quiet yet deeply bitter reflection, David's more histrionic and impassioned self-accusations of guilt and irresponsibility evoke little more than an awareness of the pathos inherent in all decisions following from casual temptations.

6

MARRIAGE AS CULTURAL CHANGE

Henry James's *The Portrait of a Lady* and Ernest Hemingway's *A Farewell to Arms*

Some of the major modern elegies for marriage are James's *The Portrait of a Lady* (1881), Hemingway's *A Farewell to Arms* (1929), Fitzgerald's *Tender Is the Night* (1933), and Updike's *Too Far to Go* (1979). The first two are discussed here and the others in the next chapter. Taken as a whole, these novels chart a broad spectrum of the marital relationship that stretches from desperate personal unhappiness, the early death of one of the partners, emotional and geographical separation, on through divorce. Significantly enough, none of them elects to memorialize a long, happy, and compatible union whose ending with death of one or both partners is the basis for mourning and celebration.

Each work points up a different way in which the modern marriage elegy develops. Taken as a group, they trace the shifting views of and attitudes toward marriage from the last quarter of the nineteenth century to the last quarter of the twentieth. Thus, for James, marriage is a sacred opportunity and enduring obligation in which the responsibility of the individual is paramount. For Hemingway, the loss of a partner by death occasions a similar kind of stoical willingness to endure what fate has dictated. The difference between the two authors lies, of course, in the nature of the union and the rationale for enduring the loss. For James, Isabel's marriage is unhappy and full of bitter disappointment but destined to continue. Hemingway's lovers, on the other hand, achieve ecstatic fulfillment until it is abruptly terminated by the death of one. In the first instance, the marriage is a moral and spiritual commitment to one's assumed obligation. In the other, it becomes a grimly philosophical recognition that even the immediate past is a cessation that can never be restored.

Fitzgerald and Updike contrast with them by tracing out the loss of a relationship occasioned by divorce. The resultant loss does not occur from either the maintaining of a legal and arbitrary connection or from the permanent separation of death. Instead, the loss experienced by the Divers and the Maples is an arbitrary and legal severance treated as inevitable given the nature of the participants and the diminished status of the institution of marriage. Dick Diver's hubristic conviction that he is capable of saving Nicole from the effects of her father's incestuous advances initiates his elegiac acceptance of defeat in a manner reminiscent of the tragic hero and even the dying god. Richard Maples, on the other hand, musingly stumbles through his marriage alternately inflamed with passion and desultorily bored by Joan, his wife. Ultimately, it is legally dissolved as a result of ennui and a spirit of mutual accommodation. The resultant impression made by both texts is that of a suppressed elegy for an unarticulated commitment to a wholly fulfilling relationship.

James's *The Portrait of a Lady* (1881) obviously encompasses much more than an elegiac perspective on a character and a civilization. Its social comedy, its tragic character analysis, its philosophical probing of self and society, and its richly detailed international theme clearly indicate that it lies beyond a single rubric no matter how complex or diversified. Nevertheless, as it moves patiently and seamlessly toward its ironically tragic finale, it becomes increasingly clear that James is reflectively contemplating the elegiac significance of death, human loss in several forms, and the inevitable twilight of a civilized world.

Indeed, even from the opening scene of the great country house of Gardencourt, the sense of pure aesthetic pleasure is depicted as reflective of a society at its full flowering but with an overtone of elegiac lament.[1] The fact that neither the house nor the civilization is likely to continue without having its tranquility disrupted by death (Mr. Touchett), illness (Ralph), change (Isabel), and moral corruption (Mrs. Merle and Osmond) is inherent in the picture drawn.[2] A casual consideration of Isabel's regard for her family home and her appreciation of her past life suggests that her role as the central character is deeply rooted in her affinity for the elegiac.[3] Her statement that "I like places in which things have happened—even if they're sad things" (I, 34) shows this. It suggests her willingness to endure the elegiac experience of sorrow, loss, and intense feelings without abandoning her sense of life's perennial promise.[4] Similarly, Isabel's appreciation of her past life, especially her childhood, produces a kind of elegiac feeling which is balanced by a willingness to welcome change of any kind. She feels pity that it is over and no longer present mixed with pleasure at being able to recall it in memory.

Moreover, the elegiac extends beyond the central character to include others. This is seen in the introductory sketch of Ralph's gradually deteriorating health from three years before the novel opens. Ralph's future is viewed with a calm elegiac acceptance as he contemplates how past events shadow the present scene. Ralph *has* survived death, although the survival is tinted with a dual recognition. First, his survival is of limited duration and, second, as a consequence, he is concerned to contemplate that fact to the full. Part of Ralph's contemplative state focuses on Isabel, whom he envies for her vigor, independence, intelligence, frankness, and her uniqueness. All of these stand in contrast to his own life's limitations of scope, venturesomeness, and duration.

This dual focus engenders a kind of double elegiac perspective overall: one for his expected but unrevealed (at least at this juncture) brevity of life, and the other for Isabel's tragic or lamentable future betrayal by spouse and friends. Ralph's imagining of loving her—as he reflects on her in conversation with his mother—has its own elegiac dimension. It consists not only in its being concealed or suppressed but also in its being unrealizable, its inability to be requited. Later during his stay in "the empty house in Winchester Square" (I, 197), Ralph again appears an elegiac figure whose life is lonely and isolated. He is pitiable because marked for a permanent spectatorial role in life. This is underscored by his marked contrast to both Isabel and Henrietta. The former is all active thinking and feeling, questioning, and theory-generating,[5] while the latter is dedicated to a vigorous, almost athletic pursuit of and desire for the social life of polite society.

James's use of characters as elegiac *figurae* is balanced by his willingness to invoke conventional elegiac natural settings as backdrops.[6] They serve to foreshadow the gradual emergence of Isabel as the preeminently elegiac creature in the novel. One of the most striking and effective instances of this is Isabel's first encounter with Madame Merle. There, the natural setting—autumnal twilight, rain, cold, wind in large trees—is sketched quickly and economically. It unobtrusively provides a sad and incipiently mournful context for Isabel's meeting with Merle at the very time of her return to her sick and dying uncle. This setting dovetails his departure from life with Isabel's innocently beginning to be drawn toward the losses she is to experience from her involvement with Osmond and his world of duplicity, betrayal, and concealed motives.

The elegiac note is also used in oblique ways to further character contrasts. Thus, Merle's protestation at her own wasted life is set against Isabel's quiet expression of condolence to Ralph at the news of his father's death. Merle deliberately construes her life as a waste of the opportunity conferred by youth in counterpoint to Isabel's qualities of frankness, genuineness, and sincerity. In so doing, Merle comes as close as she is able to the elegiac view. Yet her arousal of Isabel's sympathetic curiosity is not so much a matter of genuine sorrow as of time-tinged regret calculated to stimulate such interest. It is at the furthest possible pole from Isabel's abbreviated elegy for her uncle. Isabel's chastened, restrained, but heartfelt lament is essentially unspoken but nonetheless communicated directly. It contrasts sharply with the socially motivated utterance of Merle as well as that of Mrs. Touchett who "intimated in a few words that condolences might be taken for granted" (I, 295). This contrast sets the genuine against the fraudulent, the personal against the social. In so doing, it prepares for Isabel's final determination to honor the terms of her marriage at the expense of her self and her personal happiness. It is in this last, of course, that Isabel's full acquisition of the elegiac temper is most stubbornly insisted upon and most enigmatically acceded to by James.

A similar sort of contrast is seen when Isabel's final attitude is recalled in conjunction with her earlier assessment of her aunt for whom she "came at last to have a kind of undemonstrable pity" (I, 317). This is aroused in her because "there seemed something so dreary in the condition of a person whose nature had, as it were, so little surface—offered so limited a face to the accretions of human contact" (I, 317). Here Isabel feels a kind of unexpressed elegy for her aunt's character. Mrs. Touchett's life, while clearly defined and aggressively self-determined, is also marked by multiple losses. Through such scenic strategies, it is gradually borne in upon the reader that the novel as a whole deals with the kind of losses people suffer in merely living. It does not matter whether they do so freely (Isabel) or by being imprisoned (Mrs. Touchett) by a whole welter of conventions, attitudes, and beliefs.

Of all the losses experienced by the various characters, none, however, is as powerful or extended in duration as Isabel's. In effect, the entire first volume of the novel traces the process by which she moves to encounter them.

She begins rather hubristically by articulating a sense of her self and its individuality before arriving at a conviction of the fatality it entails. Coupled with these is her disregard of the dangers of individual pride and undue self-confidence together with her easy acceptance of the praise of others like Ralph and his father. Her remark to Caspar Goodwood as they discuss his marriage proposal and her future captures the essence of her initial attitude: "I try to judge things for myself; to judge wrong, I think, is more honorable than not to judge at all" (I, 228). This view captures the underlying dialectic in her life: self and other, freedom and restraint, independence and subjection, liberty and imprisonment, honor and dishonor. It also hints by its very directness and simplicity at the risks inherent therein. To a degree, it foreshadows the sadness and sorrow that will follow from mistakes made and recognized both by her and those who watch over or view her. That is, both Isabel and sympathetic fellow characters steadily become aware of the risks and sorrows attendant upon her attitude compounded as it of self-confidence and determined courage.

At the beginning of volume II, the complications in life arising from her initial attitude appear in two critical scenes: the juxtaposition of Lord Warburton's departure and its interruption by the arrival of Gilbert Osmond. Enveloped as she is in the silence, the sense of quietude, and the solemn spell cast by the deep stillness of the Greek sculpture in the gallery of the Capitol, she enjoys the aesthetic pleasures of the elegiac farewell to Warburton in a way that appears to argue for her having made the appropriate decision. Osmond's heightened attraction to her as a result of her having declined Warburton's proposal magnifies the reader's own quite different response to the elegiac. It increases the contrast between the candor and nobility of the rejected suitor and the deviousness and unscrupulous egocentricity of the ultimately successful suitor. Inherent here is a kind of lament or unstated regret generated by the contrast between Isabel's demeanor and James's perspective on it. Her foolish reliance on herself exclusively and on Ralph's and others' excessive praise of her is sharply outlined when set against the observed reality presented by James.

Somewhat later, when Caspar reacts vigorously to her proposed marriage to Gilbert, she is aware of the vital loss being suffered by another. Immediately it arouses in her something like guilt—"If she were not in the wrong, however, why should she desire to defend herself?" (II, 50). Further, her tears at the end of chapter 32 evidence her lamentation at the ways of the world, at having to choose, and at the terrible risks in relying on personal freedom and the individual self.[7]

Self-loss and death are intertwined in the final stage of Isabel's journey toward the elegiac temper. Her involvement in Ralph's impending demise is conjoined with her loss of admiration and respect for her husband, her acceptance of Madame Merle's past, and the latter's role in Isabel's marriage decision. Isabel's sense of perplexity, puzzlement, and apprehension at the real relations obtaining between the three of them are compounded of "a confusion of regrets, a complication of fears" (II, 159). They suggest an incipient formation on her part of an elegiac temper toward her marriage and husband, her personal decision and choice. With this, she also experiences a growing awareness of the dangers of relying completely on the self's freedom. Only with Gilbert's accusation of her interfering with Pansy's opportunity to marry Warburton does she fully see the extent of his depravity, egotism, and disregard for others.

During this traumatic experience she is also trying to cope with Ralph's precipitous decline in health, his desire to die at home, at Gardencourt, and the impact her going to him will have on her marriage. If her full understanding of Gilbert's nature is couched in Miltonic imagery of the Fall, her move to acceptance of Ralph's death is charted through an aura of elegiac natural settings and personal perspectives.[8] She sees all of his commendable qualities set against the stark fact that he is actually dying. Her sense of reflective sadness follows from her contemplating the inexorability of his death. She realizes all too well that with it she faces the loss of his personal qualities. His stoical, lighthearted attitude toward the possibility of their meeting again creates a deep pathos in her for him, one that contrasts with her admission that she is afraid of herself.

As she moves toward the elegiac temper in her own person and being, the external natural world both in England and Italy increasingly takes on an elegiac aura. Gardencourt is seen by her now as a place of elegiac qualities. Memories of deep, dim chambers, dark ivy around windows that glimmer, a place in which "no chapter of the past was more perfectly irrecoverable" (II, 296) bring tears to her eyes. The elegiac note of the novel's opening scene is raised here to a major key in which it dominates both setting and point of view.

Similarly, after the revelation of Madame Merle's close personal involvement in Isabel's marriage, Isabel takes a solitary drive. Its setting completely mirrors her final elegiac temper, which enables her both to go to Ralph in his last hours and to return to Gilbert and her marriage:

> She rested her weariness upon things that had crumbled for centuries and yet still were upright; she dropped her secret sadness into the silence of lonely places, where its very modern quality detached itself and grew objective, so that as she sat in a sun-warmed angle on a winter's day, or stood in a mouldy church to which no one came, she could almost smile at it and think of its smallness. (II, 327)

The world of old Rome, a world of ruins and silent, lonely places bears in on her a "haunting sense of the continuity of the human lot" (II, 327) in which resides the elegiac temper consciously realized.[9] Here James deploys a high rhetorical style of sonorous images to capture an emotional progression through a contemplative personal acceptance of history, physical decline amid beauty, and all that simply is and which lies beyond change. Thus, after being confronted by the Countess's horrendous disclosures concerning Madame Merle and Gilbert, Isabel is able to insist on going to Ralph "in a tone of far-reaching, infinite sadness" (II, 373). This reveals her full envelopment in the elegiac temper. Life is fundamentally sad not only because of betrayals and foolhardiness and headstrong insistence on self and freedom but because things once done cannot ultimately be altered or eliminated. The impact of history—cultural as well as personal—produces the elegiac impulse, while the effort to evade it is an inevitable fact of personal history.[10]

At the beginning of her European experience, Isabel insists that her happiness depends on her not turning away, not separating herself from "life. From the usual chances and dangers, from what most people know and suffer" (I, 187). She opts not for knowledge so much as personal conviction, which assumes she is somehow "special," ordained to risk and receive more from life than other people. But by identifying her fate with that of "most people," she endeavors implicitly to "democratize" herself, to make herself more like others rather than unlike them. In setting up this dialectic at the outset, James essentially creates an elegiac situation or temper with which to invest her actual fate. She creates by her attitude or convictions a fate fraught with tragic or sad or pitiable consequences. These she need not have encountered except for the rarity, delicacy, and protractedly contemplative nature of her temperament. Her temptation is to feel too much, to explore, contemplate, and analyze issues and concerns overly much. In this, she is like James himself, so that in a sense the novel is his confrontation with his own temptation as an artist.[11] Before the enormity of human losses, their inevitability, and incomprehensibility, even the most subtle and sophisticated of minds can do no more than stand silent and regretful. James testifies to this when he records Isabel's inability to read after Ralph's death and her lack of interest in literature. The irony inherent in James's elegiac temper applied to the *Portrait* itself resides in Mrs. Touchett's reflecting on Ralph's posthumous recognition of Henrietta's "services to literature" (II, 423).

Clearly, *The Portrait of a Lady* (1881) focuses on marriage as a legal and religious institution to be adhered to by its central character. Its author implicitly endorses this view as central to the preservation of the culture that honors it. James treats Isabel's decision as deferring the demise of a civilization that he finds inherent in the actions of Osmond and Madame Merle. *A Farewell to Arms* (1929) replaces this conviction with a wholly personal and emotional definition of the marital relationship. It sees the elegiac loss not through ironies inherent in the maintaining of a purely legal contract. Instead, Hemingway locates the elegiac in the physical loss of a sexual and emotional partner amid a civilization scarcely worthy of the name.

Both works, however, depend heavily on their settings and general conditions of life to define the reader's elegiac expectations. From the novel's very outset, Hemingway generates a seasonal elegy based on a coalescence of time of year, natural surroundings, and war seen from a distance as if by a completely detached observer. Chapter 1 focuses on a series of physical elements all passing by as if toward some multifaceted disaster compounded of death, obliteration, dirt, and disease.[12] The author creates a sense of events objectively and flatly recorded. Their observer abstains from suggesting their significance save for a final inference that the war is unsuccessful and that death is plentiful.

A year later things are *said* to be better: more military victories, more civilized, comfortable living conditions, and greater sexual normality. Yet doubt is cast on this claim by the destruction of the hitherto pristine forest of trees. The quick appearance of a cloud, the color of the sun, the grayness of the weather, and the sudden arrival of a snowstorm suggest that nature is past the stage of elegiac mourning. It is now embarked on its own destruction and is completely bereft of fruitfulness and life:

> The snow slanted across the wind, the bare ground was covered, the stumps of trees projected, there was snow on the guns and there were paths in the snow going back to the latrines behind the trenches. (6)

This scene contrasts with the greater surface human sociability—the drinking, the brothels, and the teasing conversation—that suggests the troops are adjusting to the idea and fact of war. In effect, it's almost becoming the norm of existence. Here is the first understated instance of Hemingway's irony. It sardonically suggests that human nature is such that initially it is almost unaware of the loss of the normalities of life. It is the growth in awareness of this loss and the focusing down to the deeply personal nature of the loss of a loved one that provides the elegiac culmination of the novel.

From the outset, the simple past tense used throughout coupled with the direct rendering of observed phenomena—central characteristics of the celebrated Hemingway stylistic innovations—generate an expectation that what is being narrated has an as yet unrevealed significance.[13] Else why would the narrator recollect them in this painstaking fashion? Both natural and human scenes are firmly and deeply inscribed on the narrator's memory for a reason as yet unrevealed. The sentence rhythm and images suggest that what is being recollected will prove to be a bitter memory marked by sorrow, loss, and death felt in both general and specific senses, both in personal and cultural terms.

The reliance on the past tense in the telling of the story establishes that its tragic finale has already been experienced by the narrator. The very inarticulateness of his elegiac grief sums up and consolidates what is diffused obliquely throughout the novel: "after I had got them out and shut the door and turned off the light it wasn't any good. It was like saying good-by to a statue" (355). It permeates his responses to natural settings, the war itself, and various characters all of which he also loses through separation or death. Seasonal change contrasts with the static conditions of existence in which houses and people remain the same. This juxtaposition creates in Lieutenant Henry the unreal sense of time both passing and not passing. In effect, it is the superimposition of one past upon another that creates the elegiac mood that dominates much of the novel: the past in which Catherine is alive and with him and the more recent past in which she is dead and eternally separated from him except in memory. This superimposition generates the ironic core of Hemingway's elegiac tone.

The first romantic encounter between the two occurs in chapter 6. Henry sees it as a ritualistic game requiring deceit, simulation, and evasion. For both, initially, it is part of wartime's casual, largely meaningless, sexual encounters devoid of deep emotions.[14] This is undercut by Catherine's candor in so assessing it, which is founded on her elegiac response to her former lover's wartime death. In relation to the elegy of war, she is the more deeply experienced in its personal implications.

Until Henry meets her, war for him generates only revulsion at the destruction involved and sorrow for the sudden violent loss of casual friends. Catherine's initial frankness and candor—"you don't have to say you love me. That's all over for a while" (33)—presages their own elegiac fate at the end of the novel. Ironically, there the gender situation is reversed: she is dead and he is left to mourn in silent isolation. The irrelevance and ineffectiveness of language coupled with the profound isolation of the individual self become in both scenes the defining points in the Hemingwayesque romantic marital elegy.

The casual sexual relationships embodied in his visits to the military brothels and while on leave are part of the war elegy. They serve as mementos of the lack of genuine emotional relationships that normally are a part of peacetime life. They become sardonic symbols of a loss scarcely experienced as yet but nevertheless creating a deep impact of nothingness. It is from the war elegy itself that Henry's meeting of Catherine begins to extricate him. With her, he begins to formulate the characteristic Hemingway marital elegy. It entails a virtually prescribed series or stages. First, there is the discovery of someone new and the conviction of the uniqueness and permanence of that relationship. Then, there comes a sudden, inexplicable interruption of it by the intervention of a permanent change, whether of impotence (as with Jake Barnes) or death (as with Catherine). Finally, it concludes with a disruption of the individual's life that leaves him a permanent victim of living.

In a minor but key fashion, the soldier from Pittsburgh with the hernia encountered by Henry at the side of the road serves as his counterpoint in the elegy of war. He first suggests the widespread intense repugnance felt for the war and the likelihood of death. In effect, he embodies the disdain felt by Hemingway's characters for the traditional or conventional elegiac mode of celebrating heroic elevation and the noble sacrifice of one's own life.

The contemporary (Hemingwayesque) mode, on the other hand, faces death reluctantly as something imposed rather than chosen. In wartime, this fate is intensified by its being seen as virtually inescapable. Yet the almost convulsive longing not to have to endure it is the context against which its occurrence is set. Unlike the conventional mode, this mode does not welcome or celebrate the event. Instead it confronts the event reluctantly with an attitude of almost fatalistic despair. This spirit is redeemed only by the manifestation of a determination to endure stubbornly what cannot be avoided any longer. The difference between Henry and the soldier from Pittsburgh is that the latter is willing to abrogate any personal code of conduct in order to avoid the elegiac confrontation. The former struggles to maintain a loyalty to the ethic of romantic commitment as an alternative to death.

In a somewhat similar fashion, the difference of opinion between Henry and Passini over which is worse—war or defeat—points up a related contrast. It captures the difference between survival with and without a code. Whether war ever ends or is finished, is won by victory or surrender, underscores the difference between the anti-elegiac and the elegiac attitudes toward existence. For Hemingway, they represent the difference between mere continuance of existence lacking any honor whatsoever and a minimalist honor based on an inherent truth to oneself, the personal self with whom one must live. The response of Henry and the others to the death of the nameless soldier in the ambulance embodies the neutral, minimalist acceptance of death. It is basically a nonlinguistic antithesis of the conventional or "literary" elegiac response:

> "How is he?" the Englishman called back. . . .
>
> "He's dead I think," I said.
>
> The drops fell very slowly, as they fall from an icicle after the sun has gone. It was cold in the car in the night as the road climbed. At the post on the top they took the stretcher out and put another in and we went on. (66)

This device of compressing the elegiac response anticipates the more expansive one developed in chapters 10–12. Together they conclude Henry's involvement with the elegy of war. The former enables him as an individual to recognize the intimacy of his involvement in the war elegy. With it, he becomes less a spectator and more of an actual participant in wartime death. The expansive role of chapters 10–12 delineates his continuing to share in the public, group responses to the consequences of being actively involved.

Whereas the method of compression suppresses the verbal, the expansive approach is one of evasion and substitution. How to avoid the visceral feelings of recoil, horror and terror, and fear is, in effect, part of the effort to retain the old world of the customary. In short, it deploys the conventional responses to physical wounding and the facing of death as a means of avoiding the elegiac expressions of emotion.

These three chapters explore graphically the physical surprise and shock of the wounding, the stoical, commonsense, "masculine" effort to control them, and the sense of their diminishing impact and trauma. This is seen through the characters' reliance on ordinary conversation about ordinary affairs and a teasing, joking manner over romantic, sexual matters. Both of these devices attempt to minimize the elegiac impact of physical violation, to render it somehow commonplace and an accepted part of normal experience. They also prepare for the final loss of Catherine through downplaying via a taut self-control the lesser shock of the wounding. As a result, the greater shock—her death in childbirth—achieves an even more powerful intensity. It generates an overwhelming sense of the powerlessness of the individual to reverse, alter, or modify the trauma of loss. This powerlessness, in a sense, outweighs even the fact of death.

Henry's preparation for disengagement from the elegy of war is signaled at the beginning of book 2. There, when recovering in the hospital, he first declares himself in love with Catherine. In effect, this act signals the coalescence of physical and emotional trauma and their convergence in the anticipation of death. The chief difference is that the wounding brought him consciously close to death, whereas the committed declaration of love brought him to face death directly only in retrospect and during the narrating of his farewell both to war and to love. This difference in awareness heightens the irony of his final situation. Pleasure, fulfillment, and self-realization become the medium by which death and loss of the most searing and personal order is experienced. In determining to bid adieu to military arms, he chooses to welcome love of another person as providing a renunciatory escape from war and death. Only retrospectively does he recognize that love apparently entails its own loss through the death of the beloved. Chapters 13 and 14 juxtapose the pleasures of love against the pain of war. The first consummation of their recently declared love stands against the doctor's probing of his wounds for metal fragments. This occurs in a way that almost ironically declares the situation to be a *liebestod.* Thus, in the next chapter the major's kissing Henry on the forehead symbolically captures the association of war and death with love and loss.

During the summer Henry and Catherine's courtship is marked by simple physical pleasures enjoyed with other people. Dining, pleasant surroundings, attentive friends and acquaintances, and casual physical contacts in social situations make the unusual situation of war appear almost like the ordinary one of peace. The tranquility they experience together gains in poignancy both through its retrospective narration and the stylistic suggestions that it is transitory and fleeting. It stands as a tranquil interlude amid an ultimately disastrous situation that is cast not so much as unusual as the customary consequence for people of this generation and historical milieu.

During this phase of their relationship, they start to carve out their personal definition of marriage as something radically different from those of the state or the church. Both institutions' elaborate formalities hold out the threat of arbitrary separation of the principals. Her claim that he is her only religion and that they can consider themselves married privately is deeply paradoxical. For the very concept of marriage entails public ceremonies of at least a minimal order as well as legal and institutional sanctions. This paradox invests their relationship with a certain hubristic quality. They are daring both time and fortune by claiming a permanency for their relationship that neither of them can ensure. Indeed, her stated importance of the relationship functions as a prelude to the elegiac finality of her death and his confrontation of desperate and irretrievable loss.

The novel's elegiac quality, of course, includes more than the death and loss suffered by the two principal characters. It possesses also a sense of the pathos and sorrow enveloping their conviction that escaping from a world of war is a simple matter. Such an escape, they think, is one that can be handled simply, directly, and personally. Thus, being happy and in love is enough for Catherine. Hedonism, emotional satisfaction, and personal commitment represent the entirety of expectations in life, or so she says. The simplicity of her viewpoint and the directness of her statements (particularly in chapter 18) generate a touching impression of vulnerability, which augurs the elegiac experience that ends the novel. The aura of impending disaster is generated by her easy simplicity of outlook, which arouses apprehensions that she is misreading their situation.

At the same time, Hemingway shrewdly counters their rather simplistic outlook on the chances of survival in the world they currently inhabit. Her naïve faith in love is offset by her later, more austere and fatalistic statements. Thus, she remarks that her fear of rain is due to her sometimes seeing herself dead in it. This functions as a foreshadowing of the novel's last scene in the hospital. The persistence of the rain at the end of chapter 19, after she has stopped crying, provides a foreboding glimpse of the truth of her apprehensive claim that "nobody can help themselves" (135).

Similar remarks and responses combine to narrow down their future prospects to an elegiac fate. One is her somber comment that "Nobody is like us," and Henry recognizes that "She did not mean it happily" (157). Still another is her rejection of seeking solace and consolation in the cathedral. Her sad awareness of the uniqueness of their situation forms a choric-like commentary on their struggle to evade the war with all of its obligations. Their relationship is doomed because it faces an inescapable fate in which death, separation, and loss are inextricably joined. Further, their intense belief in their love's uniqueness follows from their focusing on themselves alone. At the same time, such a focus follows from their effort to avoid feeling love's loss is inevitable in a world dedicated to destructiveness and governed by a war that appears to be the public expression of society's deepest desires.

The paradoxical contrast in her outlook—so romantically simple as to be almost naïve, and yet deeply fatalistic—is fraught with irony. It reveals the deep, irredeemable flaw in their trust in romantic love. Out of this trust comes their effort to redefine the concept of marriage solely in terms of personal relationship. Her remark that "I'm so very happy married to you" (165) reveals both their dismissal of ordinary social conventions and their tacit use of one of them to justify an unconventional relationship. The permanency and stability inherent in the marital claim is undercut by the Marvell quotation about "Time's wingèd chariot hurrying near" (165). The quote points up the fragility of her marital claim, based as it is purely on personal desire and hope. Marvell's powerful sense of the transitoriness of life, its inevitable close, and its unavoidable state of loss ominously threatens the durability of their love. The illusoriness of their actually being married underscores the real elegiac outcome that they cannot avoid no matter what stratagems they employ.

Their parting at the station in the last chapter of book 2 serves as a prelude to the elegiac finale created by her death. By being marked by elegiac images of rain, shadows, and isolation amid crowds, it is deeply premonitory. Thus, his loss of Catherine is ironically compounded by his abandonment of his seat to the wounded captain. His gesture of surrender signals his acceptance of the need still to comply with the military code of warriors. To this extent, he is still engaged in and with the war even though his focus is now on romance, love, and the illusory prospect of living. At the same time, his surrendering his seat also underscores the consequences—the diminishment of existence—of any experience of loss. Here, his loss is more than his separation from Catherine. It also entails his temporary relapse back into the wartime world of military hierarchy, the concerted weight of the opinion of others, and the general sense of personal frustration that it contains.[15]

Book 3 submerges Henry once again in the world of war. Only this time the minutiae and the continuance of the war slowly conspire to crystallize his intent to escape it. Now, he is determined to isolate himself and Catherine in their own individual world of love, pleasurable sensations, and honest direct emotions and feelings. Thus, at this point Rinaldi's war-weary cynicism and skepticism about existence become the diametrical opposite of what Henry now desires. Rinaldi's penchant for a pervasive irony that dissolves everything into an unrelenting simplification of choices and opportunities leaves no room for the personal commitment so valued now by Henry.[16]

Yet his desire to leave the war behind is not simply a personal decision quickly and easily arrived at. Events at the front also play a significant part in bringing him to recognize that that "was not my show any more. . . . That life was over" (248–49). Thus, the preparations for the full-scale retreat of their forces represent a significant war loss for Henry and the others. The retreat arouses a kind of sadness and regret that lies somewhere between the conventional elegiac grieving with its rhetorical expostulation and the tacit inarticulateness of his final elegy for love. His response to the retreat is his elegy for the war and relies on his skepticism about words as obscene, lacking in dignity, and basically meaningless. Only with their final meal is the elegiac note ostensibly dispersed. There, a kind of gallows humor, mock gaiety, and confidence about the immediate future is coupled with an ironic sardonic deflation of their happy expectations.

Less general than the implications of the retreat and of a more personal order is the death of Aymo. It occasions a limited elegiac response from Henry that develops both the dignity and the pathos of the corpse:

> I looked back. Aymo lay in the mud with the angle of the embankment. He was quite small and his arms were by his side, his puttee-wrapped legs and muddy boots together, his cap over his face. He looked very dead. It was raining. I had liked him as well as any one I ever knew. I had his papers in my pocket and would write to his family. (229)

Even more immediately bearing on his own fate is Henry's escape from the battle police and the prospect of his being shot.[17] Both signal to him the consummate stupidity of the war and of those only indirectly involved in fighting it. Anger at the war and what it brings is coupled with his regretful farewell to those still involved, to "the good ones, and the brave ones, and the calm ones, and the sensible ones" (248). In so doing, Hemingway testifies to the dual threats and values both of the war and of his new life founded on love.

Henry's need to escape from the forces of war and society testifies to their negative connotations. Yet his regrets at the loss of comradeship also bespeak his recognition of the values they have conferred on his life. At the same time, his conviction that "there were many places" (249) to which he and Catherine could escape betrays that their sense of love and marriage as simply being together is an unlikely one. On the one hand, "I had made a separate peace" (260) is his most direct statement of his new, hoped-for relationship to the war and his old life. On the other hand, his fullest assessment of his actual relationship to them is found in his recognition of its interim function or role:

> Then I realized it was over for me. But I did not have the feeling that it was really over. I had the feeling of a boy who thinks of what is happening at a certain hour at the schoolhouse from which he has played truant. (262)

Here Henry senses that his official desertion from the war and his joining Catherine is only a temporary interlude from the actuality of existence. Implicitly he sees that responsible isolation, not joint irresponsibility, is the ultimate fate of human beings during wartime. Thus, ultimately the elegy for love exists not so much apart from the war elegy as enveloped within and subject to its pressures. Both are linked together just as illusions and dreams are in the real world. It is in the interaction of the two elegiac modes with their antithetical aspirations that Hemingway achieves his most complex assessment of the difficulties in living a normal life while engulfed in a world of war.

Book 4 charts the interrelation of the sorrows of war and love. Thus, the couple's first night together in the hotel at Stresa initially stresses a celebration of their emotional, if not legal, marriage. The setting emphasizes quiet, light, cheerfulness, and excitement. Its primary focus is the "feeling that we had come home, feeling no longer alone, waking in the night to find the other one there, and not gone away" (266). Offsetting this epithalamion is the rain outside and Henry's somberly ironic and flatly declarative elegiac assessment of life and (implicitly) of their future:

> If people bring so much courage to this world the world has to kill them to break them. . . . It kills the very good and the very gentle and the very brave impartially. (267)

This assessment, by its calmness and level of unequivocal generalization, gives the celebration the quality of a temporary interlude. In so doing, it reinforces the feeling that personal happiness is a rare commodity destined not to last.

Several of the elements in book 4 gradually deepen the sense of the lovers' illusory conviction of being able to escape war and death. A pall is cast on their celebration by the threat of Henry's execution for military desertion. This is intensified by the simplistic, shortsighted, self-deluded, and immature responses they use to control their concern. These consist of joking about it, making love, and by simplifying their conceived solution to the dilemma. By envisaging a relatively easy escape to a safe land and by simply not thinking about the problem, they postpone the ultimate confrontation. No matter how human and desperate these responses are, they do not assuage the underlying unease felt by both about their ultimate fate. This is seen in Henry's sense of isolation and separation that results from his desertion and leaving the war behind them. He endeavors to "explain" it away as due to Catherine's presence. His love for her, he feels, completely blots out all other forms of reality or existence, but of course it cannot.

In a similar but starker fashion, the Count's claim that love is a religious feeling provides an implicit rationale for Catherine's death and the temporary, incomplete nature of their love.[18] Henry's basic outlook, however, is resolutely secular rather than religious. He cannot subordinate his own convictions to those of an institution such as the Church. Nor does he believe in the existence and relevance of God to human affairs. The billiard game with the Count, which Henry loses, is their joint ritual. It substitutes for divine worship in that both are essentially waiting for the end with a quietly felt sense of the inescapability of mortality.

Once Catherine and Henry are in Switzerland, with its promise of geographical escape and freedom, book 5 starts in a minor key marked by an idyllic natural setting of peace, tranquility, and beauty. Such a setting ostensibly mirrors the hope inherent in their love and the impending birth of their child. Yet the winter season suggests a hiatus in their life rather than a movement toward freedom, escape, and fulfillment of their dream of perpetual happiness. The setting is one of crystalline hardness and clarity of outline, of natural, pristine beauty, and of stern and bare living conditions. It quietly undercuts their courageous but desperately romantic, almost sentimental, conviction of the possibility of a separate peace. It does so by suggesting they are living withdrawn from both society and reality while dominated by a quiescent, spectatorial attitude. They exist with a kind of calm-before-the-storm perspective that is underlain by a foreboding that the perfection, quiet serenity, and peacefulness cannot last for long.

The first overt sign of the intrusion of the external world comes with Catherine's raising the desirability of legal marriage in view of the child's impending birth. For the first time, one of them entertains that in a peacetime, conventional world an actual legal marriage may be preferable to a solely personal, emotional commitment. Their romantic dream of togetherness independent of legal and social practices and conventions is further implicitly questioned. Catherine reveals that she is still sufficiently bourgeois not to want to couple a legal marriage ceremony with her obviously pregnant condition.

The inadequacy of their dream of personal independence from the strictures of society is even more chillingly underlined by the doctor's concern over the narrowness of her hips. In an almost predetermined fashion, this physical fact foreshadows the difficulty of her delivery. In turn, this institutes their anticipation of the elegiac response to birth and her death. This anticipatory pathos is intensified by their mutual protestations that each lives only when the other is present. Similarly, their playing chess, a game predicated on reason and shrewd strategies, is the very opposite of their approach to their romantic relationship. Obliquely, the game suggests their total concentration on each other is an emotional evasion. This is seen in the stormy weather currently dominating the outside world that they are soon to face in the finale of their relationship.

Both of them in different ways hint that they are aware in an increasing, though still dim, fashion of not really having escaped into a personal freedom of romantic love. Henry's lying awake "for quite a long time thinking about things and watching Catherine sleeping" (321) conveys a kind of fateful apprehension of the future on his part. In a related fashion, Catherine's assertion that "we live in a country where nothing makes any difference" (323) embodies a compressed dual irony. On the one hand, it indicates a realization that their illusion of being beyond the ordinary consequences of actions, decisions, and choices is soon to be refuted by her delivery and death. On the other hand, it underscores the brutal reality inherent in the war. Truer than they yet realize is the fact that they are subject to forces more powerful than individual wishes or desires can control. The same sort of bitter irony of recognition is contained in her teasing, joking claim that "I want to ruin you" (325) and Henry's equally frivolous agreement. Once again they are trying to evade the tragic complexities of their situation. While more than human enough, their efforts are also inadequate to the occasion.

The persistent rain of the penultimate chapter brings back the overt elegiac motif of sorrow, emotional depression, and dissolution. Moreover, such ominous weather counters Henry's brief anticipation of spring, birth, and their isolation from society, freedom from the war, and exclusive involvement with each other. In doing so, it increases the sense of the growing futility of such dreams. The specific identification of the year as 1918 implicitly and ironically contrasts the end of the war and death with the anticipation of birth, the creation of a family, and the perpetuation of their separate peace. The elegiac rain brings a deeply ironic foreshadowing to their situation.

This foreshadowing continues even during the onset of spring. Thus, Henry tranquilly engages in simple physical pleasures such as boxing. All of these get their focus and value from his being with Catherine on a quiet, daily basis. Yet their being together generates a feeling of living in slow motion as they approach some unforeseen but nevertheless dimly apprehended crisis of loss and separation. The culmination of their physical togetherness—the impending birth of their child—makes fully explicit this commingling of pleasure and pain in both of them:

> We knew the baby was very close now and it gave us both a feeling as though something were hurrying us and we could not lose any time together. (332)

This realization contains a *carpe diem* motif that recalls the earlier Andrew Marvell theme of the inexorability of the passing of time. It also implies a new, barely conscious awareness that their romantic absorption with one another is insufficient to make them immune from time, the world, and human society.

The elegiac farewell to their romantic life together is initiated by chapter 41's concentration on a ritual of pre-delivery details. These arouse the reader's apprehension, coupled with a subterranean conviction that the outcome must be elegiac in character. Otherwise the details would be superfluous and irrelevant to the dramatic and narrative action. This conviction is heightened by the extended duration of the delivery—approximately nine hours—that presages the likelihood of complications. Catherine's remarks—while subject to the birth anesthetic—about death and dying immediately raise the possibility of Henry having to face the elegiac occasion and of how he is to do so. His being sent out of the room by the doctor creates a temporary separation suggesting the imminence of its becoming permanent. This is intensified by his frenzied, out-of-control apprehensions concerning Catherine's likelihood of survival. They move finally to a convulsive, almost hysterical self-interrogation:

> But what if she should die? She won't die. But what if she should die? She won't. She's all right. But what if she should die? She can't die. But what if she should die? Hey, what about that? What if she should die? (342)

The logic of the elegiac process moves from his anxious contemplation of death to her capitulation to the delivery pain. In effect, her acceptance of it moves her death from possibility to probability: "They've broken me. I know it now" (345). Similarly, Henry's indifference to the actual birth of his child confirms the unreality of their becoming a family. With this, the achieving of an existence beyond their individual selves is blighted and the trap of romantic love closed permanently. Only with the nurse's disclosure that the child was born dead—strangled by his umbilical cord—does Henry accept that Catherine too will die. In doing so, he extends his pre-elegiac reflections to include all the deaths in the world. Hers via childbirth, the many gratuitous wartime deaths he has encountered, and even Rinaldi's syphilis are seen as signaling the end of sexual life. His grim assessment of her death is cast as a single instance of a universal fate, namely, that "they killed you in the end. You could count on that. Stay around and they would kill you" (350).[19] This view coupled with his extended analogy to ants on a burning log sums up the philosophical perspective engendered largely by the war. And it ends up shaping Henry's elegiac response to their romantic effort to escape the war, its implications, and consequences.

Her sudden hemorrhage initiates their final separation and loss. With it, Henry shapes his minimalist approach to the farewell inherent in the elegy: feelings of sorrow and regret; recollections of past shared memories; and the realization that language, any language, is incapable of encompassing and alleviating the experience fully. The first of these is found in his silent, secular, and essentially incoherent prayer that she not die. Ironically enough, their final words together evidence the slender and almost trivial nature of the memories they have. All they can say reflects but two things. One is their intense desire for a future containing the things that have brought them to this situation. The other is the implicit protestation of the persistence of their love for one another. Ultimately, of course, even these words are finally revealed to be powerless, useless, and irrelevant, for she dies. They are no longer able to communicate with each other, with themselves, or with others. The opportunity to say good-bye, the simplest of elegiac expressions, is lost for he cannot speak and she cannot hear. In effect, all he is left with is the world, that world he has renounced for the sake of his love, which in turn he has now lost as a palpable, living presence.

> It was like saying good-by to a statue. After a while I went out and left the hospital and walked back to the hotel in the rain. (355)

7

MARRIAGE AS THE END OF LOVE

F. Scott Fitzgerald's *Tender Is the Night* and John Updike's *Too Far to Go*

Like *A Farewell to Arms,* F. Scott Fitzgerald's *Tender Is the Night* (1933) slowly builds to a climactic conclusion of the marital elegy, one that overwhelms the hero with the losses he has suffered.[1] One major difference between the two novels lies in their historical settings, the one devoted to World War I and the other to the postwar era of Europe in the 1920s. Consequently, where death is a central focus for Hemingway's elegiac tone, it is but part of the normal backdrop of human existence in Fitzgerald.[2] For him, the concentration falls not on death but on psychic losses experienced principally by Dick Diver, his protagonist, but also by many of the other characters although in less vividly realized and less developed ways.[3]

In effect, the role of felt losses insidiously grows throughout the story of Dick, Nicole, Rosemary, and all the others in the Riviera world that Dick has created for the amusement and pleasure of his acquaintances.[4] After her first meeting with the Divers, Rosemary, for instance, is struck by the presence of a deep but dim sense of loss. She senses this loss beneath their effortless social manner with its easy graciousness and familiarity and she is curious about what lies behind it, what, in fact, was seen by Mrs. McKisco in the bathroom. Essentially, this is the contrast between what the Divers had when Dick first married and treated Nicole and what they lack now. Gone is his hubristic self-confidence in his professional skill and his personal compassion as well as her need and trust in him. At this point, the loss is neither complete nor permanent, but it is beginning to shadow their relationship fugitively beneath its social surface. Thus, when the novel opens, their marriage is starting to unravel, as it will continue to do with increasingly dire consequences for both of them.

Human loss, then, not death, is the topic on which Fitzgerald focuses his marital elegy. Hemingway balances his mourning for a dead lover against a measured, dispassionate interrogation of the minimal value of his social world. In so doing, he manages to skirt the thrust toward pathos to which his plot and characters incline him. By way of contrast, Dick is presented first through Rosemary's eyes as the master of all he surveys and the egregiously kind and generous benefactor of everyone.[5] To track such a character's fall from grace and eminence to social obscurity and personal failure could scarcely avoid the lineaments of tragedy. On the other hand, if his character should be irredeemably flawed—by hubris, weakness, a fatal need to be loved, or a willingness to celebrate and elevate the trivial—he will appear more as both an overreacher and a victim of pathos, as someone whose success and failure are both ultimately unworthy of pity.[6]

This challenge to Diver's character and his world is suggested in an early assessment of Dick's role: "It was themselves he gave back to them, blurred by the compromises of how many years" (52). Restoration of the self is obviously an admirable professional and personal goal so long as the restored self is complete. To restore less would be a savagely ironic gift.[7] Similarly, Fitzgerald's phrase about compromise suggests the presence of an ambiguity. It may refer to the compromises generated by the others through the years. Or it may allude to Dick's own compromises resulting from his relationship with Nicole and her family and its wealth. As a result of this complexity, what Dick in fact gives back to others proves to be both a blessing and a curse. It is a delightful gift as well as a restoration of a guilty conscience for past defaults in living and being. Compounding the irony is the protracted and futile effort by Dick to restore his own fundamental self. Irony and pathos ultimately fuse around him in the profoundly elegiac perspective of the celebrated dying fall scene that ends the novel.

This ambiguity of morality and character suggested by Rosemary's initial reaction is basically maintained throughout the novel. Thus, Rosemary is filled with admiration amounting almost to adulation for Dick's social manner:

> The enthusiasm, the selflessness behind the whole performance ravished her, the technic of moving many varied types, each as immobile, as dependent on supplies of attention as an infantry battalion is dependent on rations, appeared so effortless that he still had pieces of his own most personal self for everyone. (139)

So unrestrained is her assessment that one is led both to accept and to question his achievement. On the one hand, it does mark him out as superior to most men. Yet, on the other hand, it may be no more than a social skill, one that may or may not be identifiable with a truly civilized cultural or moral attainment. Further, the psychological riskiness of appearing to apportion out one's personal self in such a fashion renders facadelike the social control exercised.[8] As Fitzgerald himself knew, it is like living on one's financial capital; sooner or later, it will be exhausted. And yet at this very moment, Fitzgerald endeavors to counter the potential diminution of his protagonist as a dramatic and heroic figure. Thus, another side of Dick is revealed when he presents his assessment of Abe North: "Don't you know you can't do anything about people?" (140). Here he calls attention to the ultimate impossibility of changing, persuading, or materially affecting people. With this, his casual disentangling of himself from the ultimate problems of others and his aura of cold, hard self-sufficiency asserts itself and so blunts or dulls the pathos about to envelop him.[9] The remark is set against his private experiences with Nicole as the ultimate test case. Thereby, it attains a quality of composed, almost tragic awareness of the futility of altering another person's destiny or self-determined fate. When applied to his case, it creates a balance between the tragic and the pathetic. Such a position, indeed, captures the elegiac temper's full sense of both the acceptance of loss as the end-point of human life and its regret that it could not be otherwise.

As if to underscore Dick's deflection from a purely pathetic role while still denying him true tragic status, the novel briefly attends to Abe North as a figure of almost pure pathos:

> They stood in an uncomfortable little group weighted down by Abe's gigantic presence: he lay athwart them like the wreck of a galleon, dominating with his presence his own weakness and self-indulgence, his narrowness and bitterness. All of them were conscious of the solemn dignity that flowed from him, of his achievement, fragmentary, suggestive and surpassed. But they were frightened at his survivant will, once a will to live, now become a will to die. (144–45)

Abe mirrors in a generic way many of Dick's capabilities as well as his ultimate fate.[10]

The difference between them is encapsulated in their contrasting relations with Nicole. She likes Abe and he has an intense love for her, a fact that provides a counterweight to the relationship of Dick and Nicole. The latter relation is sanctioned socially, legally, and domestically and ultimately moves from the tragic to the pathetic to, finally, the elegiac. The Abe-Nicole affinities are socially or publicly unrealized and conclude in an essentially ironic fashion with their gradual alienation from one another. Implicit in this is Fitzgerald's perception that unrequited and requited loves alike are doomed. Abe, thus, functions as an elegiac yet pathetic prelude to the major collapse and withdrawal of Dick from Europe and high society when he has lost any relevance to their world. Finally, in the last third of the novel, Dick comes to hide all of his sociopsychological lights under a variety of baskets. That is all he has the strength or energy to do since he has exhausted his entire emotional capital on Nicole and her world.[11] In the beginning, he is capable of willing their joint withdrawal from self-absorption; in the end, he cannot even will his own withdrawal from self-reflection.

In a similar fashion, Fitzgerald underscores in a minor key the novel's elegiac motif by introducing death in a variety of forms. None, however, are allowed to usurp the centrality of human losses as its theme. Thus, Rosemary's mother has attended the peaceful deaths of several people. Mary Wallis shoots a man—presumably over a broken love relationship—in the railway station. Briefly glimpsed are gold-star mothers "who had come to mourn for their dead, for something they could not repair" (162). Jules Peterson, the black businessman involved in one of Abe's drunken escapades, is murdered, anticipating Abe's own violent death in New York. All of these consort to point up death's ubiquity. Their several fates also suggest with quiet, understated irony something about death that is too often overlooked. In point of fact, it is not always—perhaps rarely—accompanied by the sorrow, grief, and lamentation inherent in the conventional elegiac response.

Actually death's role in the novel is not to inspire the elegiac. Instead it allows the sudden incursion of traumatic violence into the Diver world dedicated as it is to amusement, pleasure, and self-absorption while protectively isolated by wealth, social position, and professional status. It provides "echoes of violence" that "entered into all their lives" (147). These echoes call into question not only their lives but also the relevance of the traditional elegy. This is especially the case when set against the various kinds of loss addressed in the novel—sexual innocence (as with Nicole), moral and psychological maturity (as with Rosemary), personal dignity (as with Dick), and professional achievement (as with Abe).

Living, Fitzgerald recognizes, is as much attended by loss as it is by death. The chief difference between them is how the recipient of or witness to the loss responds. Rosemary's failure to grow, Abe's capitulation to alcohol, and Nicole's gradual movement toward becoming a hard, self-absorbed woman like her sister, Baby, all produce scarcely any regret or sorrow.[12] It is only Dick's futile struggle to reclaim his personal dignity and the worth of his life that Fitzgerald invests with the elegiac aura of regrettable loss. What Dick loses is himself as a person of great compassion and considerable professional promise. To others, he embodies the loss of a psychological and social yardstick capable of an unending supportive interest in the individual, the loss of an ideal figure in their significantly less than ideal world.

The relationship between Dick and Nicole consists of the ambiguous power source in their mutual attraction, the tensions inherent in it, and its final dissolution. It is caught early on in their fantasy set to specific pieces of popular music. These capture their falling in love, their quarreling in which "finally one of them had gone and left the other crying, only to feel blue, to feel sad" (26). This pattern conveys a romanticized sense of love as concluding, almost as a mock elegy, with loss and sorrow and yet pleasure. Loss of something memorable and unforgettable begets a certain pleasure when it is felt to be doomed to pass away into merely a fond bittersweet memory. The music creates for them the image of young love, doomed to be lost, and yet ultimately repeated until, one hopes, achieved permanently: "the thin tunes" hold "lost times and future hopes in liaison" (26). Fitzgerald essentially creates an elegy for the flawed and crippled human being. It depends on the unconscious ruthlessness of another crippled individual in order to perpetrate the social death of the hero. With it comes the loss of his physical presence and authority in a world where he had once reigned supreme in its eyes.

In so doing, Fitzgerald assimilates one aspect of *The Waste Land* (1922). It is subtly signaled in Nicole's comment to Dick, which recalls Eliot's hyacinth girl:[13]

> I can remember how I stood waiting for you in the garden—holding all myself in my arms like a basket of flowers. It was that to me anyhow—I thought I was sweet—waiting to hand that basket to you. (48)

This allusion to Eliot's poem links Nicole to Dick in a symbolic relationship. Dick appears as the embodiment of the dying god consigned to the elegiac role of the scapegoat. In effect, Dick removes the sins of society by assuming them himself. As a result, he is both temporarily elevated by his selection and ultimately destroyed by becoming in society's eyes the complete articulation of the sinner. In Fitzgerald's world, both biographically and artistically, the consummate sinner is the personal failure, the individual who experiences the loss of self through exhausting it to benefit others.[14]

For most of the women in the novel love is allowed to entail pain as long as it is borne properly and discreetly. It's an indulgence suffered by others rather than a matter of deepest moment for the individual. Each of these women—Nicole, Baby, and even Rosemary's mother—is essentially a spectator-participant capable of compartmentalizing emotions and limiting their impact and potential for psychic damage. Dick as the admired and envied hero or leader is incapable of such emotional distancing except in his profession. That is what elegizes his separation from the group after his having initially been elevated as the supreme embodiment of this mini-culture. In both situations he is distanced from his society: first, he is raised above it as is the rising god, and then he is put below it when cast into the scapegoat role.

The sense of casual emotional and romantic diversion permeates the novel in a minor key. It continually threatens to collapse its thematic focus into an ironic perspective on the essentially less than serious Riviera world. Such a view threatens to render the Divers pathetic rather than the tragic creatures Fitzgerald primarily strives to make of them. To counter such a detached assessment becomes essential for Fitzgerald. Thus, he sets against his analysis of Nicole's past losses and consequent dilemmas a more extended rendering of the behavior and demeanor of a number of the clinic's patients. This generates a sense of the unmitigated pathos enveloping their lives and futures.

Their mental and emotional losses grow with a kind of quiet starkness that deepens our appreciation of Nicole's illness and of the enormous burden it imposes on Dick. As a result, their joint failure to achieve the perfection they embody socially and publicly creates an ultimately elegiac perspective on their lives. The sense of the futility and hopelessness of his professional task with the patients carries over to his personal challenge with Nicole and by extension the social world of which they are both a part. The difference lies in the starkness of the patients' losses and the failure of the doctors contrasted to the concealed subtleties and tangled complications never openly talked about in the Divers' world.

Like *The Portrait of a Lady, Tender Is the Night* attains an elegiac perspective through its delineation of a marriage ruined through the incompatible natures of its participants. Where the two novels differ, however, is in the motives ascribed to the principals and the actions taken to perpetuate the marriage. As Gilbert's true nature increasingly reveals itself, the legal, contractual character of their marriage is theoretically endangered. For Isabel Archer, the Christian, sacred quality of the relationship grows until it dominates her mind. For her, spiritual authority underlies the ritual of marriage and determines her view that neither divorce nor legal separation is a possible option. She moves from her original position of viewing her marriage as ideal to seeing it as a tragic mistake which, nevertheless, must be preserved because it is real. Dick Diver, on the other hand, recognizes from the outset that he is taking an immense risk in marrying Nicole, given her psychological malaise.[15] It is only his hubristic professional self-confidence and the personal temptation aroused by her physical attractiveness and financial wealth that leads him to accept the risk as one that he can control and master. Fitzgerald, like Hemingway, sees marriage as the culmination of sexual attraction and romance sanctioned not by religion but by personal desire. Consequently, they both implicitly accept the relationship as potentially of limited duration and hence as entailing physical loss or separation. Inevitably, such a view entails issues of personal justification, judgments of blame, and issues of fault finding, as *Tender Is the Night* makes copiously clear. Implicit in such issues is an inherent judgment, namely, whether primary responsibility for the dissolution of the marriage is attributed to Nicole or to Dick. This generates Fitzgerald's shifting sensibilities, which produce the inherent irony underlying the assignment of responsibility. The uncertainty as to which character is ultimately responsible modulates the novel's tone from the tragic through the pathetic to the elegiac.

Although the most powerful instance of the elegiac is found in Dick's farewell to the beach, Nicole too has her own elegiac response to her affair with Tommy Barban. The affair is seen as both frightening and determinedly impulsive. It is not a realization of another, different love but an unconscious escape into becoming another version of Baby, a hard, self-contained, and more than slightly selfish woman capable of living by and for herself alone. In Nicole's case, the elegiac response is for the loss of her role as victim for which Dick has so sedulously compensated. It has made her a figure of quiet pathos and pity, someone for whom excuses need be made and understanding constantly provided. For her, the elegiac mood is aroused by the fact that she is unaware of what she has lost and of its inherent value to her. Dick is more than the sum of his parts and attributes; he has made her what she can become both for good and ill. He has simultaneously made her strong enough to stand and live alone and selfish enough to think only of the present moment. He has taught her to set aside the past with its incestuous terrors and to concentrate on the bittersweet pleasures gained from his sensitivity to her both as a patient and as a wife.

Dick's final rejection of her sympathy and pity rescues him from being an object of sentimentality. Instead, it keeps him on the elegiac course of struggle, helplessness, and ultimate acceptance of what can no longer be avoided—his loss of himself as a human being: "I can't do anything for you anymore. I'm trying to save myself" (319). All that he has left is his intelligence, which for her exists "with substrata of truth under truth which she could not break or even crack" (319). This is what enables him to separate himself from her, to accept his irrelevance to her life now, and to face with ironic courage his elegiac farewell to the beach. The scene of his former triumphs and now of his final departure presages his entrance into a realm of lost souls doomed by their own choice of the poison of love, the desire of being loved, and ultimately of death.

Nicole's realization that "Dick had anticipated everything" (329) confirms his tragic nature. By so doing, it diminishes without destroying his pathetic status. His is essentially a conscious choice of self-destruction. He has realized from the outset both the professional and the personal risk he was running by entering into the marriage. In short, beneath the surface he saw the relationship's potential for the elegiac. When his energy is exhausted beyond replenishment, all he can do is to plan how to let the situation run its course in the most ritualistic or formal way possible. That is why his farewell to the beach is a reprise of his life and achievements there. It is compounded of a whole host of dramatic gestures. These include: a final sociability with the servants and children; an ironic substitutive effort to "seduce" an old friend, Mary North, into thinking he is really and truly serious in what he is saying, thinking, and feeling; an almost parodic effort to elevate his creation of the beach into a true social achievement valuable in and for itself; and a tragic ability to compel Nicole still to want to join him. All of these unite in an elegiac scene that joins the trivial and marginally valueless with the profound and essentially important.[16] It is a patently human effort to secure an achievement capable of resisting the passage of time, the changes of human personality, and the disintegration of society while at the same time recognizing the folly of the effort and its misguided focus.[17]

The tone and the perspective taken toward marriage in John Updike's short story collection *Too Far to Go* (1979) are basically more ironic or flatly declarative than elegiac in the traditional sense. This is clear from the author's foreword as well as from the stories themselves:

> That a marriage ends is less than ideal; but all things end under heaven, and if temporality is held to be invalidating, then nothing real succeeds. The moral of these stories is that all blessings are mixed. (10)

This generalization about time's inevitable role in human affairs is both accurate and too easy as a justification. As a dispassionate assessment of the nature of human existence, it is unexceptionable. Nevertheless, it tempts the individual to acknowledge too readily that his responsibility to counter this nature vigorously is both limited and bound to be unsuccessful. In short, Updike's rationale claims to prove too much by suggesting that no marriage may be temporally successful and able to thwart the emotional loss and legal separation of divorce.

From the very first story, "Snowing in Greenwich Village," an inherent likelihood begins to emerge that the Maples' marriage—here only in its first year—will founder. Neither Richard nor Joan is an exceptional individual. Instead they are quite ordinary persons with more than their share of flaws and inadequacies. His include a tendency to posture, to endeavor to be more than he is, linked with a deeply hidden feeling of sexual guilt. Hers consist of a childlike desire to be delighted, overly so, by the stories and experiences of others, a somewhat artificial naïveté and ingenuousness, and at the outset at least, a less than attractive appearance. Together these traits suggest an essential lack of harmony in temperament and outlook. In addition, they betray an unwillingness or inability to modify their shortcomings so as to preserve the marriage indefinitely. At the outset, then, Updike subtly and quietly promotes an elegiac feeling for the likelihood of the marriage's ultimate demise.

In effect, the remainder of most of the stories charts aspects of the relationship as it crumbles slowly and inexorably. By the end, the marital ideal is destroyed, if not totally then certainly thoroughly.[18] "Wife-Wooing" provides a snapshot of family life after seven years of marriage. It reveals Richard's penchant for self-inflation and play-acting. Thus, his sexual arousal is stimulated by his thoughts about *Ulysses* as well as the imitation of Old English verse with its heavily repeated pattern of alliteration. For him, sex is always initiated by a series of role-playing fantasies. They begin first with literature and then move on to his imagining himself as a primeval hunter or food-gatherer and then to the role of a contemporary cultured individual who can intellectually entertain by attaching sophisticated symbolism to the human anatomy. The most extreme of his fantasies is, of course, his linking of cathedral rose windows to the female vagina.

By playing with these fantasies with a quietly amused irony and self-indulgence, Richard elevates himself psychologically above his wife. At the same time, he affects a certain sense of boredom at their ostensible ability to "sense everything between us" (33). In turn, this leads to his reflection that "courting a wife takes tenfold the strength of winning an ignorant girl" (33). The story focuses implicitly on Richard's frustration over his unsatisfied passion and his dissatisfaction with Joan's ostensible remoteness from his desires. Sexual discontent is, then, the first sign of loss to occur in the marriage. Its systolic-diastolic movement through the rest of the stories gradually elevates it to one of the major chords in the slowly but inevitably developing elegiac view of the relationship.

A more complex and sobering glimpse of the realities of marriage is found in "Giving Blood," which picks up the narrative two years later. Here the sexual malaise has moved from the privacy of Richard's consciousness to a jealousy verbally expressed by both principals. But it plays a secondary role to their almost unconscious struggle for primacy, authority, and control in (and of) the relationship. He openly criticizes her smugness and sexlessness while pretending to accept what he regards as her stupidity. In response, she takes the high road in their argument by simply requesting silence so that he is the one who feels in the wrong.

The inherent savagery of their verbal exchange is dramatically offset and the tension relieved by a commonplace event. Richard and Joan are required to complete hospital forms prior to donating blood for a distant relative. This creates a shallow companionability through their joking over the experience. For Richard, the bloodletting becomes a richly fanciful experience, an impressionistic, colorful, imagistic assimilation of doctors, deities, and kinds to the Maples' everyday lives. In so doing, it charts the gradual ebbing of their mortality. By presenting Richard's imaginings in a markedly inflated manner, Updike points up his penchant for exaggerating situations. In so doing, Updike forestalls the contemplation of human mortality being enveloped in the traditional elegiac lament. Instead, he makes it part of an ironic comedy focused on a single individual's character flaws.

After they have shared the blood donation, in a brief and unexpected moment, Richard suddenly declares his love for Joan simply and apparently authentically. This act arouses a sense of the broad scope of actual marital relationships. They extend, the story suggests, from bitter, more or less irrational bursts of anger and resentment and irritation to simple, heartfelt declarations of commitment. Both of these are regarded as typical and capable of being psychologically reconciled. At the same time, concern is aroused in the couple about the stability and enduring nature of such relationships especially since so much has been said of a critical, personal, almost hateful order.

Ironically enough, this speculation deepens as their ostensible verbal reconciliation is brought to a head by a sense of its being a fantasy. His anger at lacking money to pay for their lunch and her retreat into a composed foreshadowing of their fate with the words "we'll both pay" (58) augurs ill for their future. Her phrase foretells their ultimate separation and divorce by transferring the level of discourse from the financial to the emotional. Its overtones clearly imply that Updike construes marriage quite differently from the other writers considered here. It is neither James's notion of permanent spiritual commitment, Hemingway's conception of unique romantic feelings precariously set against traditional and institutional boundaries, or Fitzgerald's sense of it as a heroically futile sacrifice of one party for another. Instead marriage for Updike manifests itself as an all-too-human, relatively casual engagement of two basically dissimilar individuals. Their relationship is destined to wear out and is so recognized by the society of which it is a representative part.

This drift toward dissolution, loss, and physical separation reaches another level in "Twin Beds in Rome." Here, frustrations and quarrels are not so much an integral part of the marriage as they spell the likelihood of its ending. Why, when, and how to terminate it becomes the topic of extended conversations, debates, and arguments. For them, the concept of marriage no longer entails sexual gratification and emotional fulfillment (Hemingway), indentured psychological transformation (Fitzgerald), or personal, spiritual exploration (James). It is essentially a habit producing "a painful, helpless, degrading intimacy" (59). Thus, despite their passionate desire to break free from one another, they are still bound together by "marital habit," so that at this point "their marriage could not die" (60).

Marriage is not something to which they see themselves bound regardless of personal feelings of the sort James envisages. Nor is it a physical and emotional passion terminable only by premature death, much less a hubristic sacrificial gesture as it is with Hemingway or Fitzgerald. All of these perspectives occasion, to greater or lesser degree, overt elegiac responses by the participants and their authors. Instead, for Updike, marriage is a relationship almost completely deprived of the heightened values that allow for an elegiac recognition of its passing. For the Maples, only the habit of sharing a bed remains as something of value, marginal and almost purely practical though it is. Richard's plaintive remark that this habit "seems sort of sad" (63) is as close to the elegiac tradition of mourning as either of them can attain at this point.

As if to point up their separation from this tradition, Updike creates out of their walking tour of Roman ruins and other famous artistic and historical settings a deliberately simulated setting of age, achievement, abandonment, death, and ruination. Compared with James's similar Italian settings, Updike's appeal to the elegiac betrays a conscious, deliberate artificiality, which underscores the gap between it and the responses of the characters. Richard's sudden experiencing of acute stomach pains reduces the monumental elegiac attitude inherent in the setting to a backdrop of trivial proportions. Richard's stomachache, not the Roman ruins, dominates the scene. In so doing, it intensifies the gulf that exists between the traditional mourning pattern of the elegy and the counter form of it developed by Updike.

It is Richard's simple, almost miraculous awakening free of pain that appears to signal the couple's farewell to marriage. Now they have a sense of being finally able to part emotionally, to live separate lives physically and legally. In so doing, they momentarily seem to recover their original ability, lost since their courting days, to be "courteous, gay, and quiet" (72). With the ostensible letting go of their marriage *relationship,* it would appear that they have reached their last "level elegiac days" (72). Yet even this truncated, foreshortened version of the elegiac attitude with its aesthetic ease and finality is called into question, "for he again grew reluctant to leave her" (72). That this response remains the dominant one in their relationship documents Updike's remark in his foreword:

> The musical pattern, the advance and retreat, of the Maples' duet is repeated over and over, ever more harshly transposed. (10)

Taken as a whole, the stories relentlessly portray the couple's ambiguous recognition both that marriage holds no transcendent reality for them and that they ought to end it. Yet one or the other ceaselessly turns away from the final decision, which would permanently consign it to the past. Nowhere is this seen more clearly than in the story that follows "Twin Beds in Rome," namely, "Marching Through Boston." These two tales polarize in latter-day Jamesian fashion the worlds of Italy and America. The former uses the art of the past as a way of ironically documenting the failure of the elegiac tradition to function meaningfully for the midcentury Maples. The latter invokes contemporary American history, as embodied in the civil rights movement, to point up a similar failure. Its contemporary setting fails completely to provide an elegiac or ironic finale to their mutual search for personal freedom and a new beginning. It also reveals the growing extent to which they no longer share a point of view but instead represent antithetical psychological and political poles. She is a devout, involved—though still somewhat naïve—activist while he is an ironic mocker and pseudoreactionary. While she lives by and for abstractions, he sees them all as "phantasmal" (77). In effect, this polarization suggests that neither an aesthetic tradition nor a sociopolitical cause can summon up the elegiac mourning associated with the ending of a marriage and the loss of a once powerful and personal relationship.

The next two stories, "The Taste of Metal" and "Your Love Just Called," introduce sexual infidelity as a real option and alternative to marriage. At last, it forms part of the Maples' behavior as well as their conversation. Expressions of verbal jealousy are replaced or augmented by two related forms of behavior. One is a series of secret surreptitious actions indicative of their individual inclinations. The other form consists of various ingenious and self-serving efforts to disguise or justify these actions as socially acceptable. Richard's tentative and casual attraction to a woman recently separated from her husband is made part of a new convention of infidelity, separation, divorce, and remarriage. It is resolutely anti-elegiac so far as the conventional formalities of mourning for the end of a marriage are concerned. Thus, his embrace of Eleanor after the automobile accident is marked by its accidental and incidental character, its casual, thoughtless quality. In so doing, it testifies to the historical shrinkage of the solemnity and importance of marital relationships in midcentury American society.

Adding to this aura of easy acceptance of the idea of infidelity within marriage is Joan's and their neighbor Mack's efforts to justify their embrace. They portray it as a casual gesture of companionable affection well within the moral bounds of their society and its practices. Sexual jealousy is both summoned up and thwarted by verbal protestations that deny wrongdoing, guilt, and even shame. Only in "Eros Rampant" is it explicitly revealed that Joan and Mack were in fact lovers briefly. Their denial of this adds deceit to the casual marital actions that are deemed acceptable to this society and its inhabitants. The issue here is not so much how we assess this mode of behavior—that is, whether acceptable or not—for the marital relationship. Instead it is the fact of its signifying a profound shift in the role of infidelity. From the original elevation of sexual jealousy as a genuine threat to their relationship, it now becomes a kind of play-acting and psychic projection.

The fact that Richard and Joan continue to quarrel the next day indicates two things. First, the prospect of infidelity clearly serves as a substitute for deeper tensions in their relationship. Second, and perhaps even more significant, as a result, quarreling itself has become their means of communication. Paradoxically enough, arguing serves to extend their relationship by a kind of negative contact. What began as a kind of joking, teasing, barbed affection between them in the end stands as a stark, silent challenge to their knowledge of each other.

"Waiting Up" and "Eros Rampant" in a sense constitute companion stories, for in them the infidelity is not a matter of wishing or speculation but a known, confessed fact for both Richard and Joan. The first of these tales probes with a dispassionate irony their ostensibly different yet inherently similar responses to his extended affair with the wife of a neighbor. The crux of the societal shift in attitude is contained in Joan's visit to the neighbor couple to discuss the matter. Richard's staying at home points up the gender and role contrasts he notes as having transpired from when he was a child to his life as an adult. This generates a sense of both dramatic and profound historical shifts in the two societies and their values.

It also creates an ironic recognition in Richard's mind of the indecisiveness enshrouding his actions. Thus, he is dually aware of both the impact of the loss or absence of his marriage partner and of his awareness of his own infidelity with a neighbor and friend. His reaction is less one of guilt than puzzlement at how he can have both feelings—of loss and betrayal—at once. Updike here points up a further significance to the casualness and apparent social acceptability of infidelity. It eliminates for the Maples the possibility of sexual relations figuring into any elegiac attitude toward their ostensible love and actual marriage. Because fidelity matters so little now, its loss can no longer form part of the intense mourning pattern of the conventional marital elegy.

Gradually, however, their sharp critique of the other couple modulates into an implicit criticism of each other. They both begin by disdaining the other couple's belief in human perfectibility, in understanding and compassion, and in talk and discussion as a problem-solving method. Soon, however Joan's continuing but confused indignation is set off against Richard's self-centered concern with *his* feelings and desires: "it's you. . . . I seem to want most" (121–22). This effectively shows the extent to which they are an integral part of their society even as they level legitimate criticisms against it. One concludes that if she is going to be angry, then she should be much angrier. Similarly, if he is going to engage in extramarital affairs, he should decisively face the full consequences of his behavior rather than resort to wavering efforts both to risk and retain his marriage.

Updike starts to unfold here a novel elegiac attitude toward marriage. He concentrates on the individual psychology of the characters, their emotional losses through change, time, and history of the familiar and the habitual with all of its reassuring, soothing, stable qualities. It is the loss of the ordinary, not the extraordinary, that is the focus of his marital elegy. He concentrates on the quiet, protracted diminishment of a once-central relationship rather than, as with Hemingway, its dramatic and sudden termination by death. In effect, for him the elegiac becomes a normal and anticipatable if not inevitable phase of living with another person. It is something not to be exaggerated or exalted or tragically mourned over publicly but something to be endured and lived through in as controlled a manner as possible.

"Eros Rampant" extends the motif of infidelity still further by revealing Joan's own repeated and flagrant participation in it. As the title indicates, the story's setting is the many forms of love in the domestic world. These include the differing passions of the individual children, the pets' attractions, and the parents' involvement with each other and with others. The very spectrum of kinds of love indicates the impossibility of its being permanently localized into a single emotional and sexual relationship.

Such a perspective dissolves the likelihood of the marital elegy attaining either the height or intensity found in its traditional forms. The elegiac too, like so much else in mid-twentieth-century life, is de-escalated, de-emphasized, and rendered smaller and less unique or valuable than it has been in the historical past. His multiple ironies, however, indicate that Updike's concern is not to contrast the present with the past in order to decry it. Instead, he suggests that a resolute clinging to the past is a product of nostalgia. At the same time, a single-minded embracing of contemporary attitudes of the sort exhibited by Richard's mistress and her husband is also faulty. It rests upon a thorough dismissal of the past. In effect, by completely disdaining history as a conspectus of time-tested forms of behavior, it proves itself hopelessly shortsighted.

The next story, "Plumbing," casts the growing disintegration of their marriage into a longer perspective. It emphasizes one's view of time as being a recalling of the past coupled with the wish to avoid the future. The old plumber insistently recalls the ways of the past in terms of his profession's changing practices. Implicitly, this bears in on Richard both the differences between then and now and the persistent strength of past ways of doing things. The vital importance of plumbing to their dwellings embodies the necessary nature of the values inhering in the older, traditional concepts of marriage. As a result, it creates an interrogative perspective on his behavior and attitudes toward the institution now. The elegiac sadness inherent in such a view provides a somber and sobering backdrop. It summons up a simultaneously nostalgic and ironic view of the life of the family, the conducting of a marriage, and the impending dissolution of both:

> What are they saying, what are these violent, frightened people discussing? They are discussing change, natural process, the passage of time, death. (150)

Seen as an immediate context for the very next story, "Plumbing" functions almost protophilosophically. That is, it draws attention to the larger issues underlying the tacit and almost subterranean elegiac chronicling of the slow dissolution of the Maples' marriage. "The Red-Herring Theory," on the other hand, views the institution of marriage from a personal, quasisociological standpoint expressed by Joan. She observes that every man has both a mistress and a red herring that distracts suspicion from the mistress. The whole story wraps their marriage in devastating irony bearing on their loss of any actual remaining *relationship.* All that remains is subterfuge, concealment, and ostensible verbal candor. The disappearance of their original relationship, Updike suggests, is profoundly elegiac. Ideally, marriage constitutes the closest connection possible between two people and yet they, the Maples, are quite unaware of this. They are part of a situation—one that is implicitly elegiac—that embraces loss, change, severance, and (at least metaphorically) death. Yet they remain essentially unconscious of the fact. And in this very unconsciousness lies the contemporary nature of the marital elegy. The Maples have grown accustomed bit by bit to diminishing the elements initially constituting the relationship. Trust, fidelity, friendship, honesty, and communication are simply verbalized until the only remaining link between them is the social facade of convenience and habit. Only through the shadow nature of this façade is there any sense of the implication of these losses.

"Sublimating" merges the comic and the pathetic so as to capture the impact of the atrophying of their elegiac perspective on their marriage. Here, after being married for eighteen years, they decide to give up sex with one another because it is "the only sore point in their marriage" (165). Richard's purchase of a cabbage as a snack is pointedly ridiculous and so underscores the comic nature of their reasoned sexual decision. Back of both decisions—abandonment and acquisition—one feels a profound but remote pathos for the insistent solemnity visited on foolish and trivial human actions and convictions. Against their pledge of abstinence stand their mutual infidelities. Both have become habitual and commonplace events countenanced as part of ordinary, normal life and marriage.

Their ability to view the present nature of their marriage as elegiac has atrophied almost completely. Updike presents this in a scene that reverberates with a combination of pathos and irony. The scene opens as the dreary round of ordinary domestic activities comes to an end with their return from a dinner with a couple very like themselves. Alone, they focus fugitively on death: she on being dead, and no one being much concerned; he on his funeral, and whether or not his other women would join his wife in mourning him. Both can see it as no more than a personal and individual matter: he sees it as enhancing, she as diminishing. This contrast starkly testifies to the extent of their personal alienation from one another. Finally, tentatively and without conviction, they try to convince themselves that their sexual abstinence from one another has given them a far broader perspective. They struggle to feel it has made them aware of an eternity of death. This awareness they ludicrously think can generate a conservation of energy capable of being transformed into a major historical event like the Crusades. This is but a momentary, transitional state devoid of depth of implication and barren of sustained significance. Even their imagined deaths fail to provide a sustained ground for a consciously elegiac view of their marriage.

Their inability to get beyond their oscillatory pattern of behavior is starkly set forth in "Nakedness." It consists simply of clinging to and recoiling from one another. They do not strive to change their responses to each other, to face past individual imperfections, and so to remake their marriage. Here, the brief intrusion on the beach of two nudists with their affected naturalness makes both of the Maples aware of the inevitable dissolution of their family, the passage of time, and the onset of death. Later, Richard contemplates nakedness generally and recalls several memories. He remembers it first as an innocent act, then as a sexual one, and finally, as a series of representations in art, literature, and popular culture. These memories form for him a kind of elegy for his personal, aesthetic, and cultural past. They arouse a reflective thoughtfulness about the concept of nakedness—starkness of being, self, and body—which both physically and mentally underlies the marital state. Its gradual dissolution generates his ambivalence, uncertainty, and hesitation over its passing. Unlike the conventional marital elegy, Updike's response is not one of intense or inconsolable mourning. In its place is a rueful, reflectively sad sense of the passing of something once valued—perhaps mistakenly, perhaps regretfully, perhaps anticipatory of a new freedom—which is no longer.

As they confront one another's nakedness while preparing to sleep, Joan's saying "no" is a rejection, a declination to accept and participate in their mutual psychic and marital nakedness. She is saying that it is too late. They are too old, too alienated or at odds with one another, to risk stripping themselves of their shared immediate marital past with its infidelities, cruelties, criticisms, and personal differences. Even at this point, the past functions differently for the two of them. For him, it produces memories that in being past arouse a certain fond nostalgia and regret and a hope that in their being recalled, they are not wholly or irretrievably lost. For her, the memories are buried and subsist silently as a rejection of nostalgia and an assuming of decisiveness. Richard's response testifies to his belatedness, his remaining anchored in his marital past while recognizing the changed and therefore exciting nature of the relationship. Now *he* is the one who, apparently for the first time, feels "thrilled, invaded" (191). Their gender roles have been reversed since she becomes by her negative response the one in control who is able to deny or avoid penetration and consummation. Her rejection of the force of nostalgia and the past seals the inappropriateness of the tradition of elaborate mourning patterns and rituals for the marital elegy.

It is with "Separating" that finally the replacement for these patterns emerges clearly. Here the Maples enact a new pattern for midcentury marriage elegies. It consists of elaborately repeated advances and retreats, betrayals and counterbetrayals, overtures and rejections enacted by both of them. Essential to the process of their legal and physical separation is the fact that it is protracted. In addition to this pattern's being extended over much of the relationship, it is also diversely and repetitively painful. As such, it is regarded almost as if it were a decision and action out of their hands to control. They continue to quarrel, even over how to tell the children of the separation. At the same time, Richard recoils from his new and bitter realization that the end of the marriage spells not only release from but also loss of Joan. Even more bitter and surprising for him is the recognition that it entails also the loss of and separation from his children. When he tells his oldest son of the separation, the boy's response turns the whole prolonged decision process into an almost silent elegy jointly felt by father and son:

> In his father's ear he moaned one word, the crucial, intelligent word: "*Why?*"
>
> *Why.* It was a whistle of wind in a crack, a knife thrust, a window thrown open on emptiness. The white face was gone, the darkness was featureless. Richard had forgotten why. (211; Updike's italics)

The impulse to protract the relationship continues even after it has been emptied of essential significance. For in the next story, "Gesturing," it appears that even after they have decided on a separation, it has not extended beyond his having moved out. She has still been feeding him; they have been spending evenings together, usually arguing, and often making love. Finally, Joan asks Richard to leave town and to take an apartment in Boston. The story then traces out the connections between Joan, his wife, and Ruth, his mistress, and in so doing limns in its irony for his future. The new relationship is already vaguely unsettling and irritating. It too will grow familiar, habitual, and convenient, and with this will start its own decline. Through this irony, Updike reveals what for him is the elegiac act adhering to marriage in the mid-twentieth century. Divorce is not simply the end of a relationship but the beginning of another, which too is basically doomed to exhaustion and dissolution and disappearance.

In the novels such as *Couples* and the Rabbit series, marital repetition and disintegration are seen as part of the larger elegiac fact of human aging and ultimately dying. The short stories, however, concentrate, as here, on the episodic aspects of the marital elegy. And one of them is found in Richard's final momentary perception about Joan. Despite their separation and the impending loss of their marriage, he will never lose his memories of her physical gestures—a combination of body and mind—for somehow they will persist even after death. What he recognizes implicitly is that personal, intimate memories are the very basis on which the marital elegy exists. They enable it to persist obliquely and almost subterraneanly despite societal inclinations to diminish the permanence or significance of the formal legal and religious relationship.

The implications of the marital elegy's reduction to individual memories are spelled out in the final two stories, "Divorcing: A Fragment" and "Here Come the Maples." The fact that the first of these is a self-declared fragment embodies Updike's basic approach to the marital relationship and how and why it is elegiac. He sets against the conventional expectations of marriage the midcentury realities. Thus, permanent existence, personal fulfillment, and companionability throughout life are confronted by limited but repeated duration, the generating of multiple frustrations, and finally the creating of irreconcilable alienation.

Taken all together, this bifocal vision with its rough edges compounded of the ideal and the real creates a bittersweet elegy. The earlier, traditional expectations of the relationship are seen from a drier-eyed, more ironic, and less committed perspective reflective of midcentury society. In effect, the memory of these expectations with their rhetorically inflated and exaggerated laments over the cessation of a marriage generates a profound if subliminal regret for the loss of something nostalgically still valued.

On the other hand, what Updike calls up is a complex memory of a past ideal value and the death of an actual relationship begun in hope and concluded with regret and a silent sorrow. Superimposed on one another, past and present become not a seamless continuity but a collection of individual memories separated by unremembered details. The most important of these obviously is his initial forgetting to kiss the bride. Loss, incompleteness, futility, and illusion are the elements shaping and dominating the marital relationship for Updike. It is the recognition of this that prompts the elegiac attitude toward it in the midcentury. Such recognition is as much a matter of memory, belatedness, and closure as Richard's now remembering to kiss his no-longer bride and wife, Joan. Significantly enough, their divorce is finalized against an equally elegiac perspective on war.

2

CULTURAL AND PHILOSOPHICAL ELEGIES

8

MODERNISM ON CULTURE AND HISTORY

William Faulkner's *Absalom, Absalom!* Ford Madox Ford's *Parade's End,* and Others

Modernism in general brings to culture and history a deep and thoroughgoing elegiac attitude that mingles nostalgia and acceptance of the changes wrought by time. Thus, T. S. Eliot and Ezra Pound, for instance, range from prehistory to the contemporary world in generating their elegiac assessment of culture and history. In contrast, William Faulkner and Ford Maddox Ford foreground their cultural vistas more single-mindedly. They focus on different eras from the recent past and their philosophical values, both of which are eroding but with integrity. For Faulkner, the locus of loss is the Civil War, which he views bi-focally. Thus, the Sartorises, Compsons, McCaslins, and Sutpens are cast as they actually saw themselves and their contemporaries and also as their historical successors came to construe them. Consequently, his elegies of patrimony like *The Sound and the Fury* and *Absalom, Absalom!* employ myth and anti-myth. They do so in order to meditate on why and how the human mind requires both for it to be aware of its past.

Thus, in *Absalom, Absalom!* Quentin Compson stands as the inheritor of an idealized heroic myth of the Confederacy, while Shreve McCaslin occupies the role of skeptical interrogator of the South's heritage and mores. Together, they fuse as narrative explorers of an ethos that is dead but not gone:

> both thinking as one, the voice which happened to be speaking the thought only the thinking become audible, vocal; the two of them creating between them, out of the rag-tag and bob-ends of old tales and talking, people who perhaps had never existed at all anywhere, who, shadows, were shadows not of flesh and blood which had lived and died but shadows in turn of what were (to one of them at least, to Shreve) shades too, quiet as the visible murmur of their vaporizing breath. (303)

Ultimately this dual identification with their prime human subjects, Henry Sutpen and Charles Bon, leads them to an ambivalent awareness of the Confederacy hegemony. This is an awareness reverberant with an elegiac mood of regret, recognition of folly, and the inevitability of both:

> They both bore it as though in deliberate flagellant exaltation of physical misery transmogrified into the spirits' travail of the two young men during that time fifty years ago, or forty-eight rather, then forty-seven and then forty-six, since it was '64 and then '65 and the starved and ragged remnant of an army having retreated across Alabama and Georgia and into Carolina, swept onward not by a victorious army behind it but rather by a mounting tide of the names of lost battles from either side—Chickamauga and Franklin, Vicksburg and Corinth and Atlanta—battles lost not alone because of superior numbers and failing ammunition and stores, but because of generals who should not have been generals, who were generals not through training in contemporary methods or aptitude for learning them, but by the divine right to say "Go there" conferred upon them by an absolute caste system; or because the generals of it never lived long enough to learn how to fight massed cautious accretionary battles, since they were already as obsolete as Richard or Roland or du Guesclin, who wore plumes and cloaks lined with scarlet at twenty-eight and thirty and thirty-two and captured warships with cavalry charges but no grain nor meat nor bullets, who would whip three separate armies in as many days and then tear down their own fences to cook meat robbed from their own smokehouses, who on one night and with a handful of men would gallantly set fire to and destroy a million dollar garrison of enemy supplies and on the next night be discovered by a neighbor in bed with his wife and be shot to death. (345–46)

In Ford's case, as *Parade's End* (1950 in a single volume; published originally as four separate novels in the mid-1920s) persuasively shows, the backward glance is foreshortened dramatically so that the past is in the process of emerging from a dramatic present. Christopher Tietjens is an anachronism becoming aware of itself as such.[1] In the process, the world of which he is the consequence is defined at the precise historical moment when it functionally disappears as a social reality. Religion, class, education, region, and political conviction combine and conspire to generate a pathos that arises out of the diminishment and dissolution of a clear moral and intellectual code. Its historical adversary is a rising tide of cultural barbarism, vulgarity, and hypocrisy that is then projected as the present ever since.[2] By tracing the bulk of Tietjens's life, Ford deploys the novel as an elegiac chronicle mourning the loss of an entire culture seen through the fate of a single individual.[3] His story is one of a series of heartbreaking defeats suffered by a stubborn hero born on the cusp of historical and cultural transition. From his graduation from Cambridge through his endeavors to fulfill his manifest and redoubtable intellectual skills in the public world, his virtues and talents are undercompensated by an increasingly alien society. The same is true with his problematic marriage and establishing of a family. On a personal level, they enact his failure to adapt to the meretricious and his subsequent defeat by it. These personal and social issues are all part of his doomed cultural struggle. The intransigence he reveals in them is matched by his moral insistence on active involvement in World War I despite his age. With the same sort of determination he accepts the dissolution of his marriage, founded as it is on an almost pathologically cruel betrayal wrought by his wife.

As such, *Parade's End* compares strikingly with Woolf's *The Years*, which traces in more muted tones the dissolution of essentially the same historical period and culture. The major difference between the two novels, of course, is their authors' attitudes to the societal and cultural dissolution and the ways in which they have their characters respond. Woolf focuses on the general historical, social, and large-scale attitudinal shifts in the culture and on how its participants subtly modify their responses and continue to live. Ford, on the other hand, traces these shifts as they impact with increasingly devastating resonance in the life of one individual whose moral and intellectual code opposes and decries singly and together each one of these changes. His irony with regard to Tietjens's stubborn refusal to compromise is more subdued than his recurring elegiac regret for the losses suffered by his protagonist. The hopeless folly of such stubbornness is recognized by Ford but is not subjected directly to the corrective complaint of satire. Instead he subtly mingles his ironic awareness with the sorrowful lament of the elegy in order to center on their common focus, namely, recollecting a prior, more satisfying time and world. He does so to etch in more fully an awareness of the disparity between past and present. It is Ford's preponderance of elegiac sorrow for the loss of both individual and culture that makes his work echo so plangently and directly.

An even more extended version of this disparity occurs with another trait of the modernist elegiac voice. This trait revolves around the idea of an ideal harmony between nature and culture. It appears as a conviction expressed sometimes as an assertion and sometimes merely as an obliquely voiced hope. At some point, it feels, human society existed in a condition of ideal and archetypal simplicity that was essentially primeval as well as paradigmatic. In effect, this view represents a secularization of the prelapsarian ideal and the human struggle to regain it. As such, it is a dominant and shaping factor in the work of D. H. Lawrence, both by virtue of the immediacy of its appeal and the ambiguities of its reality.

A striking perspective on this trait is provided by the late Erwin Panofsky's essay on Poussin and the elegiac tradition in which he charts the rationale for the misreading of "et in Arcadia ego." In a curious but illuminating sense, Lawrence reverses the historical trajectory described by Panofsky. His psychologically initial predisposition is to see man's original state as "a golden age of plenty, innocence and happiness" (297). Only on closer speculation, mixed with examination of other cultures such as the American Indian and the Mexican, does this view yield to its opposite. This is the apprehension that man's origins represented, in Panofsky's words, "an almost subhuman existence full of terrible hardships and devoid of all comforts" (297).

Works such as *The Plumed Serpent, Mornings in Mexico, Etruscan Places, Sea and Sardinia,* "The Princess," "The Woman Who Rode Away," "St. Mawr," and "The Man Who Died" render in full dialectical complexity this combination of desire and reality. Dissatisfaction with the modern civilized culture in which he lives dominates the consciousness of Lawrence and his protagonists. Consequently, they are led to seek geographically remote and technologically less advanced cultures where they can experience life as an actual Golden Age. Thus, Lawrence himself journeyed to such places as Mexico and the American Southwest (we are speaking here essentially of the 1920s) in search of purer, more tranquil, more harmonious relics of earlier civilizations. He and his protagonists seek a primitive and basic life that is essentially, as Panofsky put it, "civilized life purged of its vices" (297).

At the same time, Lawrence's basic honesty to his own experience compelled him to recognize that such cultures as he could explore and such records as he could examine suggested quite the opposite. They reveal instead, as Panofsky put it, "a civilized life stripped of its virtues" (297). This perception gives particular poignancy to novels such as *The Rainbow, Women in Love,* and *Lady Chatterley's Lover.* Their disturbing power results not simply from the precarious and catastrophic interpersonal relationships of the characters. Even more it is the sense, similar in many ways to that of Ford, that the extant English civilization, which is the ground of their dramatic action, is profoundly degenerative and disintegrative. Its preservation of folk customs like Morris dancing and its memories of pre-Christian religious attitudes and rituals testify to this in two ways. First, they document the historical existence of an earlier, better way of life. Second, they are seen to be consigned now merely to fugitive reflections on what are regarded largely as quaint practices.

As a result of this basic conviction, Lawrence generates a desire for a prehistorical cultural ideal so as to root in an earlier time the possibility of a renaissance of mankind. The quest to restore such an ideal is both imaginative and actual as Quetzalcoatl, Rananim, and Taos illustrate. In each instance, however, Lawrence is forced to find such a quest to be fruitless. Ultimately, he takes the Arcadian harmony of nature and culture projected on the past as a trope of regret for unfulfilled but unquenched desire. Thus, his initial assumption that such a harmony was historically real modulates into one of imaginative capability without ever being completely discarded as possible. What was becomes what could have been, which then becomes what can be. And in making his texts the locus of the ideal, Lawrence voices his elegiac recognition of fissure as fate. The loss he laments is the gap between the ideal and the real, the absence of cultural ideal as historical actuality. Rather than the primeval existence and historical disappearance of an ideal harmony between nature and culture, this is what drives his imagination.[4]

The modernist elegiac temper is also shaped by another attitude. This one uses both the recent past and the whole historical vista of human culture as an index to how supremely different they are from the present of the twentieth century. Here, the great modernist exemplar is Joyce, although in their individual ways both Lawrence and Thomas Mann resonate with the same disquiet. All of Joyce's prose works are dominated by the awareness of this difference. *Ulysses,* for instance, documents that the present is compounded of greater historical mass, sociological density, and empirical detail than any available form or manifestation of the past. In many ways, this perception is modernism's formal inheritance from European and American naturalism/realism, from Zola, Dreiser, and Norris. Where the genius of Joyce, and the modernists in general, comes into play is in the ability to use this perception for other and broader ends than their predecessors. Modernists made it the basis for a greater measure of spiritual disquiet and uncertainty concerning the individual's specific place and role in such a temporal condition, cosmos, and society.

In *Dubliners,* the focus is on the incertitude of personal identity. Out of it emerge the characters' resultant deceptions and defense mechanisms. These are occasioned by their identities being devoid of an awareness of a past more than a generation old. The macro-continuities between realism and modernism are perhaps best seen when Joyce's volume of short stories is set against Sherwood Anderson's *Winesburg, Ohio* (1919).[5] The latter provides in a simpler and more obvious fashion the same concentration on the straitened lives of ordinary people, their hesitations, insecurities, and desperate hopes and struggles. It almost compulsively shows their longing for release into a more fulfilling realization of their natures.[6] Both works create an elegiac attitude toward the dichotomy of freedom and constriction, self-realization and self-defeat.[7] The major difference, of course, is Joyce's more muted and sophisticated ironic attitude. Alice Hindman, like Joyce's Eveline, has spent her life longing for an intimate relationship and self-fulfillment with a man. Both characters, finally, reach out only to discover that their choice is but a symbolic surrogate and not a possible reality. Eveline's final response to Frank consists of a helpless look of nonrecognition and a setting of "her white face to him, passive, like a helpless animal" (34). Similarly, Alice's final frenzied effort to escape her sterile existence collapses when she, "turning her face to the wall, began trying to force herself to face bravely the fact that many people must live and die alone" (134).[8] For both authors, personal loneliness invests life with an unassuageably elegiac sense of sorrow, loss, and pity for the waste inherent in the human condition.[9]

A Portrait of the Artist as a Young Man and *Ulysses* chart a shift away from concentrating on the minuscule human self and its struggle for definition. The latter novel in particular explicitly underlines the social multitude, the plethora of facts, and the experiential density they create. Both develop an implicit elegy for the individual through the deployment of narrative memory, protagonists' historical awareness, and encyclopedic allusions. As such, they pass far beyond the scope of Anderson's vision while still maintaining the core of sorrow and pity for the individual. Stephen and Bloom, for instance, engage in concentrated efforts to learn and establish their identities. Their efforts betray an all-consuming obsessive reaching out to their differing yet overlapping cultural pasts. In contrast to them, George Willard, Anderson's youthful protagonist, distances himself from his small town past at the very moment of leaving his home on the train:

> the town of Winesburg had disappeared and his life there had become but a background on which to paint the dreams of his manhood. (303)

His response abnegates his cultural past while Stephen's and Bloom's preserves it and increases its scope, density, and significance. For all, there is a profound loss, but with different consequences. In Anderson's case, it is founded on the character's failure to recognize his loss. In Joyce, it is based on his protagonists' persistent expanding of their personal past into history, culture, and their attendant ironies.

In so doing, Stephen and Bloom serve to point up through their contrasts in temperament and age a transpersonal sense of regret, loss, and remembrance. Their focus is on man being consigned forever to live in, although not wholly of, the present. When Bloom enters Molly's bed, two things are thrown into bold relief. One is the fallibility of believing in the individual's autonomy. The other is a muted recognition of the tranquility attendant upon "all passion spent." Both are captured with an economy that is the converse of the prodigality of narrative shown earlier in the novel. There, Joyce catechistically presents the elegiac resolution of sexual fidelity not only by but also through Bloom:

> If he had smiled, why would he have smiled?
>
> To reflect that each one who enters imagines himself to be the first to enter whereas he is always the last term of a preceding series even if the first term of a succeeding one, each imagining himself to be the first, last, only and alone, whereas he is neither first nor last nor only nor alone in a series originating in and repeated to infinity. (601)

The impersonality of the catechism mode casts an aura of inevitability over the sentiments expressed. When combined with Bloom's reflecting on the impossibility, strictly speaking, of human sexual fidelity, it creates a striking inflection of the elegiac temper. In it, the consciously realized loss of illusion is found to be concomitant with the individual's homecoming to reality.

In *Finnegans Wake,* the inundation of the self by the inescapable present is complete. It is compounded of factors inherited from the nineteenth century including a knowledge explosion as well as exponential urban and population growth. Here the normal definition of a literary work is tacitly recast. Instead of possessing one text and one language, it now has multiple languages and multiple subtexts. These, however, are neither variants nor alternative translations of each other because the epistemological ground of interpretation itself has been radically altered. William James's sensory "buzzing, blooming confusion" is now regarded as an overload of intellectual storing and processing capabilities. In *Finnegans Wake,* this results in the dissolution of the Cartesian subject-object relation and the concomitant self-other dichotomy. Joyce does not construe the self as an entity either circumscribed or circumscribable. Instead he here regards it as a process of consciousness of consciousness. In this process, the polarization of past and present is dissolved into an extended temporal spectrum that is contingent upon the narrative process. That is, the very endlessness of storytelling prevents the creation of distinct temporal worlds. In short, Humphrey Chimpden Earwicker is Here Comes Everyone is Human Condition Everywhere. The poignancy of the imperiled self in *Ulysses* is underscored by an inescapable historical myopia that always makes the past smaller, simpler, and clearer. This is replaced in *Finnegans Wake* by the poignancy of human consciousness forever committed to and limited by itself. All of its acts of awareness, no matter how diversified and multiplex, are simply a mental product. Both works subtly tease out the relationships between comedy and elegy. In them, arabesques of freedom and triumph are wrought upon a ground or backdrop of necessity and defeat. *Ulysses* achieves its version of this through the ludic dimensions resulting from the obsessive identity quests of Stephen and Bloom. *Finnegans Wake,* on the other hand, enacts a seriocomic perspective by the recurring prospect of apparently unending narratives. Such a prospect brackets or suspends the very issue of philosophical answers and positions by rendering all of them ultimately undecidable. Categorical decisions become impossible not so much because of congenital uncertainty concerning a definitive answer as of the presence of an endless number of options. This situation results by Joyce's imaginative versatility in generating linguistic attitudes that mime the almost infinite possibilities inherent in the human mind. In so doing, Joyce's last work generates an elegiac sadness over both the impossibility of endings and their inevitability.

9

BIFOCAL TIME

Virginia Woolf's *The Years* and *To the Lighthouse*

The history of the elegy, at least in English, calls attention to its inclination for philosophical reflections on human culture. Spenser and Wordsworth are the compelling touchstones for this facet of the genre. In modern times this predisposition assumes a more problematic cast due to such things as the knowledge explosion, intensified urbanization, and a deepening preoccupation with the fate of the self. The elegiac inflection of the modernist consciousness sounds an awareness that mankind now possesses an ever increased predisposition to puzzle over human attainments and goals. Its more expanded leisure time allows for more sustained reflection and introspection. At the same time, the modernist imaginative enactment of such an opportunity is studiously half-congratulatory and half-apprehensive.

Thus, in *The Years,* Virginia Woolf's characters demonstrate the relevance of leisure to elegiac cultural contemplation. But they also dramatize their and their age's largely unwitting participation in cultural decline and loss. Throughout the novel, they continue to contemplate and comment on individual and institutional absences and transformations. As elegiac witnesses of these, they memorialize the drift of both into an imperceptibly and steadily receding past. At the same time, they try to presage an auspicious future that they do not understand and of which they cannot be a part.

The authorial voice alone conveys the full consciousness of both actions. In a descriptive and narrative subtext, it casts nature as perdurable and culture as transitory so that the elegists themselves are elegized. The inescapability of time conditions the novel from the opening: "Slowly wheeling, like the rays of a searchlight, the days, the weeks, the years passed one after another across the sky" (2). At the conclusion of *The Years,* all persons have been changed utterly and a terrible beauty born. Time's power lies in creating the deceptive illusion that nothing has altered: "The sun had risen, and the sky above the houses wore an air of extraordinary beauty, simplicity, and peace" (469). Nevertheless, both the book's title and subheadings—from "1880" to "Present Day"—counter this impression. They and the novel's events recurrently lament that time is ceaselessly altering the world human beings inhabit. Nor, it is felt, are such changes likely to be for the better.

Perhaps the most sustained effort to chart this transition from the traditional elegiac impulse to a more thoroughly modern exploration of a conspectus of philosophical perspectives on the elegiac, loss, and time can be found in Virginia Woolf's *To the Lighthouse* (1927).[1] Here she amasses a detailed list of the ways in which time and loss contribute to a yet more complex and varied elegiac temper. In so doing, her approach is not so much taxonomic, much less dramatic, as it is contemplative and spectatorial. In a sense, all of her characters are observers more than they are active participants in life. This speculative review of the relations obtaining between time, loss, and the elegiac allows her to muse on possible directions, emphases, and attitudes to be explored in subsequent novels.

This can be seen from the very opening of the novel, which identifies a number of losses occurring in different people's lives. These range from those of central characters to tangential and even incidental figures. Thus, Mr. Ramsay's comparative failure to succeed as a philosopher and Lily's loss of self-control and confidence when she moves from the artist as appreciator to artist as creator are of central concern to the novel's themes. In contrast, Tansley's sense of not belonging, of not being a member of a social community, and of not having the money and resources that others possess is invested with a kind of pitying pathos not wholly devoid of contempt. In privileging abstract thought and art over social equality as important subjects, Woolf is, of course, only documenting the predispositions of modernism and her Bloomsbury intelligentsia. The same is true of her willingness to cite in a straight-faced humorous manner the old joke about the paperhanger who has lost an arm.

All of these losses do not generate the traditional elegiac mourning impulse, nor do they endeavor to do so. Instead, they shape a reflective, balanced, philosophic perspective that acknowledges the importance to the individual of loss but diminishes it by placing it in the total human context of time and absolute value. Woolf's view implicitly is that these losses are both strictly personal and ultimately reparable. As a result, they do not require nor warrant the traditional elegiac attitude.[2]

A more contemporary sense of the elegiac is hinted at in the initial description of James. He is one of those who "must let future prospects, with their joys and sorrows, cloud what is actually at hand" because "any turn in the wheel of sensation has the power to crystallise and transfix the moment upon which its gloom or radiance rests" (9). Thus, his basic temperament compels all interactions of present and future to generate an incipiently elegiac temper. At this point, however, James's mood is celebratory rather than elegiac. At least, it is until his father blights it by casting strong doubt on the realization of his heartfelt wish to visit the lighthouse. Woolf shrewdly fills James with rage at arbitrary paternal authority rather than elegiac reconciliation to actuality. This allows her to call into question the appropriateness of the traditional elegiac response to the quondam details of ordinary life.

She does this also through elliptically sketching Tansley's travestying of Mr. Ramsay's rather pompous, self-important attitude. Tansley is portrayed as an "odious little man" (26) and as but one of many academic toadies to Mr. Ramsay. This efficiently transforms him from a muted elegiac shadow over the immediate future into a comic figure virtually devoid of individuality. Mrs. Ramsay locates his absurdity in the absolute certitude with which he proclaims the immediate future. Such an attitude betrays his complete misunderstanding of the elegiac nature of the future. Whereas the past alone is firmly established, the character of the future must remain inherently undetermined. As such, its elegiac qualities are no more than possibilities. In effect, it is his own very assertiveness that transforms it and him into one of those comic absurdities who "parodied her husband" (27). The result is to circumscribe the temporal limits available to the traditional elegiac impulse.

Immediately, however, as if to acknowledge the validity and strength of the impulse within its appropriate context, Woolf has Mrs. Ramsay contemplate the sound of the ocean's waves. There she finds the dual impact of time: both supportive and destructive. With this, she gains an elegiac recognition of the ephemerality of life and its underlying terror. A few pages later Lily Briscoe also is made to perceive the sea as a symbol of time as it charts the movement from day to night and summer to autumn. For her, the sea though sad is also supportive, threatening but encouraging. The passage of time holds both the fear of the termination of the self and the satisfaction at the perpetuation of the physical universe. It undergoes constant change, but it also keeps doing so: everything ends, but nothing disappears.

The result is the elegiac temper experienced by Bankes and Lily when looking at the sea together:

> both of them looked at the dunes far away, and instead of merriment felt come over them some sadness—because the thing was completed partly, and partly because distant views seem to outlast by a million years (Lily thought) the gazer and to be communing already with a sky which beholds an earth entirely at rest. (34)

Here, Woolf projects the traditional elegiac resolution to lie beyond the human psyche and condition. It comes to rest in the whole physical universe and its apparent eternality.[3] In so doing, she opts for a philosophical perspective rather than a personal one. Her solace lies in a metaphysical perception of reality instead of a psychological transcendent conviction. She finds comfort in the abstract, universal, and impersonal, not in a deeply felt particularity embedded in a specific belief system.

This polarization of the personal and the impersonal is further explored through Mrs. Ramsay's reflections on their house and its contents. Her sense of the decrepitude of their summer furniture invokes the passage of time. It, however, does not command extended reflective attention. This is because the house and its furniture are so unrelievedly commonplace. In short, as empirical events and objects, they carry no significance apart from simply being what they are.

For Mrs. Ramsay, the house and its contents are destined for increased decay not only as the result of the passing of time but of family behavior. This last she is not prepared to correct since it largely involves her children whose growth and development are of greater importance to her than the condition of the house. This suggests that for her the passage of time into the future is more germane than its retrogression into the past. As a result, Woolf presents Mrs. Ramsay as an anti-elegiac person. She is someone centered in the immediate moment for herself and in the future for her family. Thus, her own demise can be recorded in the flat, economical, declarative manner of the journalist who records the fact without rhetorical emphasis:

> Mrs. Ramsay having died rather suddenly the night before . . . (194).

> She was dead, they said; years ago in London. . . . (She had died very sudden at the end, they said.) (204)

By emphasizing the impersonal in connection with Mrs. Ramsay, Woolf accepts in a clear-eyed fashion the limits that exist in understanding another person. This, of course, was an activity valued so highly not only by herself but also by G. E. Moore's philosophy and Bloomsbury. Because of such limits, Mrs. Ramsay's "beauty and splendour" (46) function as a mask behind which she exists inscrutably. The ultimate mystery of her existence gives rise to "stories" and rumors about conventional elegiac occasions: romantic tragedies, disappointed love affairs, and the like. Out of these, the novelist's voice is led to speculations about her character and perceptions, speculations whose unverifiability makes them uncertain. With this recognition, Woolf pushes yet further in her effort to redefine the scope of the elegiac. The elegiac inflections found in individual lives are seen often to be fictions, inventions based on speculation, produced by others. Their truth remains tantalizingly unsubstantiated yet still within the realm of possibility and so available to the imagination of both novelist and audience.

At the same time, Woolf does not disavow the effort to comprehend fully and truly the nature of another person. Indeed, Mrs. Ramsay pursues exactly such an effort at comprehension in her marriage. In it, she calculates how precisely this effort extends, and assesses the extent to which it attaches to his character a hitherto unrevealed dimension, at once heroic and elegiac. Mr. Ramsay's ability to think abstractly but only up to "Q" generates an awareness of the heroic struggle that is entailed. The struggle to avoid failing in the effort to know is a profound and largely silent form of heroism. It entails first of all a concentrated effort to attain abstract knowledge. Then, it confronts the consequent judgment of personal failure, and ultimately, the loss of even the possibility of attaining full knowledge, of knowing all that there is to know.

But viewed apart from the individual, it is elegiac as well as heroic. The inherently elegiac situation of loss, inevitable failure, and defeat is cast in both abstract and concrete terms (the alphabet, the survival of the stormy seas, and the Polar expedition). It functions not as subjective personal awareness so much as objective natural things (the lizard and the geranium). The whole builds to Mr. Ramsay's elegiac assessment of his career and his hope against hope that he is morally not culpable. He is the hero destined to fail in his quest for knowledge and yet to find solace in "the beauty of the world" (57) that he finds to reside in his family.

To this, Mrs. Ramsay functions as the elegiac consolation for his philosophic doubts concerning his abilities and achievements. These doubts persist in the face of, and are perhaps occasioned by, the inevitable shortcomings faced by the individual human being. She senses that his need for her ability to comfort provides a kind of elegiac solace for both of them. Together, need and fulfillment complement one another. This produces a sense of unity, completeness, and harmony closely resembling the conventional elegiac transformation of grief and loss into consolation and the ability to go on. Yet it is itself challenged by her inability to tell him the truth, to be candid about him and his family's needs. As a result, there is a fresh elegiac sorrow and challenge to confront.

This sense of the ongoing, persistent elegiac experience in life provides Woolf with her rationale for the redefinition of the elegiac attitude. Elegies, she intimates, tend to mislead if they incline one to regard the experience being dealt with as unique or individual and occupying a sole historical moment. Instead, the elegiac temper is persistently called upon throughout life and history to mourn, confront, and console for the vicissitudes of loss, time, and change.

Mrs. Ramsay's sense of herself as the elegiac consoler coupled with her doubts about the legitimacy and authenticity of this role implicitly raise a broader issue. In essence, it is the question of the writer's authority to formulate elegiac works as genuine expressions of deeply felt emotions. At issue is the whole Romantic rationale for elegies, of their capability to transform grief and sorrow at loss to a transcendent acceptance of death. Woolf's response to this challenge is one of transmutation rather than outright rejection. She sees the elegiac not so much as primarily a personal response to a specific occasion as a coherent philosophical attitude sustainable throughout a lifetime. It becomes a metaphysic, if you will, for the nonphilosopher. It is in this light that Mr. Ramsay with all of his lapses, insensitivities, and egoism can best be gauged. He stands as the conscious confronter of the elegiac fate: man's ultimate ignorance and the passage of time, which erodes whatever knowledge and whatever confidence in its legitimacy is possessed. As such, he is fated to be a guidepost for the safe journey of others while his very limitations prevent him from facing this crisis situation successfully.

Another difference between the two derives from Mrs. Ramsay's recognition that the world consists essentially of "suffering, death, the poor" and that "no happiness lasted" (98). This feeling reveals that her elegiac temper is that of the submerged self existing in isolation. In contrast, Mr. Ramsay affects elegiac sentiments through his statements, not through his feelings. Woolf is aware of this contrast: the one is a matter of expression, and the other a mode of perception. For Woolf, however, this polarization is insufficient as is seen by two events. One is Mrs. Ramsay's sudden and largely uncelebrated death and the other is Ramsey's subsequent, almost shameless, use of the elegiac pattern of emotions. Her creative struggle is to fuse the two into a perspective fully and persistently aware of the dualities and ambiguities of time.

To die basically without public recognition, as Mrs. Ramsay does, is to swallow up the individual moment into the eons of time past and future. The moment is that in which Woolf is convinced we all live, while the eons constitute the philosophic view of time. They serve to expunge or annihilate the moment in which the individual exists. Similarly, to call up grief and sorrow as if by rote, in the manner Mr. Ramsay does as widower, is, as Lily recognizes, to engage in a revolting brand of self-indulgence and egoism. By its very conventionality, it threatens to make time into something static, devoid of changing forms and innovations. How to avoid the shortcomings of both attitudes and to create a new way of apprehending the concepts of time and loss is the task Woolf set herself in writing *To the Lighthouse.*

In doing so, she was prepared to see loss as not simply the absence of that once possessed, as a change in time. For her, it had to be extended to include values and states never experienced by an individual character. The best instance of this is Mrs. Ramsay's rather puzzling claim to Lily that "an unmarried woman has missed the best of life" (77). Woolf risks having her pivotal character, the very core of perception and compassionate understanding, viewed as a rather smug, self-satisfied advocate of her own personal manner of life. In point of fact, she is simply rendering—admittedly from her own viewpoint and rather elliptically—a fact too easily overlooked. This is that fundamental choices in life may issue unavoidably in subsequent losses either not attended to at the time or treated as irrelevant.

Yet the relationship between Mrs. Ramsay and Lily, shifting and complex as it is, documents the ways in which they both share in the losses inflicted by the passage of time. Thus, Lily's sense of loss and deprivation occasioned by Bankes's having actually seen her painting produces a feeling of elegiac sadness. At the same time, it is surmounted by an almost sexual exhilaration at the removal of her feeling of being isolated and separated from the rest of the world. It serves as an iconic elegy for virginity of whatever sort, for not sharing or not having shared.

Similarly, Mrs. Ramsay's sense of lacking time for contemplated social projects such as a model dairy and hospital looks toward the future for relief from loss. Time here occasions postponement or deferral rather than curtailment or outright denial. It, in effect, puts the prospect of consolation in the future and so is a kind of deferred elegy. At the same time, while she looks forward to the future as a time of possible self-realization, she also fears it. This is because it also moves her children relentlessly into adulthood. And with their removal from childhood, she has to face that "Nothing made up for the loss" (89). What disturbs her is the diminishment of her parental role as her offspring become adults.

It is this very awareness of the extreme difficulty of truly judging the impact of time once and once only that leads to such a judgment's becoming a thing to be laughed, or at least smiled, over. In so doing, it is seen within the benign bifocal scope of the elegiac, as when Mrs. Ramsay glances at the window in the midst of the dinner party. There she has a dual realization. First, she senses that the room, dry land, and the assembled people represent order. Second, she more ominously perceives that the out-of-doors, the sea, and nature in general constitute uncertainty, change, and fluidity. This dual reality constitutes the ground for and of the elegiac. It fuses the sense of sadness at the necessity of loss with the sense of past, and possibly future, celebration and satisfaction at the inherent value of what is lost. It is in just this way that the whole novel's attitude is essentially elegiac. It acknowledges time's movement and its consequences as inescapable and yet not something to be railed against but only mildly regretted. This attitude is made explicit in Mrs. Ramsay's quiet philosophic reflection on the occasion of the dinner party itself:

> This will celebrate the occasion—a curious sense rising in her, at once freakish and tender, of celebrating a festival, as if two emotions were called up in her, one profound—for what could be more serious than the love of man for woman, what more commanding, more impressive, bearing in its bosom the seeds of death; at the same time these lovers, these people entering into illusion glittering eyed, must be danced round with mockery, decorated with garlands. (151)

The engagement of Paul and Minta is thus seen from the clear-eyed perspective of Mrs. Ramsay's relationship with her husband. Toward the end of part 1 her reflections on her husband's weaknesses and strengths are those of an elegist preparing to compose her celebratory farewell. She keeps turning over in her mind what can be said and what ought to be said as well as alternative judgments reflective of the subject's own view of himself. And just as Mrs. Ramsay conveys her love without saying it so Woolf conveys her elegy without stating it. The loss or failure or refusal of Mrs. Ramsay to speak her love doesn't fail to convey the reality of it. In the same way, Woolf's elegy doesn't fail to convey the reality of death and time's passing movement even though it seeks to deny or transcend it.

Part 2 moves the novel's elegiac temper from a consideration of the persistent and multiform ways in which time impinges on individual human beings. It pursues a more broadly philosophic contemplation of time and the inevitable effects it works on past, present, and future. It consists of an extended threnody on time and its movement. The trajectory it follows is from the creation of a future seen from the standpoint of a largely unknown present that is on the verge of being enveloped into an ever receding and continually growing past. This portion of the novel is marked by death, change, disintegration, nothingness, and awareness of the profound difference between past and present. And complicating this difference is the fact that it is differentiating between constantly changing temporal units. It struggles to distinguish between a past that was the present in part 1 and yet another present that was only the barely discernible future in the same section.

Part 2's ten sections combine three distinct facets. One is a sketchy, abbreviated narrative progression (Mrs. McNab and her son engaged in ordinary daily tasks); another that of quasiphilosophical reflections of a sensitive anonymous narrator (Woolf herself possibly); while a third consists of postulated comments by Mrs. McNab on similar problems or puzzles encountered in life. These function in a fashion similar to plot and counterplot in that they present radically different class levels while dealing with similar issues. Bridging these disparate levels are the passages in square brackets that chronicle the elegiac events marking the dual movements of time.[4] Simultaneously, time moves toward both individual, personal extinction and the universal, general persistence of mankind. In so doing, it underlines the implicit duality of human beings and the ironies generated thereby. The static and unchanging constitute the world devoid of persons and marked only by their existence in the past. It is also for Woolf the world of the beautiful, the aesthetic realm that constantly questions the permanency of the natural and the empirical in order to certify its persistence:

> Impatient, despairing yet loth to go (for beauty offers her lures, has her consolations), to pace the beach was impossible, contemplation was unendurable; the mirror was broken. (202)

External nature and its beauties are shattered by the fragmenting of consciousness, by being carried beyond what it can absorb.

Mrs. McNab's entrance into the abandoned Ramsay house questions the continued existence of this world. Her reiteration of her old, customary tasks, however, suggests a counter to this questioning: "after all, she had her consolations, as if indeed there twined about her dirge some incorrigible hope" (197). A stark contrast emerges between the house and Mrs. McNab. The house records the *passage* of time following upon its being deserted. She, on the other hand, persists in surviving while remembering the past and the losses it has occasioned. Time, like the Lighthouse light itself, "looked with equanimity at the thistle and the swallow, the rat and the straw. Nothing now withstood them; nothing said no to them" (208). It threatens to preside over the onset of material disintegration and chaos, the overcoming of man and civilization by nature and of artifice by rampant fertility. For Woolf, the anticipated disappearance of the house symbolizes the lapsing of civilization "upon the sands of oblivion" (209). Such a profound threat is redeemed only by human effort and apparent accident: the work of the charladies instigated by a sudden and completely unexpected request that the house be readied for a family visit. The result is a rebuilding of the family home and life, a restoration of life "from the pool of Time that was fast closing over them" (209). The precariousness of human life in the face of the steady onslaught of the destructive force of time is offset for Woolf only by a simple human determination to resist such dissolution as long as possible. Such a determination is called up arbitrarily and virtually accidentally.

That Lily should be the first arrival at the house after such a long time has passed is, however, no accident. She is identified with the arrival of peace, which is treated as a metaphysical and aesthetic rather than a military or social condition. Her arrival embodies life's gaining of significance, something that comes only with the passage of time and the onset of age:

> the voice of the beauty of the world came murmuring, too softly to hear exactly what it said—but what mattered if the meaning were plain? (213)

The voice of the night celebrates the majesty, authority, power, and beauty of the world. It manifests itself whether or not any of its inhabitants are awake (i.e., conscious) and able to listen to it. The voice is both a solace and a temptation. First, "gently then without complaint, or argument, the voice would sing its song" (214) thereby articulating its aesthetic reality. Then, by importuning "why not accept this, be content with this, acquiesce and resign?" (214), it suggests the desirability of accepting mortality. Lily's physical awakening at dawn is essentially to the duality of time's passing. Polarized are the beauty and completeness of life lived in and through time and the challenge of death, disintegration, corruption, and loss generated by time. The human being, Woolf realizes, is always witnessing a new day, which carries the disastrous threat of falling into an abyss of time. Time here is a mystery, something to come, not yet experienced, rather than something past and already experienced but without comprehension of its significance.

Part 3, entitled "The Lighthouse," attempts to articulate the meaning of the lighthouse and the past. It explores how when one has grown from a child to an adult the understanding of the past illuminates itself in the present. This occurs when one has replaced innocence or ignorance with experience or wisdom. It also marks the shift from the commonsense, ordinary empiricism of Mrs. Ramsay to the aesthetic, creative idealism of Lily. Concomitant with this is the final understanding by the narrator/artist/Woolf of the two-sided reality needed for comprehending life and death together. This reality is the elegiac temper that countenances both equally. Thus, the apparently simply question "what does one send to the Lighthouse?" (218) calls for a twofold reply. One is an empirical answer (tobacco, newspapers, etc.) and the other is an aesthetic one of meaning, coherence, community, and symbols. Facts, pragmatic usefulness to further life as survival, are balanced by "the truth of things" (219). This truth is a reverberant significance that satisfies only for the immediate moment and in different ways for different individuals. This is seen most compellingly in Lily's remembering to "move the tree to the middle" (220) of her still-to-be-finished picture. This action is her intuitive recognition that the empirical, the actual, the commonsensical must always be the center of the aesthetic vision.[5]

Against Lily in this section stands Mr. Ramsay. He represents the professional philosopher's analytical intelligence. His way of thinking threatens ruin and chaos to the intuitive perceptions of the artist. His method of viewing problems is antithetical to that of the creative mind. Also subsumed in this polarity are the male versus female attitudes and the fertile versus the virginal spirits or drives. By saying "You find us much changed" (221) Ramsay frankly insists on the recognition of the actuality of time. He stresses its movement from present to past. In so doing, he seeks to remember the past in order to chronicle and assess the prime differences between it and the present.

Lily by herself is inclined to blur over the temporal change or at least to leave it as something to be contemplated aesthetically. For her, such change is to be seen as part of a pattern rather than as a sharp fact dividing the world and perceptions in two. For her, past and present are both of equal value and dependent on each other for an understanding of the meaning of life and time.

It is only when he is occupied at an ordinary activity—like talking about and tying boots—that "thus occupied he seemed to her a figure of infinite pathos" (230). He too, she realizes, is destined to become a figure or focal point of the elegiac. Despite all of his intellectual eminence, he too, she feels, must engage in the ordinary, humdrum acts of living, all of which lead but to death and loss. Lily's perception that he "was always changing, and hid nothing" (233) links him with time in a way that opposes the elegiac lament. His is "that other final phase" in which he silently questions the other and pursues the mystery of the future "as if by curiosity" (233). It is this that places him beyond ordinary "worries and ambitions, and the hope of sympathy and the desire for praise" (233). He contemplates the past with a tough-minded equanimity amounting to a certain kind of self-satisfaction.

Lily, however, finds, through her clear recall of Mrs. Ramsay's writing letters by the sea that memory functions not simply as recollection but also as stimulation. For her, this links it to art. Each is something that can survive the immediate passage of the present into the past. Both continue to be "complete" and to stimulate the mind to a fuller, more complete, a fairer assessment—in short, a balanced judgment—of the past and its occupants. In so doing, they work as a stimulus to raise once more the question bedeviling Lily (and Woolf) of "what is the meaning of life?" (240)

This major question is answered in Lily's eyes not by a great revelation but rather by a small, daily one. What she senses now is that Mrs. Ramsay was able, occasionally and for a brief interval, to make "of the moment something permanent":

> In the midst of chaos there was shape; this eternal passing and flowing (she looked at the clouds going and the leaves shaking) was struck into stability. (241)

This suggests that the elegiac temper is the momentary insistence on stability and permanence desired and achievable by the human consciousness.

The nature of the elegiac is caught perhaps most fully in the shifting, fluctuating thoughts of Cam, James, and their father as they finally make the journey to the lighthouse. Indeed, Cam's ambivalent thoughts about her father suggest that the elegiac is somehow equivalent to the novel itself and the consciousness of its author. Cam's memory is marked by several features: its efforts to arrive at the truth about the individual, its balancing of positives against negatives, and its efforts to sum up the person's life and influence or impact. Through her, Woolf is in part trying to arrive at a just estimation of her own parents and siblings and to record a judgment about their collective past. At the same time, Cam's reaction to looking back from the sea to their house captures the anti-elegiac spirit of the young. Movement through space is like that through time: it "had put them far from it and given it the changed look, the composed look, of something receding in which one has no longer any part" (247).

This is in contrast to Mr. Ramsay's having actually seen the house. It creates in him the introspective, self-focused elegy in which he instinctively plays a dramatic part: "the part of a desolate man, widowed, bereft" (248). While his self-indulgent attitude is egocentric and mildly contemptible, it also is a common enough characteristic of many otherwise commendable individuals. Ironically enough, James's perceptions about Cam are cast in a similar elegiac mode. He sees her faltering in her determination to resist their father whom they together have cast as a tyrant. Yet while he finds her hesitation lamentable, he also recognizes it as understandable or condonable. These responses of both characters, however, are self-induced and somewhat fraudulent. This is because of their propensity to exaggerate the importance of the perceptions and events in order to elevate the self. By rendering both attitudes toward the elegiac—acceptance and rejection—Woolf incorporates a largely stylistic approach into a seminal assessing of her own past and family.[6] In the process, she creates a dispassionate version of the self-focused elegy, one, however, that mutes the self as elegiac subject.

This muting of the self is dependent on the vagaries inherent in the passage of time. Woolf is keenly aware of these vagaries. In particular, she is alert to the way events begun in the past do not follow the narrative envisaged for them in the future once it is transformed into the present. Thus, Minta's and Paul's courtship and marriage resembles Andrew's death, that of Mrs. Ramsay, and Prue's death in childbirth.[7] Each death represents a concomitant loss: that of a fine mathematical mind, of a core personality capable of taking people out of their ordinary loves, and of the ordinary expectancy of ongoing family life. They all testify to the problematic nature of controlling or predicting the future based on the present. All too frequently such predictive assumptions are contradicted when the future becomes the past. It is through the very passage of time that in Woolf's eyes the elegiac nature of life both develops and receives its plangency and persistence.

The only things to lie outside the passage of time and the impact of change are aesthetic media; people "pass and vanish; nothing stays; all changes, but not words, not paint" (267). Or so Lily the artist tries to convince herself. In articulating this prospect, Woolf strives to argue for the permanency of her own craft. At the same time, she—through Lily's uncertainty and indecisiveness—still subjects it to steely-eyed questioning. She insists on a dispassionate—almost philosophical—interrogation as to whether art really is an exception to temporal change. Ultimately, it would appear that Lily is unable fully to convince herself of the exception. In so concluding, she embodies both the consolation and the challenge inherent in the metaphysical exploration of death, loss, and time.

The casual indifference to these issues, of course, is embodied in the fisherman's boy cutting a piece out of a fish for bait and then throwing it back still alive into the sea.[8] His actions are set against Lily's passionate interrogation of life for answers. Against his obliviousness to both questions and answers, she struggles to reverse time's movement into the past. By this, she seeks to achieve the return of Mrs. Ramsay, all the while realizing its impossibility. Lily recollects her first response to the news of Mrs. Ramsay's death: seeing her as a shade, as a quasimythic figure of Demeter-like proportions. It becomes a recurring vision that requires anchoring in some immediate empirical scene which "had been part of the fields of death" (270). The inclusion of the immediate world, however, brings with it time and change so that "the vision must be perpetually remade" (270).

It is Cam, however, who recognizes, dimly to be sure, that time and its movement are a central aspect of the imagination's ability to envisage scenes and patterns. This awareness is set against the immediate stillness of the boat on the water:

> Everything in the whole world seemed to stand still. The Lighthouse became immovable, and the line of the distant shore became fixed. (272)

Similarly, it is time's presence that results in James's recognition that "nothing was simply one thing": the lighthouse is both "a silvery, misty-looking tower" and a "tower, stark and straight . . . barred with black and white" (276–77). With this, he experiences simultaneously the plurality, the stillness, and the motion of reality. This generates a context for the facts of death, loss, and the elegiac and with this "the relief was extraordinary" (279). James finally sees his father not as an antagonist and enemy but simply as an ancient object, something "very old . . . like some old stone lying on the sand" (301). And in doing so, he senses what they have in common:

> he looked as if he had become physically what was always at the back of both of their minds—that loneliness which was for both of them the truth about things. (301)

With this, James also sees the lighthouse as what it really is: a stark tower on a bare rock.[9] No longer is it a childhood impulse or a desire to visit something that then later has to be recoiled against because sought in response to his father's will.[10] No longer is it a psychological projection or an aesthetic symbol but simply a visual object that "satisfied him" (301). It creates for him a recognition that life is driven by time, the result of which is inevitably death. This awareness is one, he feels, which he shares with his father. Ultimately, then, this explains why the lighthouse is Mr. Ramsay's goal or destination, not the children's. It fuses with Lily's painting; both are an "attempt at something" (309), the one intellectual, the other artistic or aesthetic; one living, the other a contemplation of living; one pursuing time, the other resisting it. Her line drawn in the center of the painting is the same as his reaching the lighthouse.

10

PERSPECTIVES ON THE SELF

Malcolm Lowry's *Under the Volcano,* Truman Capote's *Breakfast at Tiffany's,* and Joan Didion's *Play It as It Lays*

Virginia Woolf's elegiac attitude, as we have seen, is essentially philosophic and interrogative, partly because she is endeavoring to understand time and its human implications. Other writers, however, approach the elegiac by focusing on the lost self and its consequences. In general, they combine a helpless, minimally expressed, elegiac spirit with that of a spectator witnessing a self-wrought tragedy. It is this focus that links such otherwise different writers as Malcolm Lowry, Truman Capote, and Joan Didion and such works as *Under the Volcano* (1947), *Breakfast at Tiffany's* (1958), and *Play It as It Lays* (1970). Their principal characters—Geoffrey Firman, Maria Wyeth, and Holly Golightly—are essentially devoid of a viable personal self. This lack prevents their motivating themselves to function effectively in their widely differing settings of rural Mexico, Los Angeles, and New York. All three can be seen (and have been frequently) as emotional cripples, weaklings, psychologically self-indulgent misfits undeserving of pity, sympathy, or mourning.[1] And yet they do arouse precisely such feelings. As a result, these works become, as it were, elegies for the undeserving, articulated by narrators or narrative voices scarcely able to identify the grounds for their caring for the fates of the three.

The close proximity between the narrative voices and the implicit authorial perspectives on respective characters engenders an essentially bifocal view of them. On the one hand, the narrative voices are cognizant of the moral and social flaws of the characters. At the same time, they also express a kind of reluctant compassion for the personal losses occasioned by those very flaws. On the other hand, the authorial perspectives implicitly suggest that the roots of the characters' origins lie in the natures and situations of Lowry, Didion, and Capote themselves. They are simultaneously indicting and elegizing the modern human propensity for waste, for squandering the social and psychological potential resident in the individual.[2] These authors appear to be defending, deploring, and regretting those very impulses and actions in which they themselves have participated, including those that led them to create such bifurcated fictional characters. Here we have but to list their respective fates. Lowry suffered his own long descent into alcoholism. Capote similarly declined into drug-induced travesties of his earlier demonstrations of personal self-control. Both traits consisted of *outré* and outrageous behavior accompanied by an engaging, childlike willingness to shock. And finally, Didion lapsed into a protracted fictional silence (some seven years) following publication of *Play It as It Lays*. In a sense, such a silence was virtually a consequence of her stylistic minimalism. All testify to their individual prescience in facing, however obliquely, their crucial personal problems through the creation of such characters for which both elegy and tragedy, compassion and pity are essential components.

In all three novels, the principal elegizing factors or foci prove to be threefold. First, they focus on the *self* in its most basic and essential form. Second, they explore the *values* each self espouses and adheres to, for better or ill, with almost compulsive determination. And finally, they assess the complexities of *love*, the responses to which motivate the self in its arc of existence. Because the individual selves of the Consul or Geoffrey Firman, Holly Golightly, and Maria Wyeth move toward their own losses in more or less conscious and deliberate fashion, a central crux emerges as the issue of necessity versus free will. Essentially, this crux results from the individual texts questioning why the characters elect their own destruction. Is it because of some metaphysical necessity that compels them to waste the potential or promise inherent in their individual selves? Or is it due to their exercising, either consciously or unconsciously, a kind of free will? Depending on the differing authorial perspectives taken on this question, their works assume distinctively different though related literary modes or emphases.

Geoffrey Firman treats his innermost personal self as a sovereign being, which may be argued with, struggled with, berated and pled with in endless, convoluted, and ultimately circular discussions. Each such debate or argument concludes, however, with his submission to the choices and inclinations of the self. It is allowed to follow its own course even though, as is seen with increasing clarity as the novel progresses, it proves to be a destructive and ultimately disastrous one. Geoffrey makes his rational mind the servant or vassal of his emotional or subconscious self. The latter always dictates the course of action he is to adopt. Either it argues its case endlessly and with specious sophistication, or it simply dismisses all arguments as irrelevant in the face of the overwhelming compulsion it feels to take another and yet another drink. In a sense, he appeals to and develops a cult of character. Like Othello, he sees his destruction to be determined by his essential and unchangeable nature compounded by his obsessive conviction of having been betrayed in love.[3] And yet, as the novel makes clear, however much he inclines to the role of the tragic hero, he lacks the plausibility of motive required to make his fall and death truly inevitable.[4]

If Geoffrey's self is a labyrinth of involution and evasion, Holly Golightly's is a mélange of surfaces. It is a compound of shifting, disconnected, essentially momentary attitudes and judgments surrounding a core of ostensibly simple, unchanging values.[5] The former create her "phony" exterior appearance, her madcap endearing foolishness and frivolity, her quality of never seeming to have grown up or have wished to. She is a depiction of the quintessential party girl on whose acquaintance Capote drew in developing his fictional character.[6] These traits are seen ultimately to serve as armor or a disguise for the essential personal self. She allows only the narrator to see it fleetingly because she (and her creator) hesitate to talk about or analyze it unduly. Her personal self, unlike Geoffrey's, is seen essentially from the outside, by the narrator who himself is both a fictional character and a surrogate for the author. He regards her basically as a phenomenon streaking across his path to be marveled at and silently sorrowed over because of the waste of such a vibrant, exotic, charismatic, "crazy" individual. As such, she stands in contradistinction to Geoffrey's cult of character, of brooding, monomaniacal persistence in deliberate self-destruction. In contrast, Holly generates a cult of personality, of unique individuality avoiding a variety of disasters by a kind of ad hoc resourcefulness coupled with a luck that forestalls them, for a time at any rate. In so doing, she resembles, almost mimes, the multitude of public performances of her creator.

Maria Wyeth's self most nearly resembles an onion in a continual process of being peeled. Throughout the novel, Didion shows Maria being slowly stripped of one skin of selfhood after another. And perhaps more importantly, Didion conveys a dual perspective on the process. On the one hand, there is Maria's own initial intuition, which tacitly and unconsciously assumes that the repeated skin-stripping will ultimately reach a core. This resembles Holly's values or convictions in that finally it can no longer be peeled and so is fundamentally inexpungable. On the other, there is the author's view. It sees that the process of self-divestment is wholly a matter of the number of layers of skin and that such a self is indeed expugnable. Starkly, Didion sees that in Maria's case this can come only through the physical intervention of suicide. The novel shrewdly brings these two views into line as it strings its snapshot scenes together so as to move them increasingly into focus. In stripping off her outer surfaces, Maria finds slowly that there is nothing of ultimate or paramount value in the self. Finally, she realizes that the self in its most basic form is identical with simply living itself. By facing BZ's challenge as to why one should continue to go on living, Maria answers traditional defenders of suicide. In effect, she counters their copious and ingenious arguments by her cogent and elliptical question of "Why not?" Her implicit rationale is that to cease living requires—as one sees from BZ's case—even yet more commitment, more decision making, more judging there to be some ultimate value on which one is basing the action not to live.[7] To keep on simply existing becomes for Maria the extreme of skepticism concerning the personal self. This extreme combines the classical dispassion of considered objectivity with the romantic extravagance of histrionically reaching out to waste something still felt, however subliminally, to be precious. Doing anything, even dying deliberately and by one's own hand, has no warrant, no justification, and no value.

Geoffrey the Consul sees his self as possessing some sort of almost transcendent importance, the loss of which is a virtually ceremonious disregard for the awfulness of the waste entailed. Capote's narrator sees Holly's self as a mysterious but vital core of being whose eclipse arouses regret for the loss of an exceptional and unforgettable nature. This loss stems from her personal refusal to accommodate or compromise with the ordinary world that really exists everywhere—New York, rural Texas, Brazil, even Africa. Maria, on the other hand, sees her inner, personal self as virtually extraneous to her obsessed revulsion from an external environment that she regards as thoroughly corrupt and degenerative. The self has little value for her because she sees it as something perpetually to be stripped away or else as something not to be attended to with a direct and conscious gaze. Unlike the Consul, she simply does not attend to her self as an entity for analysis and respect. Nor does she, like Holly, have a core of conscious values that, however briefly and simplistically articulated, she can equate with her personal self. For her, as has been noted, her personal self is essentially identical with living itself.

Just as the characters' personal selves are distinctive, so do their related values differ. Geoffrey's choice of drink and death is finally seen simply as a fact. No one reason is allowed to become a clear motive explaining his excessive and prolonged drinking. The various reasons advanced are as plausible as they are ultimately individually unconvincing. They include: his involvement with a wartime naval catastrophe; his personal conviction of guilt for everything from his actions to his self's responses and attitudes; Yvonne as another person with an essentially unknowable self that for him engenders an interpretational puzzle begetting suspicion and accusation; his envy, hatred, and contempt for his brother Hugh; his reliance on Dr. Vigil and M. Laruelle as drinking companions who create a miniature society or community that sanctions his excesses. These reasons or explanations are multiplied by elaborate and complex symbolic patterns and interrelated and overlapping internal monologues so dense and contradictory as to defeat the search for a clear motive founded on identifiable values. In effect, Geoffrey puts his trust in evasion of the destructive arc of the self by winding further and further into the labyrinth of analysis, explanation, and justification. He becomes the victim of his own absorption in self-delusion.

In contrast to his ostensible heightening of the multitude and inscrutability of values, Holly's commitment to her values appears simple and direct. They include personal honesty, the pursuit of a place where she will feel she belongs, and a rather quixotic search for an ideal man and love. These values are complicated by her willingness to use whatever is convenient or available, to live only for the moment, and her desire for status even if only as the quintessence of the always available party girl. All of these together make the destruction of her personal self the equivalent of her disappearance from the narrator's life. The way in which it is actually destroyed remains a mystery if not for her then for the narrator.

In the process, the focus shifts from Holly's to the narrator's values, from her concentration on the moment to his on memory. She becomes for him a fragment of a memory of past time, which is what most memories continue to exist as, namely, fragments. It is the narrator's felt loss of magic, excitement, unalloyed pleasure in his life—all of which disappear with Holly—that leaves him with a residual sadness for what will never be again. Her disappearance also arouses in him an elegiac feeling for or about himself. Subconsciously, he regrets that his youth has gone, his closeness to another human being beyond recapture, and that he has never ventured to aspire to the ideal, however unrealistic it may be. In contrast, she has bizarrely and independently fused simple idealism and stark realism to create a pragmatic idealist. As a result, the elegiac temper dominating the novel is that of the narrator rather than the principal character.

Holly carries her memories almost as a series of afterthoughts that characterize in a semirealistic, documentary fashion past moments in her life. Maria, on the other hand, is almost literally haunted by her memories so that the past lives with an even greater immediacy than her present. The memories shaping her existence include those of her father and mother and their shortcomings and frustrations; her career as a model and actress having been instigated by her father rather than by her innermost self; and recurring perceptions arrived at over time that ordinary social reality is riddled with squalor, pointlessness, and ultimate futility. All of these serve to alienate her from everyone and everything. Thus, in a sense, her endless insistence on reacting to people and situations in terms of an unexplained and largely unexamined code of personal values resembles that of Holly. The major difference is that Maria internalizes all of her struggles for freedom, values, and another—better—way of life. In contrast, Holly, like D. H. Lawrence in miniature, simply changes her venue. She continually seeks new surroundings in the effort to attain congruence between her self and her world. For Maria, alienation from rather than integration with her world and perhaps even her self is her driving goal.

Love in these works, though variously construed in each, functions essentially as the actions and motivations of the self in relation to the other. The Consul engages in a prolonged struggle, intensified to the point of physical and imaginative conflict, between his love for alcohol and for a woman, Yvonne. Both are forms of love as possession and so raise moral considerations involving the possessor-possessed relationship. Geoffrey grapples with these but only in a manner that allows him to evade honest consideration of the consequences emerging from each love. As a result, he capitulates to alcohol largely because it gives him immediate and complete satisfaction rather than the ongoing fluctuations inherent in the human relationship.

Of a quite different order is the love that figures in *Breakfast at Tiffany's*. It operates on a series of levels and sketches out a variety of kinds of love. Thus, there is the narrator's love for Holly, which is basically one of companionship. Set against it is her casual attitude toward sex between consenting adults. The friend versus lover dichotomy raises implicitly the polarization of heterosexuality and homosexuality back of which stands the author's concern to disguise the narrator's sexual preference. By so doing, he sets it against Holly's expressed willingness to entertain virtually all forms of sexuality, and her readiness to see none of them as inherently connected with love itself. The result is that in *Breakfast at Tiffany's* love is a muted factor rather than an all-consuming passion. It is a condition of mutual regard independent of any kind of sexual expression. As such, it downplays the author's implicit view of love from that historically proclaimed by his society. It, however, does so in a way that deepens the elegiac temper of the novel.

What distinguishes the nature of love in *Play It as It Lays* from the forms expressed in *Under the Volcano* and *Breakfast at Tiffany's* is that it basically entails only one person, Maria. Her single-minded concentration on self-love or love of self is as destructive as that of Geoffrey and as mute as that of Capote's narrator. It forms a sharp contrast with her society's, Hollywood's, acceptance of all forms of sexuality in practice as well as in theory. What Holly proclaims, Hollywood enacts casually and repetitively. In so doing, it undercuts the notion of love as a relationship of self and other. BZ's sadistic homosexuality, Helene's flirtation with lesbianism, Maria's casual drug-aided intercourse with the nameless actor, all point up the same motif. They testify to the irrelevance of the other and its replacement with an intense concentration on the self. Where these instances differ from Maria's essentially unconscious love of her self is in their reliance on the other as an agent of physical gratification alone. For her, the love of self is more like the narrator's love for Holly. It is a largely silent acceptance of something satisfying, undemanding, and only marginally realized at the time. But her personal self is a series rather than a substance, an onion to be peeled rather than a single core. Consequently, her love for self is basically a tacit, unconscious reliance on it as a vantage point from which to critique and recoil from her world and others.

As one contemplates the differing roles of the self, the values animating them, and the forms of love they manifest, one is compelled to ponder exactly why the three characters proceed to enact the loss of self. Do they function in accord with a metaphysical necessity that locks them into an inescapably destructive course of action? Or are they shaped by the impingement of accidental forces from the external world, in which case a cause-and-effect relationship should be determinable? As with the other topics mentioned above, the answer—if it is one—possesses such nuances as to thwart any simple response. The Consul, for instance, uses history and its multiple instances as a rationale or excuse for withdrawal of the self from the world of decision, action, and change. Thus, he repeatedly invokes the Spanish Civil War, the World War II submarine attack, his brother Hugh's liberal political views, the Fascist infiltration of Mexico, and the history of Mexico, particularly the Maximilian and Carlotta story, to warrant his paralysis in the face of change. In its place, he evades the problem of exploring the loss of self by creating an ostensible intellectual necessity but one that is in reality emotionally based in a desire for escape from consciousness.

Holly is essentially unaware of history, except her own personal one, and so she too creates necessity but out of her own immediate circumstances. She uses it either to attempt to justify her actions or to warrant flight from the most pressing of those circumstances. Either option is elected essentially for the same reason: the hope that she will find or be able to generate more appropriate circumstances to match her fugitive and changing desires. Maria, like Geoffrey, intellectualizes her response, and, like Holly, seeks to alter the world through changing her place in it. She rejects necessity as a rational consideration or factor in explaining anything. For her, all is random, disparate, and disconnected events to which the self is subjected. But so categorical is her view that her various actions and responses to experience—however disassociated, fragmentary, and unconsidered—do seem to amount to a kind of empirical, if not rational or scientific, necessity. Her conscious rejection of necessity implicitly leaves her forced to accept a cause-and-effect relationship between her past actions and present circumstances. Yet her commitment to randomness and acausality makes such a situation unacceptable. In short, her declining of necessity as an explanation amounts to her refusal to see the connection between the dissolution of the personal self and physical death by suicide.

Given the various selves, values, delineations of love, and attitudes toward their behavior developed by the three authors, their works are necessarily cast in significantly different literary modes possessing differing emphases. Thus, the Consul's death (and life) is set essentially in a tragic mode marked by a protracted struggle between preserving and destroying the self. Lowry is committed to a symbolist or modernist style consisting of intricate and multiple allusions woven into scenes that are layered with temporal dislocations, shifting memories, and internal monologues of real and imagined events. These enable him to sustain the self's hopeless struggle to exist far longer than the actual events in the Consul's life would appear to warrant. The very length and complexity of the novel allows Lowry to limn in all of the details summoned up by a shifting and fluctuating consciousness. They elevate the drama from an O'Neill-like chronicling of the progress of a compulsive drinker to an almost Shakespearian depiction of a tragic hero facing his momentous fate.

At the same time, the welter of contradictory or clashing scenes coupled with the bizarre misunderstandings involved in his death take on an ironic and skeptical cast. They reveal in a variety of ways how he deliberately creates the multiple necessities that shape his downward descent. Ultimately, his fall from grace is seen to be his own fault and responsibility despite his protracted mental oscillation between life and death. The latter is his ultimate act of evasion. By it, he endeavors both to transform himself into a tragic hero and to assure his own extinction. In contemplating the Consul in his full arc of existence, one feels an ambivalent pity for a courageous but weak man who insists on wasting a life that has wit, intelligence, and sensitivity. In so feeling, one responds to the character in the same way as to its author and creator.

Capote, on the other hand, deploys an economical rather than a rococo style to generate a muted elegiac mode. The novel's being cast as an anecdote from the life of the narrator makes it recollective rather than dramatic. It is a memory whose depiction of Holly is both initially enriching and finally saddening to him. Holly's sudden departure is viewed by the narrator as profoundly regrettable rather than tragic. Her nature is compounded of vitality, inventiveness—O. J. Berman's sense that "she's such a goddamn liar" (32)—independence, generosity, capacity to shock, and vulnerability. As such, her loss is rendered by the narrator as essentially an inevitable one. Such a view, however, is as much a conviction wrought from his nature as from hers. Ultimately, he is seen to be largely a passive recorder of events, a witness who responds to persons and events only after they have passed from the scene.

The tone with which he finally registers the fate of the cat, of Holly, and by implication of himself captures the combination of satisfaction (for the cat), sorrowful hope (for Holly), and implicit judgment (for himself):

> he [the cat] was seated in the window of a warm-looking room: I wondered what his name was, for I was certain he had one now, certain he'd

> arrived somewhere he belonged. African hut or whatever, I hope Holly has, too. (111)

His elegiac regret, then, is for the loss of her presence, the waste implicit in her disappearance, and the maturing conviction that he too has lost and wasted his own opportunity for living an active life rather than being a mere recorder of it.

Didion's literary mode is dominated and shaped by her minimalist point of view and attitude. It is designed to repress authorial convictions or at least to express them largely through character and scenic vignettes structured so as to develop ambiguous possibilities reflectively. Part of her elegiac effect is produced by the conversational rhythms of sentences that convey unstated feelings more than explicit statements and by the informal, notational, diarylike tone of narrators such as Helene. As the novel progresses and Maria's collapse intensifies, her fate appears in a dual perspective. One facet is a detached irony for the metaphysical folly of attempting to eliminate the personal self without realizing the necessity of suicide or death as a consequence. Another is a mute pathos for the relentless nature of her effort to so reduce the self.

The two mingle in the growing realization that it is the only apparent response she can make to her largely self-created situation entailing as it does death, birth, career, and marriage. "I try to live in the now and keep my eye on the hummingbird" (10) is Maria's minimalist effort at physical survival. But it is also an authorial elegiac point of view that gives a very limited chance to the effort's succeeding. Concealed therein is Didion's mute regret for the waste of a life possessed of certain assets and traits that have been almost deliberately eroded and allowed to vanish. Maria's life is a marginalized one as a result of both an incomplete and inadequate self. Hers is a self that can apprehend no existence apart from or outside of it: "I was holding all the aces, but what was the game?" (10)

In effect, Didion creates two extreme and diametrically opposite positions concerning the self. One is an elegiac awareness of the catastrophic waste inherent in the loss of an individual self. This awareness resonates with the loss's irrevocability in consciousness, regardless of whether or not a recovery of mental health occurs. Once Maria is aware of her loss of self her awareness can never be dismissed, rescinded, or forgotten. At the same time, Didion insists, her character's actions and life appall by their very thoughtlessness and indifference to the momentousness of the loss itself. The other position is a mordantly analytic and ironic sense of the terrible consequences of living wholly and exclusively within the self so that it becomes one's entire existence and world. The waste inherent in the former is intensified and compounded by the recognition that a total dependency on the personal self is as destructive as a similar absorption with the external world.

A Coda
CONTINUITY AND INNOVATION

In the preceding chapters the diversity of aspects informing the modern prose elegy has been charted with a view to underlining their thematic importance. Now it may be well to conclude with a few brief reflections that stand back from the subject to ponder why so many of our seminal authors have emphasized the elegiac. To my mind, its centrality to our culture in general can only be ignored at our peril. For the issue of loss and how we face, deal, and ultimately cope with it is likely to determine both the nature and the likelihood of our future.

The reasons for this are multiple and interrelated consisting, as they do, of numerous broad social events—two world wars, an international Depression, the Holocaust, and atomic energy among others—that have reverberated throughout much of the globe. Also shaping—though less directly—the contours of the modern elegiac temper are such things as the expansion in kinds and scope of communication, its predilection for verbal and formal innovation and experimentation, a consequently diminished sense of the size of our universe, and a radically altered notion of the nature of literature and its relation to other forms of human endeavor. All of these and most of the other losses that characterize our world are functionally elegiac in that they entail sorrow or grief, facing of loss's certitude, and seeking some kind of consolation.

Therefore, I organize this study generically rather than by a chronological or thematic progression. As I indicate at the outset, it proceeds from the familial through the marital to the cultural before concluding with the philosophical elegy. By tracing the cumulative progression of losses from familial to intimately personal ones such as endured in love and marriage and then on to broadly cultural and philosophical losses dealing with history, time, and self, I have been impelled to do two essentially contradictory things. In the face of a historically mounting uncertainty as to how a substantial consolation for human losses can be generated I have been led to question the continuing relevance of the elegiac. The very multiplicity of forms being taken by the modern and contemporary elegy raises the issue of whether they do not signal the disintegration of its role and purpose.

At the same time, the overwhelming pressures both to lament and then to confront the welter of losses encountered in life has led me to insist on elegy's cultural viability and to explore the range of new forms in which it strives to persist. In confronting such contradictory challenges, I have, of course, done no more than respond to our age's penchant for ambivalence.

The accelerated loss of life wrought by a succession of armed conflicts has joined with a host of other losses in the twentieth century to create a social climate dominated by uncertainty, insecurity, apprehension, and an increasingly grim effort to survive. This climate has consequently been reflected in a broad range of individual texts that lament, confront, and assess the sorts of consolation currently available to the range of losses commanding the attention of the modern world and reader. The diverse thematic emphases they exhibit are matched by stylistic variants ranging from the clotted symbolism of Lowry to the taut minimalism of Hemingway and Didion. In so doing, they testify eloquently to the importance of the elegiac to both the age and its literature. The modern elegiac temper's persistence through such a diverse range of styles clearly marks it as central rather than peripheral to the attitudes of both.

As we all know, classical modernism's comparative probing of diverse cultures and civilizations generated a pronounced inclination to invidiously assess a broad range of historical eras. Thus, Faulkner and Joyce lead us to assess our known past and to see it as inherently variegated rather than nationally or racially monochromatic. Dissolutions on a more daily basis of the family and families as traced by Agee, Faulkner, and Updike intensify nineteenth-century suspicions and doubts about the stability of this traditional cornerstone of social order. Its apparently growing instability (from at least the time of the Great Depression) is enshrined in such sociological phrases as *dysfunctional families* and Senator Moynihan's celebrated political axiom of *Find the Fathers*. The faltering of the family arouses broad uncertainties about the difficulties and challenges to attaining social or group maturity. Conversely, changes and concomitant losses in personal relations such as marriage and romantic love elegize the lives of individuals. In the hands of writers from James through Hemingway to Fitzgerald, trust in the permanence and security of such relationships is diminished and called into question. And even such wholly intellectual excisions and reconfigurations of philosophical notions such as time and self pursued by Woolf and Didion lead to increasingly hesitant efforts to secure a viable future.

Each of these has occasioned profound elegiac attitudes ranging from regret, sorrow, confusion, and alienation to outright despair. With them has developed the need to seek less traditional forms of authority than those employed in the past. Religious, moral, societal, and philosophical grounds of authority capable of justifying elegiac consolation have all dwindled in persuasiveness for the modern mind. As a result, the individual or personal self for a time was invoked to replace them. Its own limitations for this role are, however, clearly visible in the literary parabola wrought from, say, Housman to Berryman to Didion. What emerges is a combination of hesitancy and almost desperate determination: the former as to the possibility of there being an intellectual or spiritual or psychological ground for hope of a human future; and the latter as to the mind's stubborn persistence in articulating such a ground. Both are encapsulated in Beckett's celebrated conclusion to *The Unnamable:* "I'll never know, in the silence you don't know, you must go on, I can't go on, I'll go on" (414).

In addition to the authors and texts treated, one could obviously point to many others both great and small that bear the modern elegiac impress of loss. All such losses testify to the accelerated rate of change in the modern world: of sociopolitical change, of intellectual change, of spiritual or religious change, and of personal change. The number of such transformations has resulted in a steadily growing awareness of loss as a major and crucial factor in life. They occasion both the loss of known and conventional perspectives as well as the growth of uncertainty as to the nature of their replacements. Sorrow and regret intermingle with anxiety, dread, and fear as attitudes that predominate throughout the age. The result, culturally as well as imaginatively, is the development of a broad-gauged elegiac attitude or temper, which views life as holding out the likelihood, and perhaps even the certitude, of a series of losses. Each loss requires reactions of sorrow, courage, and determination focused on a need or search for new, or at least different, forms of support, personal, societal, philosophical, and spiritual.

In exploring such a broad subject, one can scarcely hope to include all authors deemed pertinent by individual readers, critics, and scholars. As a result, a brief personal word about choices exercised here may not be amiss.

In each instance, I have elected to balance the broad range of elegiac emphases and prose styles against a commonalty of traits that over the years I have come to identify with the elegiac temper. Thus, from my first encounter as a freshman with *The Portrait of a Lady,* Isabel Archer's marital sacrifice has continued to prove a haunting instance of the solemnities inherent in personal loss. That others may wish for texts from James's later career I do not doubt, but old affections linger stubbornly. Similarly, readers may wish I had turned, say, to *The Sound and the Fury* rather than *Sartoris* to trace Faulkner's elegiac arc. Indeed, I myself hesitated for some time over a much fuller treatment of *Absalom, Absalom!* Finally it seemed wiser to direct attention to the earlier work, which has received significantly less critical attention. Such a decision also enabled me to pay a quiet tribute to the one under whose urging I first began seriously to read Faulkner. In any event, I am confident that the choices I have made are reasonable ones, if not those that others might have made.

All the works treated here arouse a similar set of responses. Pathos, desperation, and sadness commingled with satisfaction, suffering, and release inform all the fates of Isabel Archer, Geoffrey Firman, Dick Diver, Lieutenant Henry, Maria Wyeth, and the other characters. In their diverse encounters with loss, they repeatedly testify to the follies, shortsightedness, courage, and humanity resident in mankind. They also arouse a plangent nostalgia for the past as an inevitable object of melancholy even when (as with some) they occasion doubts as to the appropriateness of elegiac lamentation. By underscoring the reverberant echoing of the past in human affairs, these texts continue to point up the precariousness of choices and decisions made in the present and the increasing uncertainties of any future currently envisageable.

As a result, to hazard future directions for the prose elegy probably requires a clearer crystal ball than lies in my grasp. Yet several possibilities suggest themselves. The very emergence of a prose form of the traditional elegy in the twentieth century, as has been demonstrated here, may be followed by yet other transformations of the genre in the postmodern era. One possibility is the defictionalizing of the elegy by making its focus the lives of actual historical persons. A much praised recent instance is John Bayley's *Elegy for Iris,* which gradually grows into a biographical elegy. Whether such a form can deal equally well with ordinary uncelebrated individuals poses a tempting challenge. It would appear to depend on history continuing to be regarded as episodic narratives composed of selected anecdotes. Signs of such an emerging form can perhaps be seen in a work like *Tuesdays with Morrie* (2002).

Another mixed prose form might follow from the current resurgence of the elegiac sequence as practiced by, say, Donald Hall, Sandra Gilbert, and Robert Pinsky. Exploring more or less disinterestedly, as they have done, the potential intellectual, emotional, and spiritual grounds for elegiac consolation would surely also tempt many contemporary prose writers. Indeed, it may already have done so if we consider Thomas Pynchon's *Against the Day* (2006) closely. By seriously reconfiguring the imminence of a contemporary apocalypse in a whole host of political, scientific (particularly mathematical), religious, sexual, national, and racial contexts, it raises the specter of a cultural elegy that focuses exclusively on a sedulous confrontation with mortality virtually devoid of lamentation and solace alike. The apocalyptic thrust conveyed by its title clearly indicates that Pynchon's concern is to forge an elegy for the loss of everything. At the same time, the determination to articulate a trust in a future that is capable of embracing the provisional and the tentative certainly appears at this historical juncture to be a growing part of the literary landscape, as the poets mentioned here demonstrate.

NOTES

1.

Loss of the Ideal: James Agee's *A Death in the Family*

1. Agee's novel and that of Updike (dealt with in chapter 2) constitute two elegiac poles—the ideal and the real—of the modern family theme. For an examination of a midpoint transition between them, see my "The Aesthetics of Survival: Tillie Olsen's *Yonnondio*" in Siegel and Halio, 99–111.

2. This broader focus is supported by Spiegel's observation that Agee initially saw the novel as being "an even more capacious family study" (217) than it actually became.

3. On the numerous similarities of detail between the novel and Agee's own biography, see Doty, 1, 3, 4, 59, 80, 92, 94.

4. Andrew Lytle, in Doty, 88, calls this the "innocent eye" technique. It is one that permitted Agee to present adult perceptions through a child's awareness.

5. See Spiegel, 217, on the stylistic difference between the prelude and the rest of the novel.

6. See Spiegel, 236–37, for a cogent but somewhat circuitous defense against critical complaints about the novel's sentimentality.

7. Cf. Spiegel, 225, on the differing relationship of Rufus to each parent.

8. On the role and significance of the movies in the novel, cf. Spiegel, 172–75.

9. They consist of scenes outside the time span of the novel as determined by the author and are so placed solely by the editors. They have an arbitrary character not subject to Agee's final judgment as author. For a vigorous critique of the editors' judgments and decisions, see Spiegel, 217–19, for details and problems connected with these interludes. They underscore the unfinished, provisional quality of the text as a whole. Specifically, they point to unsolved issues of point of view and theme that tug persistently at the reader's mind even as apparently they did for Agee himself.

10. Cf. Spiegel, 216, who sees the novel as essentially adhering to the tripartite structure of classical tragedy.

11. Cf. Spiegel, 203–206, on Agee's *The Morning Watch* and its similarities to Joyce.

12. On the role of this joke, see Spiegel, 243–44.

2.

Failure as a Loss: John Updike's *The Centaur*

1. On the centrality of storytelling to Updike's view of the artist and fiction, see my "*The Centaur*: Myth, History, and Narrative," *MFS* 20 (1974): 32–33.

2. The Hamiltons, 156–57, suggest that the novel is essentially "another Olinger story" to which the mythological material serves to provide a transcendent dimension to its the-

matic focus. In effect, this claim serves to privilege the novel's realistic dimension unduly.

3. Greiner, 106–7, traces the autobiographical dimensions of the novel, which invite comparison and contrast to Agee and his work.

4. See my "*The Centaur:* Myth, History, and Narrative," 29–43, and *Myths and Texts* (1983), 149–65. For views that stress the centrality of Peter's perspective see Mellard, 112, and Vargo, 453, who consequently slight the familial dimension of the novel.

5. Hence, as Uphaus, 42, notes, two stories, those of the father and the son, are told. He fails, however, to see how these bear on the family as a unit and so views, 43, the novel as mock-heroic rather than elegiac.

6. Uphaus, 40, equates Peter's contradictory responses to George with the literal-mythic modes of narration and so concludes, rather paradoxically, that the novel ends with the son's abandonment of the mythic.

7. Cf. Markle, 69.

8. I differ here from Mellard, 119, who thinks Peter's final perspective lies in the myth of Art. For this to be so would entail Peter not having learned by confronting the inevitability of his father's death that life ultimately brings the recognition of loss as inherent within it. Thus, art provides not a perfect, trouble-free existence but the means of accepting loss, which in the final analysis is an elegiac act.

9. See Hunt, 61, on the various narrative modes used in the novel; also Mellard, 117. It is worth noting too that Updike's use of irony and satire recalls to some degree the tradition of classical and Renaissance elegy.

10. In this, he reflects many of the concerns of modernism with what I have called the backward glance, the Golden Age, and cultural loss. These are explored more fully in chapter 8.

11. On Updike's use of pastoral elegy, see Taylor, 86–101, for an extended treatment, and Mellard, 117–18. Cf. Greiner's assessment, 107, of Taylor's claim that *The Centaur* combines pastoral elegy and the epic.

12. Cf. Greiner, 109. It should be noted, however, that Peter's discovery of love occurs too late since his father now is actually dead. This is what elegy frequently encapsulates: the belated discovery of the full, true significance of the person who, as a result of death, can be appreciated and praised only in absentia.

13. Cf. Markle, 72–76; Burchard, 63, 69; Uphaus, 33–38; Greiner, 113–14, 118. They fail, however, to bring to bear the multiple perspectives on George's obsessive fascination that Updike so carefully limns in. It is the complex of spectator attitudes that provides the full authorial perspective here.

3.

Generational Critiques: Virginia Woolf's *The Years* and William Faulkner's *Sartoris*

1. There is a sense in which her often-cited statement in *A Writer's Diary*, 78, about all of her novels being elegies, testifies to this movement.

2. See Daiches, 111–18, for a sensitive stylistic differentiation of Woolf from her predecessors. Cf. Hafley in T. S. W. Lewis, 121–22, for points concerning her relation to Galsworthy and Proust.

3. Cf. Rosenthal, 169–70.

4. Guiguet's list, 305, of eight different working titles contains at least five that in one form or another reflect Woolf's concern with time and its passage. Cf. Rosenthal, 181, for a somewhat different emphasis.

5. Cf. Hussey 1986, 116, 119.

6. See Laurence in Hussey, ed., 1991, 229.

7. Cf. Rosenthal, 171–72.

8. Cf. Rosenthal, 176–78.

9. Cf. Hussey 1986, 129, though I think he underestimates the novel's contribution to Woolf's general philosophical perspective.

10. By this I do not mean to disregard the extent to which Woolf embodies critiques of gender and contemporary historical issues of the sort discussed by a variety of critics, most notably Poresky, 219–30; Bazin and Lauter in Hussey, ed., 1991, 22–27, 32; Zwerdling, 251–52, 254–57, 274–76. Rather I want to suggest her ultimate philosophical conclusion here is a very tough-minded one that sees the temporal limitations that attach to any historical or societal attitude.

11. See Zwerdling, 166–68, on how the lie, especially one involving sexuality, was a part of the Victorian family.

12. Cf. Poresky, 216–17.

13. Cf. Poresky, 218–19, who sees the issue essentially as a public-private one cast in terms of Self set against Society or civilization. The role of the family or families in the novel is largely ignored.

14. See Leaska, 73, and Poresky, 216–17, on the significance of the name.

15. Cf. Poresky, 219–24, on the traits of the three central families. Her concern with hypostatized gender distinctions prevents her treating the family as a sociological rather than a psychological concept.

16. See Zwerdling, 162, 165, 171–72, on Woolf's sensitivity to the ambiguous nature and role of the family.

17. This elegiac tradition reaches all the way from Lady Winchilsea to Francis Thompson and includes poems on monarchs, political figures, military notables, and religious leaders, as well as poets and dramatists.

18. Hafley in T. S. W. Lewis, 116–17, 120, points out her concern with society is essentially on its changing aspect, what he calls "the social shift" rendered in the novel.

19. This, of course, is not to say that particular characters do not embody either of these responses but only that neither view is the final one of the novel. In a sense, my view is perhaps closest to that of Zwerdling, 278–79, and Rosenthal, 174, and furthest from Hafley in T. S. W. Lewis, 118, who contends that the collective future is regarded positively by Woolf. See Richter, 149–79, for an extended analysis of Woolf's techniques for dealing with time.

20. See Richter, 171–79, for a more detailed discussion of the novel's techniques of rendering the key dualities (public-private, conscious-unconscious, past-present) of the novel.

21. Blackstone, 198, suggests somewhat ingeniously that *The Years* is an inverted redaction of all her novels designed to reveal the obverse of her earlier views of family, university, and childhood.

22. See Brewster, 148, on the relation of the novel's stress on questions to Woolf's penchant for anxiety as a result of her lack of dogmatism.

23. See Poresky, 234, for a reading of this scene that emphasizes the motif of human

loneliness and its cure. My view is that there is no cure in Woolf's eyes and that this can only be shown, not articulated, hence her final perception of the limitations of language and art.

24. See Ryle, 16–23.

25. See Poresky, 225–30, 239–40, and Rosenthal, 178–80, for a discussion of their roles for several of the characters. Cf. Ruotolo, 172, 177, 183, on the Dante reference.

26. Poresky, 229, is able to see more positive implications in this scene only by not attending to the limitations in its allusiveness for the society and world as a whole. Ruotolo, 183, rightly points out Eleanor's plumbing of Dante's meaning is deferred by her until later, though he somewhat underestimates her self-deception in so thinking.

27. Cf. Rosenthal, 174.

28. See Rosenthal, 175, who points out the frequency and centrality of questions raised by the characters and their relevance to Woolf's overall philosophical enterprise.

29. Cf. Rosenthal, 173, who sees the novel as Woolf's "bleakest view of the human condition."

30. Poresky, 241, sees this scene as an emblem of psychic wholeness and androgyny rather than the more individual and limited role I attach to it.

31. This image should be set against Poresky's, 219, stress on the novel's opening with a setting sun, which she equates with the diminution of human consciousness, spiritual blindness, and the fall from grace. Rhode in Denniston faults this scene for not resisting the impulse "to transfigure death symbolically" (164) and contrasts it with Lawrence's handling of Paul Morel's mother's death at the end of *Sons and Lovers.*

32. The unraveling of the Sartoris family, of course, has its origin in a period prior to World War I, as *The Unvanquished* reveals. For a fine examination of the interplay of the Civil War, the changing natures of human loss, and the problematics of gender in Faulkner's struggle to shape a complex response to the elegiac tradition, see Arnold, 89–120.

33. In developing Faulkner's elegiac temper here, I am obviously indebted to Olga Vickery's views, 15–27, on *Sartoris.*

4.
Familial Disintegration: James Joyce's *Dubliners* and F. Scott Fitzgerald's "Babylon Revisited"

1. Schneidau, *Waking Giants,* 4–9, links Joyce's rendering of familial disintegration to the iron grip of the past on the culture as a whole. He sees Joyce's attitude toward the past as dominated by "fear and loathing" (4) in the sardonic manner of Ibsen. This perhaps oversimplifies the portrait presented in *Dubliners* by insufficient attention to Joyce's awareness of his culture's past from long before the nineteenth century.

2. The savage ironic manner Joyce takes to this spirit as articulated by lesser imitators of Yeats's Celtic Twilight is emphasized by Torchiana, 131–39. At the same time, he points out the frequency of an ambivalent tone—"both satirical and sympathetic" (14)—brought to bear on many of Joyce's characters.

3. The deaths—actual and impending—of family and city in a series of guises and forms coupled with elegiac celebration and regret provide, it seems to me, a structure for the book closer to the stories themselves than many others that have been developed over the

years, such as the *Odyssey* parallels, the moral history of a community, and the systematic deployment of symbolic patterns like the Christian movement of the soul toward alternatively sin and salvation. Cf. Torchiana, 258–71, especially for Joyce's complex relation to Dublin.

4. Two explorations of Joyce's famous phrase developing complex and persuasive elaborations of what it entails can be found in Riquelme, 94–130, and Gottfried (in Cheng and Martin), 153–69. The former concentrates on the shifting relationships between telling and experiencing selves, while the latter stresses *Dubliners*' style as a comic parody of a style prevalent in Irish society of the period.

5. Cf. Riquelme, 110–11.

6. Riquelme, 118–19, is astute in teasing out Joyce's various techniques for revealing the character's self-delusion. He fails, however, to connect that recognition with Mrs. Sinico's actual death and how both contribute to the elegiac mood.

7. For an additional basis for contrasting these two stories, see Riquelme, 120.

8. Cf. Gottfried, 155, 161, 163.

9. For an extended narratological analysis of this story, see Riquelme, 121–29. He stops short, unfortunately, of plumbing its elegiac temper.

10. Rhode in Denniston, rather idiosyncratically, finds Joyce's style here not so much to generate his individual elegiac acknowledgment of human mortality as "to cocoon us beautifully from any sense of loss or isolation" (165).

11. On Fitzgerald's gradually maturing notions of home and family, see Petry, 167–68, 178, 181.

12. Cf. Petry, 186–87.

5. The Loss of Romantic Love: Ernest Hemingway's *The Sun Also Rises* and James Baldwin's *Giovanni's Room*

1. Williams, 46, recognizes that all of the characters are dealing with loss and how to carve out a viable life for themselves.

2. Hook in A. R. Lee, 57, somewhat surprisingly suggests Jake is similar to James's Ralph Touchett by virtue of his physical limitations inhibiting more active expressions of his love.

3. On the differing critical judgments of the novel's tragic dimensions, see Williams's summary, 41–43.

4. Williams, 49, identifies this as the novel's primary theme without articulating its elegiac dimensions; cf. Baker, ed., 1972, 92.

5. Spilka in Baker, ed., 1961, 83, points out that Brett's behavior in this scene in chapter 5 stamps her as also suffering from the loss of her gender's traditional sexual role.

6. Cf. Spilka in Baker, ed., 1961, 83; Young, 88; Wagner in Nagel, 66 ; Miller in Nagel, 173–74, for a range of views on the role of the homosexuals in the novel.

7. Williams, 49, suggests Jake, Brett, Mike, and Cohn are all "paradigms of the smashed human being" produced by World War I while deftly sketching how they intrinsically differ from one another. Cf. Rovit, 159, on the novel as a cultural document.

8. Ney's career—with its incredible bravery, his many wounds including one in the

thigh, his inspirational leadership especially in rearguard actions such as that from Moscow, his failure to maintain his loyalty to Napoleon, his final betrayal and execution coupled with his ironic restoration to public favor in 1853—has a number of ironic and agonized elements of pathos that would resonate particularly with a veteran like Jake as well as with the historically cognizant reader.

9. On the role of romantic love and its consequences for the characters, see Williams, 47–48.

10. The varied and subtle uses of these diverse settings have been explored by many critics. See, e.g., Williams, 59–60; Hook in A. R. Lee, 54; Daiker in Nagel, 75, 77–70; Josephs in Nagel, 131.

11. See Baker, ed., 1961, 80, on Hemingway's own personal view of this epithet. My point here is that its use in connection with the novel draws on both the willingness of many of the characters to draw attention by posturing to their sense of being lost and on Stein's ironic intent as well as the author's skepticism concerning it.

12. Baker's, ed., 1961, 89, emphasis on Jake as a religious man and practicing Catholic seems driven largely by the need to contrast him to Brett whom he sees as a pagan. Neither Roman Catholicism nor pagan quasifertility rituals provide the sort of spiritual authority for which Jake and the novel are seeking.

13. See Williams, 56, on the limited nature of Jake's consolatory values.

14. See Hook in A. R. Lee, 54, for the polarities between the fiesta and the bullfight proper.

15. Cf. Daiker in Nagel, 75.

16. Cf. Daiker in Nagel, 78–79.

17. For some of the critical attention to this element in the scene, see Williams, 53, 63; Spilka in Baker, 91; Daiker in Nagel, 84–85.

18. Spilka in Baker, ed., 91, considers the scene to present Jake's "total disillusionment" whereas I regard it as his awareness of the elegiac temper as his final perspective on the consequences of his war wound.

19. Both Giovanni and Mearsault suffer profound isolation from others; both engage in murder; endure flight, capture, and execution, while both narrators suffer anguished contemplation of the death of another.

20. For a quite different view of his aspirations in this novel, see Johnson-Roullier, 932–56. She attends exclusively to Baldwin's attraction to Henry James and the ways in which the novel resembles or emulates modernism's approach to the past.

21. Sylvander, 48, limits the structure unduly by focusing only on its bipartite division; Pratt, 59, finds, as I do, a fourfold sequence more appropriate.

22. For a sustained examination of the theme of identity in Baldwin, unfortunately limited to the essays, see Moller, 1–189. On Baldwin's own protracted struggle with his sexual identity, see Leeming, 45–47, 53–54, 91–92, 115, 127, 358–59, 364–65.

23. Cf. Sylvander, 51.

24. Macebuh, 74, goes so far as to argue that David's response to his initial homosexual experience with Joey is inflated far in excess of what he considers to be a normal recognition of man's inherent bisexuality.

25. Macebuh, 71–72, 74, interestingly argues that David's dilemma is occasioned by his

effort to substitute human love for a more traditional relationship to God. In so doing, he sees the conflict as one shared by Baldwin, a theme he traces throughout the career.

26. See Macebuh, 72.

27. See Lash in O'Daniel, 48–52.

28. Johnson-Roullier, 940, sees the novel as focused more on David's self-deception rather than homosexuality.

29. A central difference, however, is the order in which they are placed in each novel. Faulkner first develops the rationale of inherent evil before, rather belatedly, introducing hereditary and genetic factors to explain Popeye. Baldwin, on the other hand, begins with the naturalistic, genetic/nurture aspect and only when David is completely isolated by his nature and actions does he invoke the metaphysical self-accusations of his protagonist.

30. Macebuh, 73–74, sees David's sense of freedom as spurious but ascribes it to Baldwin's latent theological and originally Christian perspective.

31. See Lash in O'Daniel, 47–55, for an interesting and cogent assessment of Baldwin's challenge to confront himself in relation to the theme of phallicism in any form as providing self-fulfillment.

32. The image of the room is seen by Sylvander, 52, as womb-like and carrying the faintest of promises of David's rebirth. Macebuh, 78, sees it as revealing David's sense of corruption. Both views may obtain depending on where in the narrative the image is presented.

33. Cf. Macebuh, 72.

6.

Marriage as Cultural Change: Henry James's *The Portrait of a Lady* and Ernest Hemingway's *A Farewell to Arms*

1. Hutchinson, 25, sees the opening garden teatime scene even more mordantly, as already embodying the dissolution of a highly civilized civilization rather than presaging it.

2. Cf. Long, 106.

3. Cf. Long, 108. See Poirier in Buitenhuis, 32, on the multiple and metaphoric forms of death to which she is subjected.

4. Cf. Poirier in Buitenhuis, 31, 32, 35; Stallman in Buitenhuis, 42.

5. See Cargill, 83; Tanner in Buitenhuis, 69, 70.

6. On the interplay of nature and civilization, see Berland, viii, 109; Long, 107, 110; Gervais, 187–88; Chase in Buitenhuis, 20; Stallman in Buitenhuis, 39, 41.

7. Cf. Hutchinson, 38; Anderson, 186–87; Van Ghent in Anderson and Mazzeo, 567; Montgomery in Buitenhuis, 60–61; Tanner in Buitenhuis, 75.

8. Cf. Long, 110; Van Ghent in Anderson and Mazzeo, 570; Porte, 12, 16.

9. See Porte, 25–29, for a sensitive reading of the second half of the novel in terms of the Virgilian *lachrimae sunt* context and tradition.

10. Cf. Berland, 99–100, 105, 124, 132–35. Gervais, 194, sees Isabel's decision concerning her marriage purely as an authorial interposing of "a ready-to-wear convention" calculated to give her a noble appearance. Anderson, too, 188, questions the legitimacy of her idea of marriage. Clearly, the issue is a vexing one for many critics. It becomes less so if one sees, as

Krook-Gilead, 97–99, preeminently does, that Isabel's conception of marriage entails personal responsibility, moral integrity, and duty as traits inherent in a civilized culture dedicated to the cultivation of taste as a moral as well as aesthetic experience. See Powers, 76–81, 99–101, for a subtle effort to assess the extent to which marital obligation, duty to her innermost nature and self, and the basic inexhaustible mystery of existence are involved in her decision. Nor should one overlook the very Jamesian possibility that her decision to return to Osmond may be yet another foolish decision calculated to endorse her concentration on her own personal desires and feelings to the exclusion of external advice or counsel. James delicately balances the moral issue of her decision—between headstrong folly and profound commitment to accepting the consequences of her actions—so as to question the very postulate of *civilization as culture,* which serves as the cornerstone of his thinking.

11. Porte, 25, argues, in effect, that Isabel as an individual is absorbed into culture and culture into art as embodied in James's novel itself. This may well be true without entailing the discountenancing of the author's own elegiac temper rendered in my stress on his recognition of the centrality of loss in the human economy.

12. For detailed treatments of this chapter, see Baker 1972, 94–96; Rovit, 92–93; Schneider in Bloom, ed., *Hemingway's Farewell to Arms,* 13–15; Williams, 82–84.

13. See Rovit, 98, 105–6; Brenner, 30–31; Merrill in Bloom, ed., *Hemingway's Farewell to Arms,* 31.

14. See Baker 1972, 116; Rovit, 93.

15. Cf. Schneider in Bloom, 19.

16. See Williams, 79, for the polarized attitudes of Rinaldi and the priest.

17. His response to this prospect is likely rooted in Hemingway's own historical awareness of the threat of summary execution in this arena of the war. See Hynes, *A War Imagined, 214,* who notes that the Italians in World War I dealt harshly with deserters after the rout at Caporetto and in general they killed twice as many as the English and French had executed from 1914 to 1920.

18. Cf. Williams, 79.

19. Baker's (1972) assertion, 100, that the plural pronoun "is nothing but a name for the way things are" is technically correct, but in ignoring its being the perspective of the two lovers, he unduly limits its elegiac implications.

7.

Marriage as the End of Love: F. Scott Fitzgerald's *Tender Is the Night* and John Updike's *Too Far to Go*

1. By so characterizing Fitzgerald's novel, the primary concentration is on the personal dimensions of Dick and Nicole's marriage. In no way is it designed to deny the larger social and psychological themes—the conflict between an older, prewar America and an emergent, postwar America, the aspirations and failures of romanticism, the bitter consequences of a naïve American optimism, and the disintegration of civilization in the face of a new and relentless barbarism—dealt with by most critics. See, e.g., Sklar, 267–68, 274, 282; Callahan, 74–77, 110–18; Way, 127, 144; Stern, 308–9, 334. These all grow out of the characters and actions of the Divers. Without them, there would be no novel; and central to their story is the slow, inevitable disintegration of their marriage, which Fitzgerald's ele-

giac temper born of his background, adult biography, and Spenglerian view of contemporary history chronicles remorselessly.

2. Thus, Fitzgerald touches on historical calamities such as the Civil War, especially Grant's career, and World War I battlefields and Gold Star mothers, as well as personal fatalities such as Abe North, the widowhood of Rosemary's mothers, and the death of Dick's father, but never in a foregrounding fashion.

3. Dick's losses have been identified as including his personal identity (Sklar, 285), his innocence (Miller, 141), his will (Callahan, 147), his moral judgment (the Kreuters in LaHood, 55), his personal authority and self-discipline (Lehan in LaHood, 68), his sense of balance (Way, 127), the ability to control himself (Stavola, 154), and his personal goodness (Stern, 374).

4. The surface triviality of his creation should not blur the fact that it is a creation conceived and brought into being by him alone and that it does engender a happiness in its occupants they do not experience elsewhere. See Sklar, 270, 274, on its utopian qualities.

5. Her ingenuous, naïve perspective is obviously not that of the author, but just as clearly Fitzgerald wishes to underscore the positive traits inherent in Dick Diver's character. See, e.g., Sklar, 269.

6. Critics such as Sklar, 277, 280–81; Miller, 141–42, 147; Callahan, 118, 126–28; Kuehl in LaHood, 14; Millard in LaHood, 34–35; and Stavola, 150, 154, in varying degrees view Dick as an object lesson essentially responsible for his ultimate demise. Others, like the Kreuters in LaHood, 54–55; Lehan in LaHood, 83 (but see also 66–67); White in LaHood, 117, 126; and above all Stern, 328, 337, 350, 365, are more sympathetic to the inherent moral complexities in Dick's character and historical situation.

7. Ultimately, Fitzgerald's irony is at Dick's expense with regard to Nicole. He does restore her to her original self, but it is not the one he thought it was, not one capable of a full romantic love for another (as is his) but the narcissistic Warren one.

8. Sklar, 268, 276, points out the facade possibilities in Dick's nature by suggesting that his first appearance on the beach is a theatrical one. For Sklar, this is an artificial world rather than one of self-created artifice in which Dick is both actor and director. My sense is that the latter view more fully captures Dick's dilemma and fate. Cf. Millard in LaHood, 34–35, on Dick as an entertainer.

9. This scene elliptically counters the critical indictments of Dick's capabilities and commitment as a psychiatrist. Intellectually he is capable of the clinician's detachment; it is only when a profound personal relationship, such as with Nicole, exists that he responds empathetically to the individual as a fellow human being.

10. See Lehan in LaHood, 62.

11. See, e.g., Callahan, 103; White in LaHood, 117, 119; Way, 129; Stavola, 154. Most critics see such an expenditure of will and energy as ill-advised and as following from a flaw or weakness in his nature. A notable exception is Stern, 328, 334, 337, 357, who sees Dick's basic values as profoundly moral and so at disastrous odds with the new postwar world.

12. Of these, only Nicole occasions any fugitive regret for what she becomes and that is more a result of her initial experience of incest and her beauty than of what she becomes. See Miller, 147. Rosemary cannot become more than what she is, and Abe will not.

13. Cf. Eliot's "La Figlia Che Piange" for its relevance here. The images of woman, flowers, and self from both poems are consonant.

14. By this, I do not intend to question the elaborate and sustained interpretations of the novel's involvement with American social and military history such as those to be found in Callahan. My point is that Eliot's concerns are with multiple cultures viewed comparatively and are more deliberately explicit than those presented by Fitzgerald. Stern, 302, interestingly suggests Fitzgerald extends the Jamesian theme to include a contrast of two Americas, the prewar versus the postwar.

15. Sklar, 272, notes that throughout, love is depicted only as unfulfilled and that this follows on World War I's exhaustion of the imaginative viability of middle-class love. Lehan in LaHood, 71, sees the collapse of conventional love mirrored in the minor characters' involvement in incest, homosexuality, and lesbianism. Dick, as White, 117, notes, is the only character for whom love of the deepest order necessarily entails heartbreak and yet who embraces that love willingly.

16. See White, 115.

17. On this dying fall scene, see Callahan, 194–96, and Stern, 374–80.

18. An even more implicitly savage view of both marriage and the elegy is to be found in Anne Sexton's "A Curse Against Elegies," which dismisses both the poetic form and the differences in personality and attitude of the speaker and spouse as equally unendurable.

8.

Modernism on Culture and History: William Faulkner's *Absalom, Absalom!* Ford Madox Ford's *Parade's End,* and Others

1. Cf. Ayers, 15.

2. Cf. Ayers, 17.

3. Ayers, 10–19, by concentrating on Ford's treatment of the changing relations between the sexes underestimates, I believe, the elegiac aspect of *Parade's End.*

4. Haegert, 115–17, argues that *The Rainbow* celebrates the future rather than lamenting the past and that its efforts to intersect its elegiac sense with historical process and change represent a concentration on the permanent in human experience rather than a lament for its losses.

5. Rideout, in Anderson, 147–48, shrewdly suggests the complexities of Anderson's realism and, implicitly, how closely it resembles Joyce's modernistic deployment of his style of "scrupulous meanness."

6. Schneidau, *Waking Giants,* 144–74, considers at length many of the similarities between Anderson and Joyce as well as Lawrence, although he perhaps is overly concerned with issues of possible direct influence.

7. Almost unique among Anderson critics is Rideout's in Anderson, 148–49, recognition of Anderson's pastoral elegiac qualities.

8. Stouck in Anderson, 181–95, correctly emphasizes the role of death in Anderson's work, but his focus is on the parallel with the medieval Dance of Death motif rather than with Anderson's elegiac attitude, which emanates from his sense of the omnipresence and omnipotence of human loneliness.

9. Fussell in White, 108–9, points out that George Willard, Anderson's quasi-artist protagonist, is unique in being able to deal with the condition of isolation and in being "a man

who joins sympathy and understanding to detachment and imperturbability." This observation underscores the inherent connection between Anderson and Joyce. If Joyce stops short of identifying the characters in *Dubliners* as grotesques, he certainly comes close to Fussell's description of *Winesburg*'s grotesques as "extremes of static and rigid over-commitment."

9.

Bifocal Time: Virginia Woolf's *The Years* and *To the Lighthouse*

1. See Knox-Shaw, 31–52, Greenwald, 37–57, and Beer, 33–55.

2. For a rather interesting treatment of the novel as a modern adaptation of the basic concerns of the elegiac tradition, see Greenwald, 23–25.

3. Cf. Hussey 1986, 116–17, for Woolf's awareness of time's traits of transience, disclosure of human deficiencies, lack of a supernatural power, and the impossibility of transcending its limits.

4. On the roles of such brackets and of parentheses, see Poole in Hussey, ed., 84–87.

5. Cf. Hussey 1986, 73–81, for an extended treatment of this scene as it is rendered both in the novel and its drafts.

6. Apposite here is Greenwald's emphasis, 37–42, 47, on the role played in the novel by Cowper's "The Castaway" as embodying her family's tendency to identify with the dead and her effort to escape it through writing the novel.

7. Ramazani, *Poetry of Mourning*, 371 n.43, suggests all of these deaths are displaced onto the vacation house, which he regards as a revision of the pathetic fallacy.

8. See Greenwald, 47, on the role of Cowper's poem in this scene.

9. On this point, as well as many others, cf. Beer's fine essay, 52.

10. Cf. Greenwald's point, 52, concerning James's relinquishing of his Oedipal attachment to his mother and his hatred of his father.

10.

Perspectives on the Self: Malcolm Lowry's *Under the Volcano*, Truman Capote's *Breakfast at Tiffany's*, and Joan Didian's *Play It as It Lays*

1. See, e.g., Cross, 33, 37, 45, 58; Day, 335, 340, 348; Hassan, 250, 253, 255; Winchell, 95, 97, 98; Henderson, 22, 23, 28, 29, 39.

2. In a very real sense, these three authors derive in this regard from Fitzgerald and, in particular, *Tender Is the Night*.

3. Cf. Tifft in Smith, 61, who suggests Geoffrey plays the parts of both Othello and Iago.

4. Critics have sought to tease out a variety of motives for him. These include an inability to love (Day, 337), his early loss of his mother and her love (Cross, 45, 50), his compulsion to preserve his own identity (Costa, 32), his loneliness (Spender in Bowker, 92), and his alienation from mankind (Pottinger in Bowker, 138). Some or all of these reasons may indeed be involved in Geoffrey's demise, but ultimately they all collapse before the question of why he fails when others with the same or similar afflictions do not.

5. Buitenhuis, 9, sees her as part of the American tradition of the isolated hero which,

he suggests, extends backward from her through James's Isabel Archer and Hawthorne's Hester Prynne to Cooper's Natty Bumpo. Cf. Hassan, 235, who treats her as an embodiment of Capote's reliance on the figure of Narcissus.

6. See Clarke, 291. Note also Clarke's suggestion that she also possesses many of the traits of her author.

7. Cf. Winchell, 98.

WORKS CITED

PRIMARY WORKS

Agee, J. *Let Us Now Praise Famous Men, A Death in the Family, and Shorter Fiction*. New York: Library of America, 2005.

Anderson, S. *Winesburg, Ohio*. New York: Random House (Modern Library), 1919.

Baldwin, J. *Giovanni's Room*. New York: Dial, 1956.

Capote, T. *Breakfast at Tiffany's*. New York: Random House, 1958.

Didion, J. *Play It as It Lays*. New York: Farrar, Strauss and Giroux, 1970.

Faulkner, W. *Absalom, Absalom!* New York: Random House (Vintage International), 1986.

———. *Sartoris*. New York: Harcourt, Brace, 1929.

Fitzgerald, F. Scott. *Three Novels*, eds. M. Cowley and E. Wilson. New York: Scribner's, 1951.

———. *Babylon Revisited and Other Stories*. New York: Scribner, 1960.

Ford, F. M. *Parade's End*. New York: Knopf, 1961.

Hemingway, E. *A Farewell to Arms*. New York: Random House (Modern Library), 1932.

———. *The Sun Also Rises*. New York: Scribner, 1954.

James, H. *The Portrait of a Lady*. New York: Scribner, 1908, Vols. 3–4, New York edition.

Joyce, J. *Dubliners*. New York: Penguin, 1993.

———. *Ulysses*. New York: Vintage, 1986.

Lowry, M. *Under the Volcano*. New York: Reynal and Hitchcock, 1947.

Milton, J. *Complete Poems*. Ed. F. A. Patterson. New York: F. S. Crofts, 1941.

Shelley, P. B. *The Complete Poetical Works*. Ed. T. Hutchinson. London: Oxford University Press, 1945.

Updike, J. *The Centaur*. New York: Knopf, 1962.

———. *Too Far To Go*. New York: Fawcett Crest, 1979.

Woolf, V. *The Years*. London: Hogarth Press, 1958.

———. *A Writer's Diary: Being Extracts from the Diary of Virginia Woolf*. Ed. L. Woolf. New York: Harcourt Brace Jovanovich, 1953.

SECONDARY WORKS

Articles cited from edited collections are listed solely under the editor's name and volume title.

Anderson, D. D., ed. *Critical Essays on Sherwood Anderson.* Boston: G. K. Hall, 1981.

Anderson, Q. *The American Henry James.* New Brunswick, N.J.: Rutgers University Press, 1957.

Anderson, Q., and J. Mazzeo, eds. *The Proper Study: Essays on Western Classics.* New York: St. Martin's Press, 1962.

Arnold, D. L. G. "In the Slow Rain Crying: Gendered Responses to Loss in Faulkner's *The Unvanquished,*" *Genre* 35 (Spring 2002), 89–120.

Ayers, D. *English Literature of the 1920s.* Edinburgh: Edinburgh University Press, 1999.

Baker, C. *Hemingway: The Writer as Artist.* 4th ed. Princeton: Princeton University Press, 1972.

———, ed. *Hemingway and His Critics.* New York: Hill and Wang, 1961.

Beer, G. "Hume, Stephen and Elegy in *To the Lighthouse,*" *Essays in Criticism* 34 (1984): 33–56.

Berland, A. *Culture and Conduct in the Novels of Henry James.* Cambridge: Cambridge University Press, 1981.

Blackstone, B. *Virginia Woolf: A Commentary.* London: Hogarth Press, 1949.

Bloom, H., ed. *Modern Critical Interpretations: Ernest Hemingway's A Farewell to Arms.* New York: Chelsea House, 1987.

———. *Modern Critical Interpretations: Henry James's The Portrait of a Lady.* New York: Chelsea House, 1987.

Bowker, G., ed. *Malcolm Lowry: Under the Volcano.* London: Macmillan, 1987.

Brenner, G. *Concealment in Hemingway's Works.* Columbus: Ohio State University Press, 1983.

Brewster, D. *Virginia Woolf.* London: Allen and Unwin Ltd., 1963.

Buitenhuis, P., ed. *Twentieth Century Interpretations of The Portrait of a Lady.* Englewood Cliffs, N.J.: Prentice-Hall, 1968.

Burchard, R. C. *John Updike, Yea Sayings.* Carbondale: Southern Illinois University Press, 1971.

Callahan, J. F. *The Illusions of a Nation: Myth and History in the Novels of F. Scott Fitzgerald.* Champaign: University of Illinois Press, 1972.

Cargill, O. *The Novels of Henry James.* New York: Macmillan, 1961.

Cheng, V. J., and T. Martin, eds. *Joyce in Context.* Cambridge: Cambridge University Press, 1992.

Clarke, G. *Capote: A Biography.* New York: Simon and Schuster, 1988.

Costa, R. H. *Malcolm Lowry.* New York: Twayne, 1972.

Cross, R. K. *Malcolm Lowry: A Preface to His Fiction.* Chicago: University of Chicago Press, 1980.

Daiches, D. *Virginia Woolf.* New York: New Directions, 1942.

Day, D. *Malcolm Lowry: A Biography.* New York: Oxford University Press, 1973.

Denniston, R., ed. *Man's Concern with Death.* London: Hodder and Stoughton, 1968.

Doty, M. A. *Tell Me Who I Am: James Agee's Search for Selfhood.* Baton Rouge: Louisiana State University Press, 1981.

Felton, S., ed. *The Critical Response to Joan Didion.* Westport, Conn.: Greenwood, 1994.

Garson, H. S. *Truman Capote.* New York: Ungar, 1980.

Gervais, D. *Flaubert and Henry James: A Study in Contrasts.* London: Macmillan, 1978.

Greenwald, E. "Casting off from 'The Castaway': *To the Lighthouse* as Prose Elegy," *Genre* 19 (1986): 37–57.

Greiner, D. J. *John Updike's Novels.* Athens: Ohio University Press, 1984.

Guieget, J. *Virginia Woolf and Her Works.* London: Hogarth Press, 1965.

Haegert, J. "Lawrence's World Elsewhere: Elegy and History in The Rainbow," *Clio* 15 (1986): 115–35.

Hamilton, A. and K. *The Elements of John Updike.* Grand Rapids, Mich.: Eerdmans, 1970.

Hassan, I. *Radical Innocence: The Contemporary American Novel.* Princeton: Princeton University Press, 1961.

Henderson, K. U. *Joan Didion.* New York: Ungar, 1981.

Hunt, G. W., S. J. *John Updike and the Three Great Secret Things: Sex, Religion, and Art.* Grand Rapids, Mich.: Eerdmans, 1980.

Hussey, M. *The Singing of the Real World: The Philosophy of Virginia Woolf's Fiction.* Columbus: Ohio State University Press, 1986.

———, ed. *Virginia Woolf and War: Fiction, Reality, and Myth.* Syracuse, N.Y.: Syracuse University Press, 1991.

Hutchinson, S. *Henry James: An American as Modernist.* London: Vision Press, 1982.

Hynes, S. *A War Imagined: The First World War and English Culture.* New York: Athenaeum, 1990.

Johnson-Roullier, C. "(An)Other Modernism: Baldwin's *Giovanni's Room* and the Rhetoric of Flight," *MFS* 45.4 (1999): 932–56.

Knox-Shaw, P. "'To the Lighthouse': The Novel as Elegy," *English Studies in Africa* 29.1 (1986): 31–52.

Krook-Gilead, D. *The Ordeal of Consciousness in Henry James.* Cambridge: Cambridge University Press, 1962.

LaHood, M. J., ed. *Tender Is the Night: Essays in Criticism.* Bloomington: Indiana University Press, 1969.

Leaska, M. *Virginia Woolf's To the Lighthouse, A Study in Critical Method.* New York: Columbia University Press, 1970.

Lee, A. R., ed. *Ernest Hemingway: New Critical Essays.* London: Vision, 1983.

Lee, B. *The Novels of Henry James: A Study of Culture and Consciousness.* London: Edward Arnold, 1978.

Leeming, D. *James Baldwin:* A Biography. New York: Knopf, 1994.

Lewis, R. W. *A Farewell to Arms: The War of the Words.* New York: Twayne, 1992.

Lewis, T. S. W., ed. *Virginia Woolf, a Collection of Criticism.* New York: McGraw-Hill, 1975.

Long, R. E. *The Great Succession: Henry James and the Legacy of Hawthorne.* Pittsburgh: University of Pittsburgh Press, 1979.

Luscher, R. M. *John Updike, A Study of the Short Fiction.* New York: Twayne, 1993.

Macebuh, S. *James Baldwin: A Critical Study.* New York: The Third Press, 1973.

Macnaughton, W. R., ed. *Critical Essays on John Updike.* Boston: G. K. Hall, 1982.

Markle, J. B. *Fighters and Lovers: Themes in the Novels of John Updike.* New York: New York University Press, 1973.

Mellard, James M. "The Novel as Lyric Elegy: The Mode of Updike's *The Centaur,*" *Texas Studies in Literature and Language* 21(1979): 112–27.

Miller, J. E. Jr. *F. Scott Fitzgerald: His Art and His Technique.* New York: New York University Press, 1967.

Moller, K. *The Theme of Identity in the Essays of James Baldwin.* Gothenburg, Sweden: Acta Universitatis Gothoburgenis, 1975.

Nagel, J., ed. *Critical Essays on Ernest Hemingway's The Sun Also Rises.* New York: G. K. Hall, 1995.

O'Daniel, T. B., ed. *James Baldwin: A Critical Evaluation.* Washington: Howard University Press, 1981.

Panofsky, E. *Meaning in the Visual Arts.* Garden City, N.Y.: Doubleday, 1957.

Petry, A. H. *Fitzgerald's Craft of Short Fiction.* Ann Arbor: UMI Research Press, 1989.

Poresky, L. A. *The Elusive Self: Psyche and Spirit in Virginia Woolf's Novels.* East Brunswick: Associated University Press, 1981.

Porte, J., ed. *New Essays on The Portrait of a Lady.* Cambridge: Cambridge University Press, 1990.

Powers, L. H. *The Portrait of a Lady: Maiden, Woman, and Heroine.* Boston: Twayne, 1991.

Pratt, L. H. *James Baldwin.* Boston: Twayne, 1978.

Ramazani, J. *Poetry of Mourning: The Modern Elegy from Hardy to Heaney.* Chicago: University of Chicago Press, 1994.

Rhode, E. "Death in Twentieth-Century Fiction." In *Man's Concern with Death,* ed. Arnold Toynbee, 160–76. London: Hodder and Stoughton, 1968.

Richter, H. *Virginia Woolf: The Inward Voyage.* Princeton: Princeton University Press, 1970.

Riquelme, J. P. *Teller and Tale in Joyce's Fiction: Oscillating Perspectives.* Baltimore: Johns Hopkins University Press, 1983.

Rosenthal, M. *Virginia Woolf.* New York: Columbia University Press, 1979.

Rovit, E. *Ernest Hemingway.* New York: Twayne, 1962.

Ruotolo, L. *The Interrupted Moment: A View of Virginia Woolf's Novels.* Palo Alto: Stanford University Press, 1986.

Ryle, G. *The Concept of Mind.* Chicago: The University of Chicago Press, 1949.

Salgado, G., and G. S. Das, eds. *The Spirit of D. H. Lawrence.* New York: Macmillan, 1988.

Schneidau, H. *Waking Giants:* Modernism and the Presence of the Past. New York: Oxford University Press, 1991.

Siegel, B., and J. Halio, eds. *American Literary Dimensions.* Newark: University of Delaware Press, 1999.

Sklar, R. F. *Scott Fitzgerald: The Last Laocoon.* New York: Oxford University Press, 1967.

Smith, A. R., ed. *The Art of Malcolm Lowry.* London: Vision Press, 1978.

Spiegel, A. *James Agee and the Legend of Himself.* Columbia: University of Missouri Press, 1998.

Stavola, T. J. *Scott Fitzgerald: Crisis in American Identity.* London: Vision Press, 1979.

Stern, M. R. *The Golden Moment: The Novels of F. Scott Fitzgerald.* Urbana: University of Illinois Press, 1970.

Sylvander, C. W. *James Baldwin.* New York: Ungar, 1980.

Taylor, L. E. *Pastoral and Anti-Pastoral Patterns in John Updike's Fiction.* Carbondale: Southern Illinois University Press, 1971.

Torchiana, D. T. *Backgrounds for Joyce's Dubliners.* Boston: Allen and Unwin, 1986.

Uphaus, S. H. *John Updike.* New York: Ungar, 1980.

Vargo, E. P. "The Necessity of Myth in John Updike's *The Centaur,*" *PMLA* (May 1973) 88 (3): 452–60.

Vickery, J. B. *Myths and Texts: Strategies of Incorporation and Displacement.* Baton Rouge: Louisiana State University Press, 1983.

———. "*The Centaur:* Myth, History, and Narrative," *MFS* 20 (1974): 29–43.

Vickery, O. W. *The Novels of William Faulkner.* Rev. ed. Baton Rouge: Louisiana State University Press, 1964.

Way, B. F. *Scott Fitzgerald and the Art of Social Fiction.* London: Edward Arnold, 1980.

White, R. L., ed. *The Achievement of Sherwood Anderson: Essays in Criticism.* Chapel Hill: University of North Carolina Press, 1966.

Williams, W. *The Tragic Art of Ernest Hemingway.* Baton Rouge: Louisiana State University Press, 1981.

Winchell, M. R. *Joan Didion.* Boston: Twayne, 1989.

Young, P. *Ernest Hemingway: A Reconsideration.* Rev. ed. University Park: Pennsylvania State University Press, 1966.

Zwerdling, A. *Virginia Woolf and the Real World.* Berkeley: University of California Press, 1986.

INDEX